19.95
5 88

MORE
CHARACTER
PEOPLE

Also by

Alfred E. Twomey and
Arthur F. McClure

THE VERSATILES

Ken D. Jones, Arthur F. McClure,
and Alfred E. Twomey

FILMS OF JAMES STEWART

CHARACTER PEOPLE

Ken D. Jones and
Arthur F. McClure

HOLLYWOOD AT WAR

Arthur F. McClure
and Ken D. Jones

STAR QUALITY

HEROES, HEAVIES, AND SAGEBRUSH

MORE CHARACTER PEOPLE

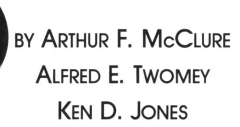

BY ARTHUR F. MCCLURE
ALFRED E. TWOMEY
KEN D. JONES

CITADEL PRESS • Secaucus, New Jersey

First edition
Copyright © 1984 by Arthur F. McClure, Alfred E. Twomey,
  and Ken D. Jones
All rights reserved
Published by Citadel Press
A division of Lyle Stuart Inc.
120 Enterprise Ave., Secaucus, N.J. 07094
In Canada: Musson Book Company
A division of General Publishing Co. Limited
Don Mills, Ontario
Manufactured in the United States of America by
Halliday Lithograph, West Hanover, Mass.
ISBN 0-8065-0876-0

Designed by Holly Johnson
at the Angelica Design Group Ltd.

This is a revised and updated version of *The Versatiles*
Copyright © 1969 by A. S. Barnes and Co. Inc.

CONTENTS

PREFACE

In two earlier volumes, *The Versatiles* (1969) and *Character People* (1976) we paid tribute to the supporting character actors and actresses who appeared in the American film from approximately 1930 to 1955. We continue our efforts with this book, which is an updated, revised, and corrected version of *The Versatiles* with additional materials. *The Versatiles* has been long out of print and many of the actors included in that work are no longer living. Many of the errors in research have been corrected. We hope that this new volume is a worthy companion piece to its predecessors. Although it certainly is not meant as a comprehensive reference volume, we hope to please those readers who loved these characters whose names always seem to be at the tip of the tongue. We remain convinced that these fine players deserve acknowledgement and their importance to the content of the American film should never be forgotten. To the character people who are still active in the films and television, the recognition has come late, but not too late for the mention that they so richly deserve. We repeat that there will be those who will label this a "nonbook" because it is a collection of brief biographies. We continue to make no apologies and once again offer up this book to readers who share in our admiration for those overlooked professional actors who so often labored in unfair anonymity.

This book is dedicated
to the many actors and actresses included herein.
To them,
our grateful thanks.

ACKNOWLEDGMENTS

The authors recognize with gratitude the help of many in the pursuit of their investigation.

Special thanks is extended to Miss Lillian Schwartz, Librarian, Academy of Motion Picture Arts and Sciences, Miss Barbara Browning, Assistant Librarian, and Miss Midori Martin for their communications and assistance in the practical implications of various phases of the study.

Serveral persons and organizations merit acknowledgment: Miss Patsy Gaile, "Hedda Hopper's Helper"; Mr. John Qualen; Salkow-Kennard, Inc.; James McHugh, Jr. Agency; The Mishkin Agency, Inc.; Walter Herzbrun Agency; all of whom supplied the authors with very useful information. It is difficult to imagine the completion of this project without the friendship and courtesy of: Mr. Frank Jones, Shelby Bourne, Robert Rothrock, and Glen Carroll of Commonwealth Theaters, Inc.; also Miss Elizabeth K. Zorn, and Mr. and Mrs. Lynn Zorn. Thanks are also due Rex Burns and Robin White, editor of *Per/Se*, who allowed us to reprint parts of an article printed in the Summer, 1968, issue of that magazine.

A very special note of appreciation is due Mr. Alan Napier whose invaluable comments and gracious hospitality contributed greatly to the investigation.

Finally, the constant encouragement and optimistic spirit of Mr. and Mrs. John V. Twomey, Judy McClure, and Nancy Jones helped to nurture the dream of scholarship and creativity in their own way.

The final resolution is our own, and the sole responsibility for all errors of omission or commission is thus established. Rupert Brooke provided the best reminder when he wrote:

Go forth, my book, and take whatever
　　pounding
The heavy fisted destinies prepare.
I know you are not anything astounding,
And, to be quite sincere, I don't much care.
Get off your overcoat, the gong is sounding.
The enemy has risen from his chair.
He doesn't look so overwhelming, but
His arm is long. Watch for an uppercut.

FOREWORD

The faces of these talented men and women may be familiar to you although you may never have known their names—they have appeared in several hundred films and major Broadway and television productions.

It is the desire of Arthur F. McClure and Alfred E. Twomey, Central Missouri State University, and Ken D. Jones to preserve this aspect of theatrical history which is so vitally important.

I firmly believe that the Hotel Clerk in *The Awful Truth*, a film I made with Cary Grant; the Judge in *My Favorite Wife*, another film I made with Cary; the old maid sister, Ellen Corby, in *I Remember Mama*; Mme. Marie Ouspenskaya, the great Russian actress, the grandmother in *Love Affair* with Charles Boyer; Ward Bond in the film made with Spencer Tracy called *A Guy Named Joe*; Charles Winninger as "Capt. Andy" in *Show Boat*; Edgar Buchanan, bathing a small baby in *Penny Serenade*; Gladys Cooper, in the *White Cliffs of Dover*, to name only a few, were as responsible for the success of these films as the stars and directors.

To see a young school girl who played a small part in the *The White Cliffs of Dover*, and in another supporting role in *Life with Father*, which we both made for Warner Brothers, become a star of the first magnitude is not completely uncommon in the motion picture business. I refer to Elizabeth Taylor, and it only proves to me that the conditioning process of actors playing many secondary roles enables them to accept the rigors of stardom should it come their way.

My enthusiasm is boundless for the character actor whether he be in motion pictures, television or a Broadway play, and I have known a production to be kept alive because of the excellent performances of these fine artists.

The first time I ever put foot on a studio lot was when I was asked to make a film test for the great Edna Ferber picture *Cimarron*. It was the story of the land rush in Oklahoma, and Sabra the heroine, a sheltered southern girl, was to marry the dashing Yancey Cravat and leave by covered wagon for the West, where she was to spend her life with her children, finally returning to Washington, D.C., as a Congresswoman to assist her beloved Oklahoma. The film embraced a span of thirty-six years for Sabra Cravat and the aging process was most important. As I came through the studio gate the morning I was to be tested, I saw a little woman who looked about sixty. I studied her clothes and especially the little black straw hat she was wearing. I went to her and told her I was making a film test and could I borrow her hat—that I would return it to her before she left her post in the wardrobe department at the end of the day.

I have always felt the portion of the test where I played the aging Congresswoman and more especially the correctness of that hat won for me that great part in a film which later was to win the Academy Award for the year.

What I am trying to say is, that for a brief time I was playing a character role in *Cimarron,* and I maintain character actors are perennial students, constantly aware of their fellowmen, and it is the awareness of these fine actors that gives a fullness to their performances, a depth that makes all the difference.

May I as a player who has worked with many of these men and women salute each and every one of them and extend my personal thanks to them for their great help.

Irene Dunne

THE ITSY-BITSY ACTORS

BY GILBERT SELDES

Gilbert Seldes, the noted film historian, very early recognized the value of the character actors in films. The following article, written in the 1930's, displays Seldes' delight and admiration for these versatile performers.

I discovered the other day, from an old photograph, that Edgar Kennedy had once been a Keystone cop and I had the same warm feeling of verification that comes over you when the man you always thought "funny" is clapped into the cooler for murder or violating the sanitary laws. With it came a sense of my own bitter insignificance, because if Edgar Kennedy had been a Keystone cop, I must have seen Edgar Kennedy at least a hundred times between 1914 and 1920, yet I hadn't, with the eagle-eye which has since been so highly praised by others, singled him out as a genius among Keystone cops. I have no apologies, but, in accordance with Kipling's advice, I offer a humble and a contrite heart. To hell with it.

Edgar Kennedy is the man who about four years ago was appearing in short comic films, usually surrounded by a group of people endowed with more capacity to irritate and annoy than any other I have seen. Edgar played golf or Edgar took a house or did any simple thing; and these harpies—men, women and children—set flies upon him, froze his water-pipes, spoiled

his stroke and otherwise made life decidedly unpleasant. What then distinguished Edgar? One thing: that his response was always the same. Beginning with something like W.C. Field's unbelief that human beings could be so despicable, he worked into a fury of exasperation, arrived at the slender edge of apoplexy and then, passing his weary hand over his bloated and impassioned face, resumed quietly the work he had been doing. It was always the same, and always good.

More recently Edgar has been playing minor parts in mystery stories, with more variety. He is still good. He is gentle, childlike, and raging like a tiger. In the movies, he gives first rate entertainment for a few moments at a time.

Except for short comics, Edgar Kennedy is not likely to be billed for movie leads, and I do not insist that he has the talent for them, only it is not the lack of talent which will stand in his way. He isn't the type. He's a largish man with a bald-

13

ish head (so he appears on the screen) and he is given to grotesquerie. The movies quite naturally do not take risks with that type so long as they have Gary Cooper and Robert Montgomery.

There are two or three dozen players like Edgar in the movies, most of them men. In fact, the only woman I recall who isn't heavily featured is that handsome, motherly and completely mahogany Negress who is everybody's maid. She must work nights getting around. The kind of thing I mean is what Edna May Oliver would have been if she hadn't imposed herself and been made into a star. Can you think of others, with her quality, who happen not to be imitating her at the moment? The men are more numerous and more varied. There are the half dozen who are usually gangsters' bodyguards, not only looking sinister, but turning in good bits of acting. There are two or three whom you will always find as assistants to the Pat O'Brien's and Lee Tracy's in their more adventurous activities. There are a couple of minor detectives and there is Paul Porcasi, the perpetual night-club owner. And a little Italian whose name I think is Armetta.

Frank McHugh is another, and of the first rank. When I first met him, McHugh had a laugh, and if someone will tell me how to transcribe the sound of a laugh with the twenty-six letters of the English alphabet, I will be grateful. For several weeks I managed a fair imitation of the McHugh laugh, but the genuine note escaped me. And the unfortunate thing is that it has been choked down McHugh's throat. Now usually when the movies discover something totally unimportant, like Dietrich's legs, they want to work it to the extreme, but directors step in and say that a pair of legs must be nursed along so that the public won't get tired of them, and Dietrich is allowed to stand on her own feet, more or less, in alternate pictures; in the others she, like the Queen of Spain, has no legs. Well, they did that to McHugh and it is months since his combination of whinny and hyena-roar has been heard. He is still amusing, because he has an innocent pan and seems to have more zest about his work than most people—the movies, perhaps because of the Klieg lights, seem to exhaust the energies of all the actors except the horses.

Charles Butterworth gets his name in lights, of course, but he is always in support. He began thinking of a nice ear of sweet corn in the midst of a sentimental solo years ago, and to all intents and purposes, he does it still. In *Bulldog Drummond Strikes Back* he was the abstracted husband who tried to sidestep Ronald Colman's activities so that he could, with all propriety, get to bed—it being his wedding night. He did it well. It may be only a fancy of mine that he could do other things also.

Roland Young is quite another matter. He is one of the few absolutely first class major actors who ever got to Hollywood and he has always built up the pictures in which he has appeared. He has even had the center of interest, although it wasn't the love interest, and he represents only Hollywood's determination not to make the best of its material in certain instances. The chance is good that after his Uriah Heep in *David Copperfield* he will be able to go into more significant parts, but my bet again is that he will do so well that they will want him only in "characters" whereas he could play anything from Macbeth to Charley's Aunt. Two to one, he gets the second before the first.

I am interested in these players of small parts and, in the case of Roland Young, of parts which the producers obviously hold secondary, because I find that I remember them much better than I do the stars and the plots and the jokes and the stunts which make up four and a half of the usual five reels. I am not alone in this. When trailers come on, you hear murmurs of satisfaction when these players are shown. You hear them notably also for Zasu Pitts who, like Miss Oliver, lifted herself into stardom and is being imitated; from mothers, for child actors who represent the same relief from the heavy stars, and from children when Tom Mix or another rider appears with a horse. (No horse, no murmurs.)

I suspect that although the movies as a whole interest their audiences more than ever, there are blank spots, wastelands, during which attention wanders, and I think I know why those infertile and unattractive spaces occur. It is because the movies hardly ever present a character; they merely present a person. And persons become tiresome, as you and I, who have met not a few, are well aware. We tire of them because we want to talk too, and you cannot assert yourself against Miss Crawford or Miss Shearer or Miss Garbo when they have the screen. (Miss West manages to make herself a character in ten seconds and is never tiresome, even if patches of her pictures may be.)

The movies might easily do character. I am not arguing from any holy artistic ground on this matter. I am, as ever and as always, just a friend of the big boys in Hollywood, telling them how to make more money. Characters sustain interest. Put a character before us and you can cut down the salaries of the plot experts by half and spend only a tenth as much on clothes and you won't need that big scene of the shipwreck. Character is the bridge between one incident and another, if you are interested in a character you are willing to wait a minute or two in order to find out what happens to him. The movies, in fact, have capitalized on this very thing because Marie Dressler appeared in pictures without exceptional plots and was for a time the top attraction of all, because she, like Miss West, created character. She was not a model for clothes and she was this side of exuding sex appeal and she out-classed the entire lot in bringing cash to the box office.

Now all these secondary players are alike in this: that you recognize something concrete, a human character, in them. Often enough it is the same character you saw three weeks ago, but that doesn't diminish your pleasure, even if it is bad for the actor to get into a rut. (After all, our friends do not change from week to week, popping up as a miserly old man one day and reformed but still attractive rakes the next.) The minor players are allowed certain human qualities which the major ones forego. They are rude, violent, ironic, mean, brutal and mocking. They say what the audience often feels, pricking the great bubble of pretensions which floats through the morals of every movie. They are disruptive elements. And they are very good company.

Some eight years ago it occured to me that what interested me most in the average movie program was the shorts. Later I went for the cartoon comedies. Since then theaters have been inaugurated for each of these types. So now I shall look forward to a movie composed entirely of the works of supporting actors. And I expect it to be good.

of the Golden Era of Movies, 1930—1955, with at least one character and perhaps more that became the real object of this historical study. The actors that repeatedly personified a particular mood, sense, attribute, or emotion have become the center of this nostalgic glimpse at the past. The character actor of the movies performed many of the same functions as stock characters in other art forms. The stock characters in any theatrical form generally remained constant. Movie character actors provided regularity and continuity to the films for audiences. It was not difficult for audiences to accept particular actors that played the stock characters with whom they had become most familiar, whether it was the drunkard, the banker, or the cracker-barrel philosopher.

The character actor is someone who appears in a *kind* of role so frequently that he practically creates the role itself. When a character actor's face is seen on a screen, it is possible to know the part he is playing. In many instances a star can be replaced by another star, but the character actor was sometimes not interchangeable with any other character type.

The expectation of seeing the familiar faces of character actors was an important part of movie going for many years. Although each character actor may have played only one role, there were so many character actors that there seemed to be an unlimited supply of parts for them to play. The character actors were often listed as "featured players," in contrast to the stars whose names were listed above a film's titles.

The period of years from 1930 to 1955 were selected because they marked the apex of the "Golden Years" of the American talking motion picture. Every studio had its own group of character actors under contract, and they were used frequently and with great versatility throughout the company's products. The studios always made an effort to cast a "type" in various featured parts. This makes it necessary to define just what was the "featured" player. These characters were often more than supporting players. Frequently they were as important to the story as the stars, but their names were listed below the titles rather than above. Many of them became entrenched in one type of role and repeated the same kind of portrayal over and over. But many character actors spanned a wide range of emotions with the versatility of their performances. These actors brought life to a given scene. Many of the character roles had little to do with the plot but their technical importance in terms of acting was considerable. The character actors were specialists in every sense of the word.

They also had the advantage of the opportunity to act much more often with the freedom to accept many roles. In addition, they could act in a flop and recover quickly to obtain a role in a film classic. A star's position was different because of the truism that he was only as good as his last movie! Dana Andrews was once quoted as saying that "The real acting parts go to the character actors."

In looking back at some of the great motion pictures produced during the period, particular roles by character actors stand out immediately in one's mind. *Sergeant York*, for all its gripping story and Academy Award-winning performance by Gary Cooper, would have proved a lot less potent without a character actress of Margaret Wycherly's ability in the role of the mother. It was her deeply lined delineation that seemed to make the whole story right. The same sort of situation occured in *Grapes of Wrath*, in which Henry Fonda starred and gave an excellent performance. But where would that story have been without Jane Darwell as Ma Joad?

Moviegoers fondly remember these characters and the types that they played in picture after picture. How often was Ray Teal seen as the local troublemaker in Western towns? Phillip Ober and Henry O'Neill consistently played executive types. Stanley Clements and William Benedict were called on dozens of times to play either bellhops, jockies, or punks. Dick Foran or Jack Haley were often seen as singing cops, and Joseph Crehan and Edward Gargan as non-singing desk sergeants. Noah Beery, Jr., and Harry Carey, Jr., were nearly always cast as the shy, likeable friend of the hero in westerns. English character actors who usually gave a picture elegance, dignity, and aristocratic snobbishness included Alan Mowbray, C. Aubrey Smith, Reginald Gardner, and Reginald Denny. Hattie McDaniel, Louise Beavers, and Butterfly McQueen were

Introduction

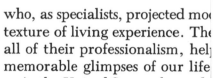

One of the most important aspects of the history of the American motion picture has been the contribution of the character actor. The character actor has had a great influence on the enjoyment provided by movies. Any American who was a steady moviegoer during the quarter century from 1930 to 1955 in many ways acquired a unique appreciation of America in our times. Such a person became, therefore, something of an authority on the current American scene. By going to the movies, moviegoers could judge character and weigh opinions in a darkened theater in the individual light of their own personal experience. Movies made during this period often have been criticised for their lack of experimentation. Many movie stories, however, if examined closely, were distinctly different in style and in the approach to character and plot. Outstanding acting was the way moviemakers departed from the development of the standard plot. The action of hundreds of movies frequently gave way to character portrayal. The emotions and thoughts of these characters were often cunningly portrayed by character actors

who, as specialists, projected mo
texture of living experience. The
all of their professionalism, hel
memorable glimpses of our life

As the United States plunged i
sion, the political, economic and
of living were reflected in the
1930's and after, the talking fi
audiences the vehicle that c
revenge, adjustment, repair of s
onciliation, acceptance." Audi
before found themselves deeply
movies with an intensity that v
measure. The trials of everday
at least temporarily put aside in
ater by identifying with the peopl
Movies, and the characters in the
some way the unconscious conflic
vidual in the audience. If a cha
toward others in a way the audi
wish to behave, the identificatio
jected. The villainous character
rejected but he was not *forgotte*

It is the identification of the m

usually seen on the domestic staff of wealthy families as philosophical servants and Mantan Moreland or Willie Best were comic chauffeurs and houseboys.

During the 1930's and 1940's every good movie and most of the bad ones, had several vivid portrayals by character actors that literally *supported* the entire production. The young stars were backed up by these very proficient actors who in turn could make the stars and the pictures themselves highly successful. In recent years, when motion pictures have aimed much of their appeal toward younger audiences, there has been a gradual but steady process of the disappearance of many good, competent character actors employed. Many of the most familiar actors are dead, while others, aging, are in state of retirement or semi-retirement. Many have moved on into other fields of employment. Motion pictures have therefore suffered greatly in a generation filled with conformity and sadly lacking in the picturesque individuality that was often supplied by a favorite character actor.

Alan Napier, a familiar face to movie fans for nearly fifty years, imparted some telling observations to the authors on the plight of the current quality and quantity of character actors in the American film.

The source who told you that things aren't what they used to be is right—the pool is depleted. And for a very good, typical American reason. There is a parallel in agriculture—the exploitation of virgin lands with no thought of replenishment. Hollywood dug deeply into the great pool of theatre-trained character actors: they are dying off and nothing is being done by Hollywood to replace them by training the young talent coming up. Aging leading men sometimes make good character actors, but not always, nor do they cover a wide field. Good character actors—little men, fat men, ugly men, come out of stock companies where the exigencies of putting on a new play every week or fortnight with a company of only 10 or 12 souls makes it necessary for all but the leads to essay all sorts of roles for which they are not obvious types. From this necessity you get acting . . . in place of the comparatively sterile practice of behaviorism.

It has been asserted on frequent occasions that the reason for the tremendous success of foreign films at the box office in recent years is the concerted effort of foreign film producers to "people their films." A splendid, example of this effort in Europe is the English movie *The Wrong Box* in which every performance is a character performance. Napier correctly maintains that the story "is a wild farce, yet every character is fantastically believable, down to the bit players." American character actors were closely studied in the Hollywood films of the 1930–1955 period. The more or less stereotypes played by these performers helped to make movies more interesting. It has also been established in many ways that there is a correlation between the time when American film studios dropped their large lists of contract players in the 1950's and the dullness of American movies1

A few American moviemakers still stubbornly make valuable use of some of the great character actors that are still available. John Ford, Frank Capra, Jerry Lewis, and Walt Disney supplemented their movie casts with some of the familiar faces of the 1930's and 1940's.

The most difficult task involved in this project was the collection of biographical data on these actors. Biographical information simply was not available for many of them. Some died years ago, while others ignored mailed requests for information. Still others have simply disappeared—vanished without a trace in many instances. In some cases it was practically impossible to track down surviving relatives who were willing to cooperate with the project.

Another sad aspect of this study was that many of these actors died during the months that it took to gather the material. Harry Antrim, William Newell, Verna Felton, George E. Stone, Nestor Paiva, Sig Ruman, Jane Darwell, Nat Pendleton, and Mischa Auer all passed away during the year of 1967 while the original manuscript was being prepared. Many others have died in the years since.

A great deal of information concerning the history of the American motion picture died with them. Most actors leave no written records or diaries concerning their careers.

19

The process of selection also proved difficult. Many times there was a fine line between what could be called featured players, supporting players, and those actors who crossed over into a degree of stardom later in their careers in movies and television. Also, there has been great difficulty in categorizing these players. It very rapidly became a problem of *who* should be included in such a work. Who should be excluded?

A study of this nature has some definite limitations and restrictions. The birth and death dates are sometimes extremely difficult to secure with a high degree of accuracy. This is due to the fact that some of these people are gone and forgotten in many instances. Another is that actors do not always keep the same birthdate throughout a lifetime, for either career or psychological reasons.

Many people have wondered why the authors undertook this compiling and writing task. Several Hollywood agents, with whom the authors corresponded concerning these people, asked why we were interested in players who were "not important in the Hollywood scheme of things." In the first place, we are certain that this is an erroneous assumption. In the second place, there is a tragic element in the loss of so many of these faces that were so familiar to a generation of moviegoers. As these people drift away unrecognized from the movie industry either by entering other vocational fields or by dying off, a great part of the history of the American motion picture fades away and will never be able to be reconstructed adequately again.

It is our modest hope that by reading through these pages a pleasant thought from the past may be awakened. Many readers who pick up this book will be people too young to remember the "Golden Age" of the talking film. Yet television, with its insatiable appetite for movies as entertainment fare, has created a whole new generation of movie experts. Regular viewers of these shows on television will recall with great affection these players who helped to strike a familiar chord or oftentimes, mirror a nostalgic facet of their own lives. The word "nostalgia" is taken from the Greek word "nostos" which means to "return home." Movie fans are by definition creatures that are motivated by a wistful or sentimental yearning to return to some real or romanticized period that is irrecoverable in the past. It is hoped that this work may help to make such a journey an enjoyable one. And then, perhaps, the character actors will be assured a place in the history of the American film.

PART 1
BIOGRAPHICAL SECTION

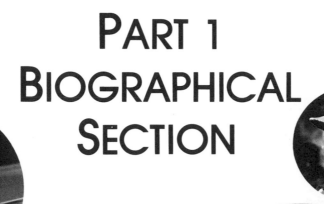

IRIS ADRIAN *(1912–)*

Iris Adrian was born in Los Angeles, and began her professional career as Ziegfeld girl in *Hot Cha* (1930), and *Ziegfeld Follies of 1931*. She

Iris Adrian, with Jack Benny and Frank Fontaine.

became the dancing partner of George Raft on a personal appearance tour and made her first movie at the age of 19, *Rhumba*, in 1934 with Raft, Movie roles included gangster's moll, wise-cracking blonde, chorus girl, dumb waitress or secretary, or street-walker. She frequently appeared on the *Jack Benny Show*. Films include *Stolen Harmony, Roxy Hart, Lady of Burlesque, Paleface, Once a Thief, That Darn Cat, Blue Hawaii*, and *The Odd Couple*.

FRANK ALBERTSON *(1909–Feb. 29, 1964)*

Frank Albertson was born in Fergus Falls, Minnesota. He had many roles in films and plays in a career that spanned 35 years, Among his many films were *The Farmer's Daughter, Men Without Women, Connecticut Yankee, They*

Frank Albertson

22

Made Me a Killer, It's a Wonderful Life, and *The Hucksters.* His last film role was that of the mayor in *Bye-Bye Birdie.*

SARA ALLGOOD *(1879–Sept. 13, 1950)*

Sara Allgood was an Irish-born actress who had a long career with the Abbey Players in Dublin before entering motion pictures in 1929. She appeared often in the role of a mother. Films in

Sara Allgood with George Sanders in The Strange Affair of Uncle Harry

which she appeared included *Blackmail,* the first British talking picture, made in 1929, *That Hamilton Woman, How Green Was My Valley, Mother Wore Tights, Mourning Becomes Electra, Jane Eyre, The Spiral Staircase, My Wild Irish Rose, Roxie Hart,* and *Lydia.*

MORRIS ANKRUM *(1897–Sept. 2, 1964)*

Morris Ankrum was a native of Danville, Illinois, and attended the University of Southern California where he received a degree in law. He founded the little theater at the University of California in Berkeley while serving as an associate professor of economics. He was a director of the Pasadena Playhouse for many years. Films include *Desire Me, Tales of Manhattan,*

Buck Benny Rides Again, Harvey Girls, Joan of Arc, My Favorite Spy, Apache, Vera Cruz, and and *The Damned Don't Cry.*

Morris Ankrum, with Barbara Stanwyck in Cattle Queen of Montana.

HENRY ARMETTA *(1888–Oct. 21, 1945)*

Henry Armetta, a native of Palermo, Italy, came to America as a stowaway at the age of 14. He started as a pants presser at New York's famed

Henry Armetta

Lambs Club and became acquainted with Raymond Hitchcock, who gave him a bit part in the stage production of *Yankee Consul*. After several years in stock he went to Hollywood in 1923. Armetta played in more than 125 pictures, specializing in comedy character roles. His portrayals of the excited, gesticulating Latin were familiar to film fans everywhere.

SIG ARNO *(1895–Aug. 17, 1975)*

Sig Arno was born in Hamburg, Germany. He became an important comedian and character actor in German theater. He left Germany in 1933 when the Nazis came to power and played in several European countries. He arrived in the U.S. in 1939 and played in musicals, light operas,

Sig Arno

and films as well as being a successful portrait painter. His favorite film role was that of the headwaiter in *Time Remembered*. Films included *Song to Remember*, *This Thing Called Love*, *Two Latins from Manhattan*, *Two Yanks from Trinidad*, *Palm Beach Story*, *Bring on the Girls*, *His Butler's Sister*, and *Up in Arms*. He often portrayed waiters, haughty butlers, and effete bon vivants.

EDWARD ARNOLD *(1890–Apr. 26, 1956)*

Edward Arnold was probably Hollywood's most popular and versatile portrayer of official characters. During his long career he was often cast as a congressman, a senator, a mayor, or a judge. Born Guenther Schneider, in a tenement on New York's Lower East Side, he went to school at the East Side Settlement House and in an amateur production there he played Lorenzo in *The Merchant of Venice*. In later years Ar-

Edward Arnold as Diamond Jim Brady in Lillian Russell.

nold wrote a book on his life, *Lorenzo Comes to Hollywood*, which harked back to his first role. After a career on Broadway, Arnold was offered the opportunity to succeed Francis X. Bushman as star at Essanay Studio in Chicago. He accepted the offer and appeared in more than forty pictures. Arnold continued on the stage in important productions, but in 1932 he returned to pictures. Some of his biggest pictures, prior to his signing a long-term ccontract with MGM in 1940, were *Rasputin and the Empress*, *The*

White Sister, Diamond Jim, Sadie McKee, Sutter's Gold, You Can't Take It with You, and *Mr. Smith Goes to Washington.* Later pictures included *Idiot's Delight, Johnny Eager, Mrs. Parkington, Nothing but the Truth, The Devil and Daniel Webster, Dear Ruth, The Hucksters, Command Decision,* and *Honest John Horner.* Arnold was at one time president of the Screen Actors Guild.

PHIL ARNOLD *(1909–May 9, 1968)*
Phil Arnold was born in Hackensack, New Jersey, and appeared in many amateur contests around Bayonne, New Jersey, in which he "won them all." His first professional engagement was at the Strand Theatre there. In the mid-1920's he joined the famous Gus Edwards Revue in which he performed single, double and flash acts. He also appeared in night clubs and danced at the Roxy Theatre in New York, as well as appearing as a featured dancer in hit musicals including *The Girl Friend* and *Virginia* at the Palace Theatre. In the 1930's he went to Hollywood to appear in movies. His credits include *King of the Turf, Sis Hopkins, Buffalo Bill Rides Again, It's Always Fair Weather, The Court Martial of Billy Mitchell, Illegal, Killer*

Phil Arnold, as Zerbo in TV series Cowboy G-Man.

at Large, A Star Is Born, Kentucky Jubilee, Men of San Quentin, Jet Pilot, My Gun Is Quick, The Jazz Singer, Damn Yankees, and *Studs Lonigan.* His favorite roles were as Congressman Fiorello LaGuardia in *The Court Martial of Billy Mitchell,* and as Zerbo in the *Cowboy G-Man* series on TV.

CHARLES ARNT *(1908–   )*
Charles Arnt was born in Michigan City, Indiana, and obtained a degree in geological engineering at Princeton University in 1929. Arnt was also president of the Triangle Club. He played a featured character role on New York stage in *Knickerbocker Holiday* with Walter

Charles Arnt, center, looking over Tyrone Power's shoulder in That Wonderful Urge. *Left, Arlene Whelan and right, Norman Leavitt*

Huston. His facial appearance even as a young man made him in demand in Hollywood to play old men, eccentrics, and other types much his senior. Films include *Reunion, The Falcon's Brother, Paris Calling, The Great Gildersleeve, Bride for Sale, Cinderella Jones, High Wall,* and *Hollow Triumph.*

JOHNNY K. ARTHUR *(1883–Dec. 31, 1951)*
Johnny K. Arthur was a native of Scottsdale, Pennsylvania. After more than 25 years on the stage he came to Hollywood in the 1920's and was an outstanding comic in silent pictures. Films included *Twenty Million Sweethearts, Many Happy Returns, Traveling Saleslady, The Hit Parade, Exiled in Shanghai, Pick a Star* and *Danger on the Air.*

Johnny Arthur, third from left with Paul Kelly, Judith Allan, Steve Clemento and Leroy Mason in It Happened Out West.

ROSCOE ATES (1895–Mar. 1, 1962)

Roscoe Ates was a rubber-faced comedian who literally stuttered his way to stardom even though he had cured himself of stammering at

Roscoe Ates

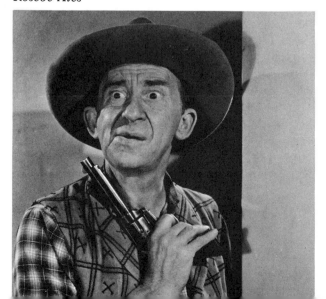

an early age. His stutter and pop eyes made him a comically appealing figure to film audiences, and was known among actors as a "scene stealer." Ates' best known role was that of a ranch roustabout in Western pictures. Some of the films in which he appeared include *Gone With the Wind, Cimarron, Alice in Wonderland, Untamed, The Champ, Captain Caution,* and *Merry Wives of Reno.* His last screen appearance was in Jerry Lewis' *Errand Boy.*

LIONEL ATWILL (1885–Apr. 22, 1946)

Lionel Atwill was born at Croydon, England, and embarked upon a theatrical career in 1905 after studying architecture. In 1915 he came to the U.S. and appeared as Lily Langtry's leading

Lionel Atwill, right, with Lester Mathews in Lancer Spy.

MISCHA AUER *(1895–Mar. 5, 1967)*

Mischa Auer was born in St. Petersburg, Russia. He came to the U.S. in the 1920's to live with his grandfather, Leopold Auer, the famed music master who taught Zimbalist, Heifetz, and Elman. Interested in the stage, he did small roles on the New York stage and arrived in Los Angeles in 1928 when he made his motion picture debut in *Something Always Happens*. Auer later gave an outstanding performance in Universal's *My Man Godfrey* and afterward was in great demand by the studios. He was usually cast as eccentric artists, or thin-blooded European noblemen. Films included *Lives of a Bengal Lancer, Clive of India, Winterset, You Can't Take It with You, Sentimental Journey, Sofia, For You I Die,* and *Destry Rides Again.*

IRVING BACON *(1893–Feb. 5, 1965)*

Born in St. Joseph, Missouri, Bacon entered films in the 1920's after a brief career on the stage. He is best remembered for his playing of com-

man in New York and on a national tour in *Mrs. Thompson*. He went to Hollywood in 1932 and specialized in villainous roles. Films included *Silent Witness, Mark of the Vampire, Captain Blood, Last Train from Madrid, The Great Waltz, Mr. Moto Takes a Vacation,* and *Son of Frankenstein.*

Mischa Auer

Irving Bacon

edy roles. His motion picture credits included *Good Sam, It Happened One Night, State of the Union, Half Way to Heaven, Woman in Hiding,* and *One Way to Love.*

FAY BAINTER *(1893–April 16, 1968)*
Fay Bainter began her acting career at the age of six with stock companies in her hometown of Los Angeles. She began her film career at the age of 41. Four years later she won The Best Supporting Actress Academy Award for her role of "Aunt Belle" in *Jezebel*. The same year she was nominated for Best Actress for *White Banners*. She was best known for her motherly and faithful wife roles. Her films included *Make Way for Tomorrow, Mother Carey's Chickens, Young Tom Edison, Our Town, Journey For Margaret, State Fair, Give My Regards to Broadway* and *The Children's Hour*.

GEORGE BANCROFT *(1882–Oct. 2, 1956)*
The "smiling villain" began his screen career portraying the menace in many of Tom Mix's westerns in 1925. Born in Philadelphia, he enterred the U.S. Naval Academy and served under Admiral Dewey in the Spanish American War.

George Bancroft, center, with James Cagney and Humphrey Bogart in Angels with Dirty Faces.

After leaving the navy he operated a nickelodeon then turned to acting. While in vaudeville he had an act with Fred Allen. He then turned to the legitimate stage, appearing on Broadway in *Paid in Full, The Trail of the Lonesome Pine,* and *Sun-Up*. Musical comedy followed with Bancroft (singing baritone) featured in *Papa's Boy, Cinders,* and others. There then followed his long career in silent and talking motion pictures. He retired from pictures and turned to ranching

in 1942. Among his film credits were *Mr. Deeds Goes to Town, Thunderbolt, Blood Money, Angels with Dirty Faces,* and *Submarine Patrol*.

GEORGE BARBIER *(1864–July 19, 1945)*
A veteran actor of more than 100 screen roles, noted on the screen chiefly for his portrayal of businessmen and fathers. Originally, Barbier prepared for a career in the ministry but became interested in acting while appearing in a seminary pageant. His early acting career took place

George Barbier, with Brenda Joyce in Marry the Boss's Daughter.

in the theatre where he played several hundred stage roles. He first appeared in films beginning in 1930 and subsequently appeared in productions for all the major studios. Some of his many films included *The Crusades, Million Dollar Baby, The Return of Frank James, Marry the Boss' Daughter,* and *Weekend in Havana*.

ROY BARCROFT *(1902–Nov. 28, 1969)*
Playing heavies most of the time, Roy Barcroft appeared in more than 200 film credits with such stars as Bill Boyd, Buck Jones, Gene Autry, Roy Rogers, John Wayne, and Bill Elliott. Born into a family of Nebraska pioneers, he did not turn to acting until he was 35 years old. His first pic-

Fay Bainter

ture was *Mata Hari* (1930), being cast as a soldier extra. He liked it so well he decided to make it a career. Though he had no favorite role he enjoyed playing villains the most. In his own

Roy Barcroft

words, "Give me a good dirty-bearded part where I can drop my 'ing's and sleep on a jail cot." A few of his many films included *The Spoilers, Man Without a Star, Oklahoma, Montana Belle, Old Overland Trail* and *Rogue Cop*.

Trevor Bardette

TREVOR BARDETTE *(1902–Nov. 28, 1977)*
A graduate of Oregon University and Northwestern University, Bardette intended to be a mechanical engineer but was sidetracked into drama through course work while in college. He began his acting career in New York in a musical called *Flossie*. Various other stage engagements continued until 1936 when he went to Hollywood and took up a screen career. Cast usually as a heavy, he was killed over 40 times in pictures. An outstanding event which he recalled from his childhood days was winning a $10 prize for writing an essay on the evils of tobacco, only to be caught behind the schoolhouse smoking corn silk with a bunch of other boys. A few of the many screen credits include *The Big Sleep, None Shall Escape, Tomorrow I Die, Topper Returns, Apache Trail, Dark Command,* and *The Moon Is Down.*

VINCE BARNETT *(1902–Aug. 10, 1977)*
The son of Luke Barnett, the greatest ribber of his day, Vince began his career as a "stand-in" for his father. His success prompted him to leave Carnegie Tech, where he was studying aero-

Vince Barnett

nautical engineering, and strike out his own. Ribbing professionally led to New York and the *Earl Carrol Vanities* in 1926–27, then across country to Hollywood. Barnett had comedy parts in over 150 motion pictures including *Scarface, The Virginian, Big Town After Dark, Little Miss Broadway, Joe Palooka in the Knockout, Big Jack, Princess O'Hara, The Killers, Black Fury, Tiger Shark,* and *The Big Cage.*

FLORENCE BATES (1888–Jan. 31, 1954)

Variety was the spice of life for Florence Bates. She was engaged in nine different careers in her lifetime. Born in San Antonio, Texas, Miss Bates received her basic education there and then went on to college. She was involved at one time or

Florence Bates, with S. Z. (Cuddles) Sakall in Lullaby of Broadway.

another in teaching, law (admitted to the bar in 1914), managing of an antique shop, oil drilling, bakery managing, and acting. While en-

rolled at the Pasadena Playhouse she was picked for a role in *Rebecca* and clicked immediately. Following her film debut she worked in numerous films, playing various types of dowagers, with a spattering of dialect characters. One of her cardinal theories of life was: "Never underestimate the intelligence of an opponent, an audience, or a child. Whenever you do, you get your come-uppance and you jolly well deserve it." Included in her many film credits in addition to *Rebecca* are *Tuttles of Tahiti, Hudson's Bay, The Chocolate Soldier, The Moon and Sixpence, My Heart Belongs to Daddy, Saratoga Trunk, The Mask of Dimitrios, Kismet, The Secret Life of Walter Mitty,* and *The Brasher Doubloon.*

LOUISE BEAVERS (1902–Oct. 26, 1962)

Louise Beavers, best known as "Beulah" for the TV show, was born in Cincinnati. The family moved to Pasadena, California, in 1913 where

Louise Beavers, with Sir Guy Standing in Annapolis Farewell.

she finished high school. She became a personal maid to Leatrice Joy, then a star. In 1926 Miss Beavers left Miss Joy and joined a *Ladies' Minstrel Troupe.* Studio scouts saw her and she was given a part in *Uncle Tom's Cabin.* Following this appearance she worked steadily in pictures. Miss Beavers had parts in *She Done Him Wrong, Ladies of the Big House, Dr. Monica, Merry Frinks,* and *Imitation of Life.*

31

DON BEDDOE (1888–)

Don Beddoe spent most of his boyhood in New York and later Cincinnati where his father was head of the voice department at Cincinnati Conservatory of Music. Beddoe graduated from Cincinnati, specializing in journalism, and he also

Don Beddoe

did little theater work. His first professional job was with Stuart Walker's repertory company and his Broadway debut was with Spencer Tracy in *Nigger Rich*. Like many other recruits from the stage Beddoe had an early experience in silent pictures and made his talking debut in *There's Always a Woman*. His pictures include *Golden Boy, Men Without Souls, Blind Alley, The Doctor Takes a Wife, The Best Years of Our Lives, The Farmer's Daughter, Cyrano de Bergerac, Calcutta* and more recently *Pillow Talk, The Boy Who Found a Million*, and *Texas Across the River*.

ALFONSO BEDOYA (1904–Dec. 15, 1957)

Bedoya made his film debut in the Mexican movies where he became a favorite character actor with no less than 175 pictures to his credit. His American film debut occurred in the part of *Gold Hat*, the giggling bandit chieftain in *Treasure of the Sierra Madre*. Born in the village of Vicam in the Mexican state of Sonora, he spent

Alfonso Bedoya, in Streets of Laredo.

his first fourteen years roving all over Mexico. He was sent to Houston, Texas, to attend private school, but finding it dull, quit school. He then went to work at various odd jobs until returned to Mexico City by his brother. When finally old enough to make his own decisions he entered acting. His quick success proved his decision to be correct. Other films in which he appeared were *The Streets of Laredo, The Big Country, Border Incident, Ricochet Romance*, and *Man in the Saddle*.

ED BEGLEY (1901–Apr. 28, 1970)

Ed Begley was born of Irish immigrant parents in Hartford, Connecticut. He started doing an amateur act at the age of nine, did the end man in minstrel shows and dramatic work with small community groups. He applied and was accepted at radio station WTIC in Hartford, performing with a dramatic stock company. After ten years of doing every conceivable type of role he accepted a job as announcer on the Blue Network station WNBC in Hartford. In September of 1943, he stormed the citadels of New York radio, stage, and television as well as dubbing foreign films into English. In 1947 he went to California and was involved in film work while commuting to New York until his death. His many films included *Boomerang*, *Deep Waters*, *Sitting Pretty*, *Street with No Name*, *Sorry, Wrong Number*, *The Great Gatsby*, *It Happens Every Spring*, *Backfire*, *Stars in My Crown*, *Tulsa*, *The Turning Point*, *Boots Malone*, *The Green Helmet*, and *Deadline U.S.A.* His favorite roles were as Boss Finley in *Sweet Bird of Youth*, as Debbie Reynold's father in *The Unsinkable Molly Brown*, and as Juror #10 in *Twelve Angry Men*.

High School. In 1935 he appeared as the tousled office boy in the Fox picture *$10 Raise* starring Edward Everett Horton. From 1935 to 1950 Benedict appeared in over 150 pictures, serials and two-reel comedies. In addition to his first screen role, his role as office boy in *The Witness Chair* in 1936 is among his favorites. Among his many film credits are *Doubting Thomas*, *Ramona*, *Libeled Lady*, *Laughing at Trouble*, *Hold That Coed*, *King of the Newsboys*, *Ox Bow Incident*, and the *East Side Kids* series, and the *Bowery Boys* series.

William Benedict, front center, with David Gorcey, Harris Berger, Hally Chester, Charles Thomas, and Frankie Thomas in Little Tough Guys in Society.

Ed Begley, in The Unsinkable Molly Brown.

WILLIAM "BILLY" BENEDICT (1917–)
William Benedict is a native of Haskell, Oklahoma, and was raised in Tulsa. He studied dancing at an early age with Irene Frank and the was active in school plays at Tulsa Central

RICHARD BENNETT (1873–Oct. 21, 1944)
Born in Deacon's Mills, Indiana, Bennett attended schools at Logansport and Kokomo and made his first stage appearance at the Standard Theater, Chicago, in 1891 as Tombstone Jake in *The Limited Mail*. His first Broadway appearance was in the same play at Niblo's Garden later that year. He was the father of Constance,

Richard Bennett, left, with George Raft in If I Had a Million.

Joan and Barbara Bennett, all of whom won screen success. He began his film career in 1913, and played in upward of 50 motion pictures, usually between stage engagements. His career was marked by tempestuous happenings and his ad-lib speeches in front of the curtain won greater applause than many of the plays in which he acted. Of Hollywood he said, "It is not a business but a madhouse."

Clem Bevans, in Rim of the Canyon.

CLEM BEVANS (1879–Aug. 11, 1963)

Bevans was born in Cozaddale, Ohio,, attended school in Columbus. After working in several amateur shows, in 1900, he joined Gracie Emmett in a vaudeville sketch. After several seasons with Miss Emmett he joined Nellie McHenry and later R.E. Johnston in various productions. Subsequently he played stock, light opera and then tried burlesque. After several shows on the Broadway stage and traveling the leading vaudeville circuits he went to Hollywood in 1935 where

he played his first motion picture role as Doc Wiggin in *Way Down East*. Bevans appeared in innumerable parts on the screen including *Big City, Of Human Hearts, Abe Lincoln in Illinois, 20 Mule Team, Thunder Afloat, She Couldn't Say No, Sergeant York, Happy Go Lucky, Woman of the Town, Grissly's Millions,* and *Night Work.*

Abner Biberman

ABNER BIBERMAN (1909–June 20, 1977)

Abner Biberman's ambition was to direct comedy. But somehow he found himself committed to acting. He was born in Milwaukee and moved to Philadelphia, at an early age. In Philadelphia he became in apprentice in Jasper Dieter's Hedgerow Theater. Following parts in Ibsen, Shaw, O'Neill, he moved on to New York where he worked with the Group Theater. Following his stage debut he went on to write, direct, and coach dramatics. His many pictures include *Gunga Din, The Rains Came, Zanzibar, Strange Conquest, Elephant Walk, Gay Vagabond,* and *Knock on Wood.*

Herman Bing, in Adventure in Manhattan.

Sidney Blackmer, left, with Jack Lemmon in How to Murder Your Wife.

HERMAN BING *(1889–Jan. 9, 1947)*

Bing was born in Frankfurt, Germany, and received an education along musical lines. At the age of 16 he joined a stock company from which he went into vaudeville and then into a circus as a clown. He then became interested in silent pictures and learned the production end under F.W. Murnau. For several years he served as assistant to Murnau, Borzage, John Ford, Schertzinger and others. In 1927 he turned to acting, with such success he became in immediate demand as a characterr actor. His American film debut was in *A Song of Kentucky*. His penchant for dialects resulted in his playing in more than a score of pictures, among them *The Merry Widow, 20th Century, Call of the Wild*, and *Where Do We Go from Here?*

SIDNEY BLACKMER *(1895–Oct. 5, 1973)*

Blackmer, a prolific performer, was graduated from the University of North Carolina. While trying to crack the Broadway stage, he accepted acting jobs at Ft. Lee, New Jersey, and other silent film centers, appearing in such serials as *The Perils of Pauline*, and *The Million Dollar Mystery*. He sang on radio and in television took part in DuMont's first dramatic program. Blackmer's latter-day career as a film heavy began with *The Cocktail Hour* in 1933. In *This Is My*

Clara Blandick, left, with Lee Patrick in The Nurse's Secret.

Affair in 1937 began the Teddy Roosevelt era. Blackmer played Roosevelt 14 times with many opportunities to do more. His busy film career led to roles in *Sweethearts and Wives, Count of Monte Cristo, The Little Colonel, In Old Chicago, Trade Winds, Duel in the Sun, My Girl Tisa, Song Is Born*, and *Rosemary's Baby*.

CLARA BLANDICK *(1881–Apr. 15, 1962)*

Miss Blandick was a veteran of the stage for a quarter of a century before her screen debut. Henry Duffy, a director, brought her to Hollywood in the late 1920's. Her first role was in MGM's *Wise Girl*. She is probably best remembered for playing the role of Judy Garland's aunt in *The Wizard of Oz*, and Aunt Polly in *Tom Sawyer*. Other motion pictures in which she appeared were *Stolen Life, Pillow of Death, People Are Funny*, and *Claudia and David*.

Eric Blore, in Quality Street.

ERIC BLORE *(1887–Mar. 1, 1959)*

Eric Blore was a "gentleman's gentleman" on the stage and screen for fifty years. His combined lifted eyebrow and petulant pout became a trade mark that made him world-famous. Born in London, he left college to enter the business world. After two years he gave up the business world for the stage where he achieved a solid reputation in London and New York. With the purchase of *The Gay Divorcee* by RKO, Blore was brought to Hollywood which was quick to

35

appreciate his talents. He appeared in more than 75 pictures from 1933–1955 a few of which included *Flying Down to Rio, Diamond Jim, Smartest Girl in Town, Breakfast for Two, Swiss Miss, The Boys from Syracuse, Road to Zanzibar, The Moon and Sixpence, Two Sisters from Boston, Abie's Irish Rose, Fancy Pants,* and many of the *Lone Wolf* series.

MONTE BLUE *(1890–Feb. 18, 1963)*

Monte Blue, born in Indianapolis, spent his early years in an orphanage and during his pre-film days, worked as a coal miner, lumberjack, cowboy, and circus roustabout. In 1915 he was hired by D.W. Griffith as a script clerk, stunt man and actor. He appeared in several of Griffith's films. He remained active throughout the silent era and successfully survived the transition to sound where he received calls for character roles. With many screen credits, he alternated, in recent years, between film and TV roles, acting as a special envoy for the Shrine Circus. His many film credits included *College Rhythm, High Wide and Handsome, Cocoanut Grove, Panama Hattie, Thousands Cheer, Two Sisters from Boston, Easy to Wed,* and *My Wild Irish Rose.*

Monte Blue

ROMAN BOHNEN *(1901–Feb. 24, 1949)*

Short, stocky and blue-eyed, Bohnen was one of the most versatile of character actors both on the screen and in the legitimate theatre. He first arrived in Hollywood in 1937 and made his first appearance in the movie *Vogues of 1938.* Bohnen was one of the driving forces behind the con-

Roman Bohnen, center, with Joe Sawyer in Kazan.

troversial Actors Lab, in whose production of *Distant Isle* he died while on stage. He is perhaps best known for his role as the father in *The Song of Bernadette.* Other pictures in which he appeared were *Of Mice and Men, The Hairy Ape, Two Years Before the Mast,* and *Best Years of Our Lives.*

Mary Boland, with Charlie Ruggles in Boy Trouble.

Beulah Bondi, in So Dear to My Heart.

MARY BOLAND *(1880–June 23, 1965)*

Noted for character parts in which she played a fluttery dowager or a zanily doting mother,

Veda Ann Borg

Alice Brady, with Charles Winninger in Goodbye
Broadway.

Mary Boland's career included silent movies,
talkies, and stage roles. Miss Boland was born
in Philadelphia. She began her acting career in
Detroit while still a teenager. She served her apprenticeship as an actress in a number of cities
and in touring the country. Her New York debut
took place in 1905. It was not until 1919,
however that she played her first ladylike scat-
terbrain. Following a long run in *Face the Music*
she went to Hollywood. Many films followed,
including *Ruggles of Red Gap*, *Here Comes the
Groom*, *Pride and Prejudice*, *People Will Talk*,
The Women, *Julia Misbehaves*, and *One Night
in the Tropics*.

BEULAH BONDI *(1892–Jan. 11, 1981)*
Beulah Bondi played little Lord Fauntleroy
when she was seven, and thirteen years later was
playing a grandmother. She was an "old lady"
on the stage after that. Miss Bondi was born in
Chicago into a family with no theatrical tradi-

tion. Her mother trained her in elocution and
suggested the possibility of a stage career. Her
first stage appearance was in Valparaiso, Indiana, in *Little Lord Fauntleroy*, at the age of
nine. After leaving college (Valparaiso University, BA and MA) she went into stock. She
reached Broadway in 1925 in a play called *Wild
Birds*. A succession of roles followed, one of
which led to Hollywood as Mrs. Jones in *Street
Scene*, and with the exception of several plays
on Broadway and some television remained
there. She has found wide diversity in her
characters, even if they had all been old. A few
of her picture credits included *The Gorgeous
Hussy*, *Mr. Smith Goes to Washington*, *Our
Town*, *One Foot in Heaven*, *Watch on the
Rhine*, *Our Hearts Were Young and Gay*, *So
Dear to My Heart*, *The Snake Pit*, and *Track of
the Cat*.

VEDA ANN BORG *(1919–Aug. 16, 1973)*
Born in Roxbury, Massachusetts, Miss Borg had
never been on stage or radio when signed to the
movies. She was a New York model until Paramount tested her and signed her to a contract.
Her first major role was that of Vivian Blaine's
showgirl friend in *Guys and Dolls*. Other films
included *Three Cheers for Love* (debut), *Big
Town*, *Confession*, *Mother Wore Tights*, *One
Last Fling*, *Bachelor and the Bobby-Soxer*, *Forgotten Women*, and *Three Sailors and a Girl*.

ALICE BRADY *(1892–Oct. 28, 1939)*
Born in New York City and graduated from a
convent, Alice Brady arrived professionally with
a great theatrical tradition behind her. She made
her debut in her father's production, *The Balkan
Princess*. After that she appeared in most of the
Gilbert and Sullivan productions, becoming a
dramatic actress for the first time in *Little
Women*. She later appeared in a number of stage
plays and films including *Goodbye Broadway*,
and *Young Mr. Lincoln*.

EL BRENDEL *(1891–Apr. 9, 1964)*
El Brendel, a Swedish-dialect comedian parlayed
his expression "yumpin yiminy" into fame. His
career encompassed virtually every facet of show
business during its 51 years. He was actually born
in Philadelphia and attended the University of

El Brendel, with Jane Withers and Leah Ray in The Holy Terror.

Walter Brennan, in Red River.

Pennsylvania. His theatrical career was launched in 1913 in vaudeville. Later he left the variety stage for several years of Shubert musical shows. Brendel turned to the silent screen in 1926 and to talkies in 1929. He was best known for his role in the 1931 film *Just Imagine*. Among other movies in which he appeared were *Meanest Girl in Town*, *If I Had My Way*, *Captain Caution*, *Gallant Sons*, *Paris Model*, and *Beautiful Blonde from Bashful Bend*.

WALTER BRENNAN (1894–Sept. 21, 1974)
Walter Brennan held the distinction of being the first film actor to win the Academy Award three times. Brennan's background and education pointed toward anything but acting. Born in Swampscott, Massachusetts, he graduated with a degree in engineering. While at college he became active in theatrical activities. He then decided to concentrate on the theatre and went into small-time musical comedy and vaudeville, touring the east and mid-west. After service in World War I, raising pineapples in Guatemala, and real estate speculation in Los Angeles, he was signed by Samuel Goldwyn to play the role of Jenkins in *The Wedding Night*. His next role was in *Barbary Coast*. From then on, Brennan scored time after time in pictures such as *The Texans*, *Meet John Doe*, *Sergeant York*, *Pride of the Yankees*, *North Star*, *Home in Indiana*, *Nobody Lives Forever*, *Dakota*, *Scudda Hoo, Scudda Hay*, *Blood on the Moon*, and his Oscar pictures, *Come and Get It*, *Kentucky*, and *The Westerner*.

Felix Bressart, second from left, with Alexander Granach, Sig Ruman and Edwin Maxwell in Ninotchka.

FELIX BRESSART (1895–Mar. 17, 1949)
Born in Eydtkuhnen, Germany, and educated in Berlin, Bressart made his stage debut in 1914 in *Twelfth Night*. Before coming to the United States in 1936 he appeared in some forty German films. For many years he was under contract to MGM and seen in a long list of pictures, notably *Ninotchka*, *Crossroads*, *Comrade X*, *The Seventh Cross*, *Greenwich Village*, *Above Suspicion*, *Mr. and Mrs. North*, *Bitter Sweet*, *Escape*, *Edison the Man*, and *A Song Is Born*.

HARLAN BRIGGS (1879–Jan. 26, 1952)
A veteran stage actor, Briggs began his film career in 1935 when, with Walter Huston, he went to Hollywood to make the picture *Dodsworth*, the play in which they had appeared on

38

Broadway for three years. Among the many films in which this character actor appeared were *Dodsworth, Mad Holiday, A Family Affair, Live, Love and Learn, Riding on Air, Reckless Living, A Man to Remember,* and *The Mysterious Miss X.*

HELEN BRODERICK *(1891–Sept. 25, 1959)*
Miss Broderick began her acting career at the age of fourteen, as a chorus girl. Born in Philadelphia, she was educated in the public schools of that city and Boston. Her parents did not want her to follow the theatrical tradition of the family, but she never considered any other career. At an early age she became one of Ziegfeld's famed Follies beauties. Later she appeared in such Broadway hits as *The Band Wagon,* and *As Thousands Cheer.* Miss Broderick arrived in Hollywood in 1935 for a role in *Top Hat,* star-

Helen Broderick, in Nice Girl?

Harlan Briggs, left, with Humphrey Bogart and Patrick O'Moore in Conflict.

ring Fred Astaire and Ginger Rogers, and stayed on to become a well-known comedienne and character actress. She was cast in many films including *Fifty Million Frenchmen, Top Hat, The Bride Walks Out, Swing Time, Smartest Girl in Town, Meet the Missus, The Rage of Paris, The Road to Reno* and *Stand Up and Fight.*

J. EDWARD BROMBERG *(1903–Dec. 6, 1951)*
Bromberg was a veteran actor of both stage and screen. He started his career as a silk salesman, candy manufacturer and laundry worker. He then studied acting under Leo Bulgakov of the Moscow Art Theatre and commenced his acting career in 1926 in the Greenwich Village playhouse. His career continued on the stage until

J. Edward Bromberg, left, with Andrew Toombes in Fair Warning.

1936 when he went to Hollywood. He was signed by Fox and appeared in many films. He returned to the Broadway stage on several occasions. His film credits include *Under Two Flags, Seventh Heaven, Rebecca of Sunnybrook Farm, Suez, Jesse James, Arch of Triumph,* and *A Song Is Born.*

Lillian Bronson

LILLIAN BRONSON *(1902–   )*
Lillian Bronson, born in Lockport, New York, trained for her career by playing almost every part available in campus dramatics at the University of Michigan. After graduation she went to New York where she studied at the American Laboratory Theatre. This led the way to Broadway, summer stock, and the Spring Festival at Ann Arbor. Her first film was *Happy Land* in 1943 and subsequently has been featured in over 78 films, including *A Tree Grows in Brooklyn, The Next Voice You Hear,* and *The Hucksters.*

EDWARD BROPHY *(1895–May 27, 1960)*
With poppy eyes and extremely mobile features, Edward Brophy usually portrayed the earthy, but not too scrupulous character. A part typical of Brophy was that of the ward-heeling politician in *The Last Hurrah.* Born in New York, he was educated at the University of Virginia. He appeared in his first film in 1919 in New York and went to Hollywood in 1929. For a time he

Edward Brophy, in Thin Man.

was in the production end of the business, but in 1934 began acting again. He appeared in the original *Thin Man, The Great Profile, Calling Philo Vance, The Falcon's Adventure, It Happened on Fifth Avenue, Sweetheart of Sigma Chi* and countless other films.

NIGEL BRUCE *(1895–Oct. 8, 1953)*

Though Nigel Bruce appeared in over 70 films, he was best known for his portrayal of Dr. Watson in the *Sherlock Homes* series. He also characterized the doctor in radio from 1938-45. The son of a Scottis baronet, Bruce was born in Ensenada, Mexico. He was educated in England where he debuted on the London stage in 1920. Dozens of plays followed and he was established as a "Colonel Blimp" type of comedian. Bruce made his screen debut in England in 1928, play-

Nana Bryant, with Otto Kruger in Counsel for Crime.

Nigel Bruce, right, with Basil Rathbone in The Hound of the Baskervilles.

ing in four pictures and his first American motion picture, *Coming Out Party*, in 1934. His long list of film credits includes such pictures as *This Above All, Hudson's Bay, Charge of the Light Brigade, Lillian Russell, The Rains Came, Trail of the Lonesome Pine, Kidnapped, I Was a Spy, Rebecca, Becky Sharp*, and *Exile*.

NANA BRYANT *(1888–Dec. 24, 1955)*

Miss Bryant's career spanned 50 years, from touring stock companies to television. She appeared on Broadway between 1925 and 1935 in some of the outstanding musicals and comedies. From 1935 on, when she went to Hollywood, she appeared steadily before the cameras with time out for roles in *Roberta* and *Song of Norway* and later on the television program *Our Miss Brooks*. Included in her many screen roles were *A Feather in Her Hat, Crime and Punishment,*

One Way Ticket, Lady of Secrets, Panic on the Air, The Lone Wolf Returns, Blackmailer, Meet Nero Wolf and *The Private War of Major Benson*.

EDGAR BUCHANAN *(1903–April 4, 1979)*

Edgar Buchanan was born in Humansville, Missouri. When he was seven his family moved to Oregon. After attending the University of Oregon he followed in his father's footsteps and became a dentist, graduating from North Pacific Dental College. From 1929 to 1937 he was the head of oral surgery in Eugene, Oregon. Buchanan moved his practice to California and joined the Pasadena Community Playhouse and gave up dentistry at the age of 36 to become an actor. The popular, gravelly voiced actor made his first film in 1939. He is probably best remembered as Uncle Joe on television's "Petticoat Junction," but also had the title role on "Judge Roy Bean," was Hoppy's sidekick, Red Connors, on "Hoppalong Cassidy" and was Deputy J.J. Jackson on "Cade's County." His films included *Penny Serenade, Renegades, Any Number Can Play, Cheaper By the Dozen, Shane, Move Over, Darling, McLintock!*, and *Benji*.

LESTER ALVIN "SMILEY" BURNETTE *(1911–Feb. 16, 1967)*

"Smiley" Burnette made nearly two hundred western movies. Born in Summurn, Illinois, he made his movie debut in 1934 and went on to

Edgar Buchanan.

42

become one of the highest paid western entertainers. He made 81 movies with Gene Autry, providing comic relief, and in addition wrote over 300 songs, more than half of which were used in movies in which he appeared. His most popular pieces were *My Lazy Day*, *My Home Town*, and *Hominy Grits*. He was also a sidekick to Roy Rogers in seven pictures and appeared in many with Charles Starrett in the *Durango Kid* series. In recent years he played the railroad engineer in *Petticoat Junction* on TV.

"Smiley" Burnette in Ridin' the Outlaw Trail.

Charles Butterworth, with Carole Landis in Road Show.

CHARLES BUTTERWORTH *(1899–June 13, 1946)*

Charles Butterworth made a career on the stage and in motion pictures characterizing the man who couldn't make up his mind, the vacillating, indecisive sort of follower-of-the-crowd. Born in South Bend, Indiana, and graduated from Notre Dame, Butterworth turned to newspaper reporting. He was attracted to acting but found acting jobs scarce and continued with newspaper work. He was finally signed by Richard Herndon to play in *Americana*. Butterworth was then featured in several Broadway musicals: *Alley Oop*, *Good Boy*, *Sweet Adeline*, and *Flying Colors*. He made his film debut in *The Life of the Party* in 1930, and went on to appear in over thirty films including *The Cat and the Fiddle*, *The Magnificent Obsession*, *Swing High, Swing Low*, *The Boys from Syracuse*, *Let Freedom Ring*, *This Is the Army*, and *Follow the Boys*.

SPRING BYINGTON *(1886–Sept. 7, 1971)*

Colorado Springs was Miss Byington's birthplace. Her parents were nontheatrical and left her orphaned at an early age. She started her career at age fourteen in Denver as a member of the famed Elitch Garden Stock Company. There followed a series of one-night stands with touring troups. Finally, George S. Kaufman and

Spring Byington, with Frank Morgan.

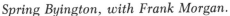

Marc Connelly cast her for her first New York hit. After some 30 New York plays, Miss Byington made her motion picture debut in *Little Women*. Her many picture credits inluded *Mutiny on the Bounty, Ah Wilderness, Dragonwyck, Singapore, Angels in the Outfield, B.F.'s Daughter, My Brother Talks to Horses, In the Good Old Summertime, Big Wheel, Walk Softly, Stranger*, and *It Had to Be You*. In recent years Miss Byington also appeared in televison on *December Bride* and *Laramie* as a star and co-star of those series respectively.

LOUIS CALHERN (1895–May 12, 1956)

Louis Calhern was one of America's most distinguished actors of both stage and screen. His many roles as a wise and witty raconteur dressed like a Wall Street broker with his theater-trained voice kept him in constant demand in films for many years. His films included *Affairs of Cellini, Count of Monte Cristo, Last Days of Pompeii, The Life of Emile Zola, Juarez, Notorious, Annie Get Your Gun, The Asphalt Jungle, Julius Caesar, Executive Suite, The Student Prince, The Prodigal, Blackboard Jungle*, and *High Society*.

Louis Calhern, in Invitation.

JOSEPH CALLEIA (1897–Oct. 31, 1975)

Joseph Calleia was one of the most versatile and colorful actors in films. A native of the island of Malta, Calleia was most famous for his portrayals of villains with homicidal tendencies and as Mediterranean nationals. After a successful career as a singer on the European/Broadway concert stage, he made his motion picture debut in 1935. His first portrayal in films was as Sunny Black in *Public Hero No. 1*. Among his favorite roles were the Inspector in *Algiers*, El Sardo in *For Whom the Bell Tolls*, Fuseli in *Golden Boy*, Father Loma in *Full Confession*, and Nick the Greek in *Riff Raff* with Jean Harlow. His other films include *Juarez, Marie Antoinette, Gilda, The Cross of Lorraine, Iron Mistress, Underwater*, and *Littlest Outlaw*.

HARRY CAREY (1878–Sept. 21, 1947)

Harry Carey probably made more movies than any other star or feature player in pictures. He played in the first western movies ever made, filmed on Staten Island. Before and after talk-

Joseph Calleia

Harry Carey

Richard Carle

ing pictures his career had a number of ups and downs, with recurrent comebacks in films that set him up as one of the most "re-discovered" actors in Hollywood. Most of his parts were those of the kind of men who made the West. His pictures included *Trader Horn, Slide Kelly, Slide, The Last Outlaw, Kid Galahad, Mr. Smith Goes to Washington, The Shepherd of the Hills, Parachute Battalion, Sundown,* and *Air Force.*

RICHARD CARLE *(1871–June 28, 1941)*
Born in Somerville, Massachusetts, Richard Carle was on the stage in America and England before entering pictures in 1916. Among his many pictures were *Moonlight in Hawaii, The Devil and Miss Jones, One Night in the Tropics, Seven Sinners,* and *The Dangerous Game.*

ALAN CARNEY *(1909–May 2, 1973)*
Alan Carney was one of the screen's top character impersonators. His first screen break came as The Crunk, the slow-witted but loyal bodyguard to Cary Grant in *Mr. Luck.* Among his other films were *The Girl Rush, Step Lively, Seven Days Ashore, Radio Stars on Parade,* and *Zombies on Broadway.*

JOHN CARRADINE *(1906–   )*
John Carradine is a super villain who is equipped with a lean and saturnine countenance and a vibrant voice that drips with menace. Although a trained Shakespearean actor, he built much of his film career upon his ability to portray men of psychopathic irregularities. His portrayal of the preacher in *The Grapes of Wrath* is unforgettable. Among his other films are *Kidnapped, The Hound of the Baskervilles, Brigham Young, Stagecoach, Winterset, Hurricane, Garden of Allah, Fallen Angel, House of Frankenstein,* and *Captain Kidd.*

LEO CARRILLO *(1881–Sept. 10, 1961)*
Leo Carrillo was born in Los Angeles. He was a descendant of California's first governor. His early careers included that of a newspaper cartoonist and a monologist in vaudeville. He made his first Broadway appearance in 1915 and his first film in 1928. Carrillo played a variety of roles but was at his best when the role called for fractured English. He became well known to generations of youngsters as "Pancho" in the Cisco Kid TV series as well as films opposite Duncan Renaldo. His films included *Men Are Such Fools, Viva Villa!, Manhattan Melodrama, The Gay Desperado, City Streets, Blockade, Fisherman's Wharf, Chicken Wagon Family, Lillian Russell* and *Danger in the Pacific.*

Alan Carney

John Carradine

Leo Carrillo in Under Western Skies.

Ben Carter, kneeling at center, with Clarence Muse, Hattie McDaniel and Ernest Whitman in Maryland.

LEO CARROLL *(1886–Oct. 16, 1972)*

Born in Weedon, England, Leo G. Carroll had a long and distinguished career as a character actor. His film portrayals through the 1930's and 1940's were usually as extremely shy and timid Englishmen. His long list of film credits included *Barretts of Wimpole Street, Rebecca, Waterloo Bridge, Clive of India, Spellbound, A Christmas Carol, Wuthering Heights. The Paradine Case,* and *Tower of London.*

ANTHONY CARUSO ( )

Anthony Caruso is one of the screen's finest portrayers of Italian gangsters, Mexicans, Latins, and occasionally Arabs. His first break in the movies was in 1940 in *Johnny Apollo* starring the late Tyrone Power. Caruso was cast as a mobster.

Leo G. Carroll

Anthony Caruso, left, with Will Rogers Jr.

BEN CARTER *(1911–Dec. 10, 1946)*

Ben Carter was a wide-eyed Negro comedian with a brush of crinkly black hair which gave him an air of perpetual surprise. He was with CBS three years on the *Happy-Go-Lucky* radio hour. His pictures included *Little Old New York, Gone With the Wind, Safari, Maryland, Chad Hanna, Tin Pan Alley, Ride on, Vaquero, Crash Dive,* and *The Harvey Girls.*

WALTER CATLETT *(1889–Nov. 14, 1960)*

Walter Catlett made his film debut in 1929 and for many years was characterized as a fidgety, google-eyed comic in scores of roles. He was once described as a "low and wonderful American comedian." He made his New York debut in 1911 at the Lyric Theater in *The Prince of Pilsen.* Florenz Ziegfeld signed him for *Sally* and he played in that show with Marilyn Miller for three seasons. He appeared in films ranging from

Walter Catlett, in Henry, the Rain Maker.

heavy drama such as *A Tale of Two Cities*, to heavy comedy such as *The Inspector General*. His other screen credits included: *Up in Arms, Mr. Deeds Goes to Town, Riverboat Rhythm, I'll Be Yours, Look for the Silver Lining, Dancing in the Dark,* and *Friendly Persuasion*.

Paul Cavanagh with Phyllis Barry in Shadows on the Stairs.

PAUL CAVANAGH (1888–Mar. 15, 1964)
Paul Cavanagh often portrayed British gentlemen, but also was frequently cast as an unsavory villain. Born in Chislehurst, Kent, England, he was active on the stage in both Europe and America before receiving a Hollywood contract in 1938. Among his films are *Humoresque, Madame Bovary, The Desert Fox, Hollywood Story, Mississippi Gambler, Flame of Calcutta, Man in Half Moon Street,* and *Woman in Green*.

HOBART CAVANAUGH (1886–Apr. 25, 1950)
Born in Virginia City, Nevada, Hobart Cavanaugh was the son of a railroading engineer. He was educated in San Francisco schools and at the University of California where he studied engineering. Among his school friends were Walter Catlett, Charles Ruggles, Lou Holtz, and William Gaxton. After a successful stage career he accepted a film contract in 1932. During the next seventeen years he appeared in 120 films. He was in constant demand, particularly for character roles of the "milquetoast" variety, of which he made a specialty. Often appearing as a henpecked husband or a harried bookkeeper, his face was familiar to millions of moviegoers. His last screen appearance was in *Stella*, in which he played an undertaker. Among his other pictures were *I Cover the Waterfront, Captain Blood, Midsummer Night's Dream, Margie, Driftwood, Best Man Wins, Kismet,* and *Two Against the World*.

Hobart Cavanaugh, in Rose of Washington Square.

WILLIAM CHALLEE (1912–   )
William Challee planned to be a newspaper reporter, but activities around Chicago, Illinois, theaters created a taste for show business. His first important Broadway play was the title role in the Jed Harris production of *Wonder Boy* in

William Challee, in Seven Days in May.

which he was featured with Gregory Ratoff. He was brought to Hollywood in 1943 to appear in *Destination Tokyo* with Cary Grant and John Garfield. Challee has appeared in many roles since, his favorite roles being those of reporters and gangsters. His pictures include *Boomerang, Deadline at Dawn, Nocturne, Days of Glory, None but the Lonely Heart, Sea of Grass,* and *The Seventh Cross.*

LON CHANEY Jr. *(1906–July 12, 1973)*
Like his famous father before him, Lon Chaney Jr. was one of the screen's greatest "monsters."

Lon Chaney Jr.

Among his favorite roles were a classic portrayal of Lennie in *Of Mice and Men,* and the ill-fated Lawrence Talbot—"The Wolf Man." Other films included *Son of Dracula, The Mummy's Curse, One Million B.C., Life of Jesse James, High Noon,* and *Union Pacific.*

GEORGE CHANDLER *(1902–)*
Born in Waukegan, Illinois, George Chandler turned vaudevillian at seventeen but still graduated from the University of Illinois. He arrived in Hollywood in 1927 and made his first feature film, *Floradora Girl* with Marion Davies. Chandler has played in hundreds of films and was cast as "Uncle Petrie" in the *Lassie* series on TV. He has played a large variety of character roles, and is seen quite often in the role of a newspaper reporter. Chandler has also held numerous offices in the Screen Actors Guild. His films include *Strange Conquest, Black Angel, Perfect Stranger, Pretty Baby, Island in the Sky,* and *The High and the Mighty.*

George Chandler, left, with Charles Laughton in The Girl from Manhattan.

BERTON CHURCHILL *(1876–Oct. 10, 1940)*
Berton Churchill was widely recognized as one of Hollywood's most versatile players of small parts. He was most often cast as a bluff, hearty

businessman or as a pompous, smalltown "leading citizen," the easy prey of conniving strangers from the big city. After a Broadway career, Churchill's film career began about 1929, and in the intervening years he appeared in literally hundreds of roles. In 1932 alone he was in 34 pictures and in 1934 he was seen in 29 different parts. Some of the motion pictures in which he had parts were *American Madness, Public Deb No. 1, Nothing but the Truth, Friends of Mr. Sweeney, False Faces, The Way of All Flesh, I Am a Fugitive from a Chain Gang, The Cowboy and the Lady,* and *Sweethearts.*

Berton Churchill, center, with Chick Chandler and Joan Davis in Sing and Be Happy.

EDUARDO CIANNELLI *(1889–Oct. 8, 1969)*

Eduardo Ciannelli obtained an M.D. degree in his native Italy. His father operated a health spa and wanted one of his sons to become a doctor. Eduardo, the youngest of four sons, did not follow up his career in medicine. He sang in grand opera and came to the U.S. after World War I. Ciannelli appeared in several musical comedies, such as *Lady Bill* and *Rose Marie.* There followed swiftly a series of stage acting successes including *Front Page, Reunion in Vienna,* with the Lunts, *St. Joan,* with Katherine Cornell, and *Winterset.* It was his outstanding success in the latter that caused RKO Radio to bring Ciannelli to the West Coast when they purchased screen rights to the play in 1936. He was equally successful in the film version, and went immediately to Warner Brothers to play the gangster menace in Bette Davis's starring vehicle, *Marked Woman.* There followed a long suc-

Eduardo Ciannelli with Virginia Bruce in Society Lawyer.

cession of excellent films in which Ciannelli played a wide variety of roles, but more often with the accent on villainy. Among his most significant pictures were *Gunga Din, For Whom the Bell Tolls, A Bell for Adano, Strange Cargo,* and *Zanzibar.*

FRED CLARK *(1914–Dec. 5, 1968)*

Fred Clark originally planned to become a doctor, and received a degree in psychology from Stanford University. He decided to try an acting career and was given a scholarship to the American Academy of Dramatic Art. Emerging from the Academy, he achieved many roles in Broadway shows, summer stock, and little theater work. After a stint in the U.S. Navy in World War II, he went to California to resume his career. He was signed by Michael Curtiz for the role of the detective in the film *The Unsuspected,* which starred Claude Rains and Joan Caulfield. Clark followed this up with *Two Guys from Texas* and *Ride the Pink Horse.* Among his other films are *Sunset Boulevard, How to Marry a Millionaire, Court Martial of Billy Mitchell, The Solid Gold Cadillac,* and *Miracle in the Rain.*

49

Fred Clark, center, with Charles McGraw and Audie Murphy in Joe Butterfly.

George Cleveland, right, with Lon McCallister in The Boy from Indiana.

GEORGE CLEVELAND (*1885–July 15, 1957*) George Cleveland was best known to the American public as the gruff but goodhearted "Gramps" on the *Lassie* television series. Born in Nova Scotia, his career covered 58 years of stage, vaudeville, motion pictures, radio, and TV. He came to Hollywood to appear in the motion picture *Mystery Liner* with Noah Beery, Sr., and appeared in more than 150 pictures in the years that followed. His films included *Mother Wore Tights, Albuquerque, Wistful Widow of Wagon Gap, Miss Grant Takes Richmond, Carson City,* and *Cripple Creek.*

E.E. CLIVE (*1883–June 6, 1940*) Edward Clive was born in Wales and was master of the various dialects of the British Isles. He toured extensively in the provinces after taking up a stage career at the age of 22. He moved to the United States in 1912. After several years on the Orpheum Circuit he operated the Copley Theatre, Boston, and later produced plays at the Biltmore, Los Angeles, and the Hollywood Playhouse. His picture work was largely confined to British characters. Among his best known films were *Bulldog Drummond, Charlie Chan in London, Captain Blood, Lloyd's of London, Night Must Fall, The Last Warning, Cain and Mabel, Kidnapped, Gateway,* and *Submarine Patrol.*

E. E. Clive

Andy Clyde

Lee J. Cobb in They Came to Rob Las Vegas.

ANDY CLYDE (1892–May 18, 1967)
Andy Clyde was a native of Blairgowrie, Scotland. He emigrated to the United States and appeared after 1929 in many feature films. In his comedy parts he mainly specialized in American rural types,, and was seldom cast as a Scot. Clyde played in many Westerns including the *Hopalong Cassidy* series. His other pictures included *Annie Oakley, Abe Lincoln in Illinois, This Above All, The Green Years, Unexpected Guest, Abilene Trail, Arizona Territory*, and *Road to Denver*.

EDMUND COBB (1892–Aug. 15, 1974)
Edmund Cobb was the grandson of Kansas Senator Edmund G. Ross, who later served as the Governor of the Territory of New Mexico. Cobb, who was born in Albuquerque, had some

Edmund Cobb, right, with Jimmy Wakely, center, and Robert Woodward left, in Gun Law Justice.

early stock and vaudeville experience, but made his first movie in 1910 or 1911. He has the distinction of having played a bit in the first serial ever made, and then many years later worked in the first sound serial made. He played in many serials over the years and made more than a hundred two-reel westerns for Universal.

LEE J. COBB (1911–Feb. 11, 1976)
Lee J. Cobb was born Leo Jacoby on the lower East Side of New York City. He was considered to be a child virtuoso on both the violin and the harmonica but an injury ended his musical career. When he was sixteen he decided to become an actor. Cobb played small parts at the Pasadena Playhouse and eventually landed on Broadway. In 1937 he started his 39-year film career. In 1954 he was nominated for Best Supporting Actor for his role in *On the Waterfront*. In spite of his long career, he is best remembered for creating the role of Willy Loman in *Death of a Salesman* on Broadway and as Judge Garth on *The Virginian* television show. Included among his films were *Golden Boy, The Song of Bernadette, Johnny O'Clock, Call Northside 777, The Left Hand of God, Twelve Angry Men, The Brothers Karamozov, The Four Horsemen of the Apocalypse* and *In Like Flint*.

CHARLES COBURN (1877–Aug. 30, 1961)
Charles Coburn enjoyed a unique place in the American theater motion picture as "the living, talking, cigar smoking, monocled and mannered image of the stage's own aristocratic culture, and Old School Gentleman, American in every fibre." His first picture role in 1938, as Doc Shingle, the beloved medical vagabond in *Of Human Hearts*, established Coburn as a distinguished acquisition to pictures. *Made for Each Other, Vivacious Lady, The Constant Nymph, Kings Row* and *The Devil and Miss Jones* provided him with a wide and significant variety

Charles Coburn, in The Doctor and the Girl.

of roles. His role in *The More the Merrier* in 1942 won for him the Academy Award for the best supporting actor of the year. His other films included *Idiot's Delight, Edison, the Man, George Washington Slept Here, Rhapsody in Blue, The Green Years, The Paradine Case, Green Grass of Wyoming.*

CHARLES COLEMAN *(1885–Mar. 7, 1951)*
Charles Coleman was known as "Hollywood's butler." Born in Sydney, Australia, he was Pauline Frederick's leading man while still on the stage, and toured the United States and Australia with her. Coleman played the role of a butler in more than 100 screen productions in his 25 years in Hollywood. One of his most prominent roles on the screen was that of the family butler in the first Deanna Durbin picture, *Three Smart Girls*. His other films included *Becky Sharp, Kitty, The Stork Club, Cluny Brown, Magnificent Rogue, Never Say Goodbye, In High Gear*, and *Pilgrim Lady*.

CONSTANCE COLLIER *(1878–Apr. 25, 1955)*
Constance Collier had a seventy-year career as an actress, producer, director, playwright, and dramatic coach. She was in the movies for over thirty years. Her early movies included D.W. Griffith's 1915 production *Intolerance*, in which she made her film debut. One of her later and most famous roles was that of the alcoholic aunt in *Kitty* with Ray Milland in 1946. Her other films included *Shadow of a Doubt, Peter Ibbetson, Professional Soldier, Girl's Dormitory, Little Lord Fauntleroy, Wee Willie Winkie, She Got What She Wanted, Stage Door, Perils of Pauline, An Ideal Husband*, and *Whirlpool*.

RAY COLLINS *(1889–July 11, 1965)*
Ray Collins was best known for his role of Lt. Tragg in the *Perry Mason* TV series. Collins, a native of Sacramento, California, started off his extensive and theatrical career playing in stock and repertoire in nearly every city on the Pacific Coast before invading New York in 1921 to become one of the leading fixtures of the Broad-

Ray Collins

Charles Coleman

Constance Collier, left, with J. Edward Bromberg, Simone Simon and Herbert Marshall.

way stage. Later he devoted himself to playing on the radio for twelve uninterrupted years. It was during this period that he met Orson Welles and played on many of Welles' radio programs. When Welles began his own Mercury Theater of the Air, Collins went with him, and appeared in most of Welles' shows, including the famous *War of the Worlds*. His screen career began in Welles' production of *Citizen Kane*. Collins gave a memorable performance in the role of Boss Jim Geddys. His second film role was an equally electrifying portrayal of Jack Amberson in Welles Mercury Production for RKO in *The Magnificent Ambersons*. His other pictures included *The Seventh Cross, The Hitler Gang, The Heiress, Francis, Summer Stock, Desert Song, Bad for Each Other, The Desperate Hours*, and *Never Say Goodbye*.

JIMMY CONLIN *(1884–May 7, 1962)*
Jimmy Conlin sparked many motion pictures with fine character as well as comedy portrayals after he went to Hollywood permanently in 1932. Previously he had been a vaudeville

Jimmy Conlin, in The Great Rupert.

headliner on the Keith and Orpheum circuits. One of his best movie roles was that of a race track tout in Harold Lloyd's *Mad Wednesday*. Conlin made his screen debut in 1928 with a Vitaphone short called *Sharps and Flats*. He also appeared in the first all-talking feature, *Lights of New York*. He appeared briefly in early television as a featured performer in *Duffy's Tavern*. His films included *The Great McGinty, Dorian Grey, Miracle of Morgan's Creek, Rolling Home, Tulsa, The Hucksters, Knock on Any Door, Summer Storm, Fallen Angel*, and *Mourning Becomes Electra*.

Walter Connolly, in The Great Victor Herbert.

WALTER CONNOLLY *(1887–May 28, 1940)*
Walter Connolly was a celebrated stage and screen actor who played a wide variety of roles. Born in Cincinnati, Ohio, he had a successful Broadway career until 1932. Hollywood pro-

Hans Conrie

ducers tried for years to persuade Connolly to appear in films, but he consistently refused. However, in 1932, Harry Cohn, president of Columbia Pictures, induced Connolly to spend the summer months in Hollywood. His first picture was *The Bitter Tea of General Yen*, followed by *Man Against Woman, Washington Merry-Go-Round* and *No More Orchids*. In 1933 he signed a long term contract with Columbia and was assigned to such major productions as *It Happened One Night, Twentieth Century, Whom the Gods Destroy, Broadway Bill*, and *The Captain Hates the Sea*. Other films included

The Good Earth, Let's Get Married, The League of Frightened Men, First Lady, Penitentiary, Four's a Crowd, Too Hot to Handle, Huckleberry Finn, and *The Great Victor Herbert*.

HANS CONRIED *(1917–Jan. 5, 1982)*

Hans Conried was born in Baltimore, Maryland. He started his acting career in radio, where he was a master of dialects. Although thoroughly trained in Shakespeare, he seemed to be more at home with comedy. He made many Broad-

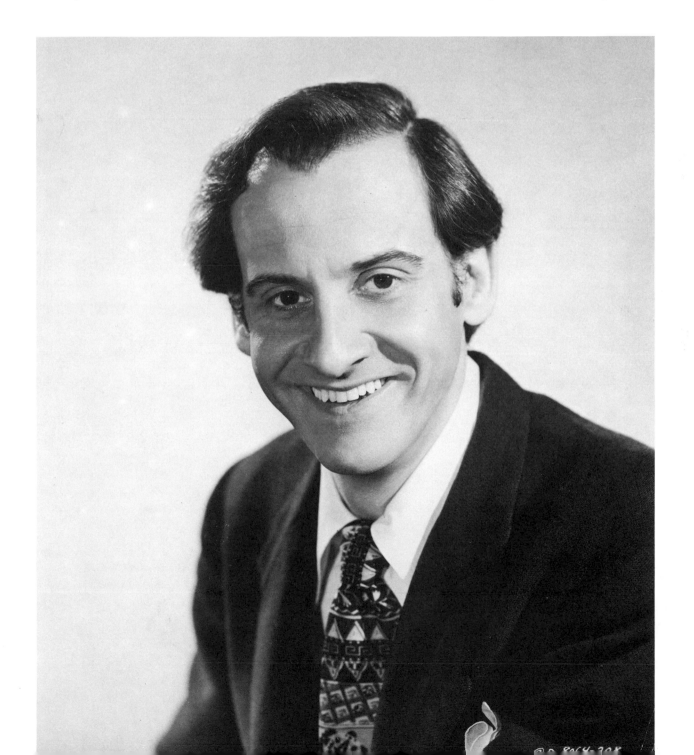

Frank Conroy, *right, with Charles McGraw in* The Threat.

Melville Cooper, *left, with Freddie Bartholomew and Jackie Cooper in* Two Bright Boys.

Ellen Corby

Gladys Cooper

Pedro de Cordoba, *right, with Fredric March and Steffi Duna in* Anthony Adverse.

George Coulouris, *center, with Howard Freeman and Anthony Quinn in* California.

way appearances and started his film career in 1938. He was featured in more than 70 films. On television he was the host of "Fractured Flickers" but he was at his best as Uncle Toonoose on "Make Room for Daddy." His films included: *It's a Wonderful World, A Date with the Falcon, A Lady Takes a Chance, My Friend Irma, The Birds and the Bees, Robin and the Seven Hoods*, and *The Shaggy D.A.*

FRANK CONROY (1890–Feb. 24, 1964)
Frank Conroy was featured in many Hollywood films in the 1930's and 1940's. Born in Derby, England, he started his film career with the *The Royal Family of Broadway* in 1930, and *Ann Carver's Profession* for Columbia in 1933. Other films included *Call Me Wild, West Point of the Air, Such Woman Are Dangerous, The White Angel, The Last Days of Pompeii, The Gorgeous Hussy, Wells Fargo, Lady of Burlesque, All My Sons, For the Love of Mary, The Snake Pit, The Threat*, and *Naked City*.

GLADYS COOPER (1888–Nov. 17, 1971)
Gladys Cooper typified superlative elegance, which for years created great demand for her in better-quality films. Miss Cooper was one of the reigning beauties of the London stage during the years of World War I. She came to Hollywood in 1940 after a long and successful career in the British stage and screen. Her first role in Hollywood was a part in *Rebecca*. She was featured in many pictures including *Kitty Foyle, That Hamilton Woman, Song of Bernadette, The White Cliffs of Dover, The Secret Garden, Madame Bovary*, and *Now Voyager*. In the latter, a film starring Paul Henreid and Bette Davis, Miss Cooper won an Academy Award nomination.

MELVILLE COOPER (1896–Mar. 29, 1973)
Melville Cooper played butlers in a number of his motion pictures. He came to the screen in 1934 in *The Private Life of Don Juan*. Cooper, a native of Birmingham, England, had an astonishing versatility in films. In *Pride and Prejudice*, he played Mr. Collins, who successfully wooed Greer Garson, in the role of Elizabeth Bennett.

In *Scotland Yard* he was Penny, a cowardly slacker and in *Rebecca* he was the coroner. He also played such parts as a British naval officer in *The Sun Never Sets*, a swindler in *Two Bright Boys*, and a jailbird in *Charlie Chan in New York*. He also played crooks and men about town, but in spite of all this diversity, his butler characterization perhaps stands out most. His other films included *The Scarlet Pimpernel, Holy Matrimony, Red Danube, Father of the Bride, It Should Happen to You*, and *Moonfleet*.

ELLEN CORBY (1913–)
Ellen Corby, a script girl for over twelve years, decided in 1942 to devote her full time to acting. She appeared in a number of pictures, but her biggest cinema chance came as Trina, the lovelorn Norwegian in *I Remember Mama* in 1948. By the end of the 1950's Miss Corby was one of the most familiar character actesses on the screen and TV. She gained her greatest fame as Grandma Walton on television's popular "The Waltons." Her films include *Cornered, Indiana Summer, Bachelor and the Bobby-Soxer, Living in a Big Way*, and *Trouble Shooters*.

PEDRO DE CORDOBA (1881–Sept. 16, 1950)
Pedro de Cordoba, who frequently portrayed a priest on both the stage and screen, was also a noted Catholic layman in private life. Born in New York, he was at one time president of the Catholic Actors Guild of America. Mr. de Cordoba was on the stage for many years with such stars as Katharine Cornell and Jane Cowl. His films included *The Crusades, Captain Blood, Anthony Adverse, Garden of Allah, For Whom the Bell Tolls, Keys of the Kingdom, San Antonio*, and *Blood and Sand*.

GEORGE COULOURIS (1903–)
George Coulouris is best remembered by film goers as a villain. His films include *All This and Heaven Too, Lady in Question, Citizen Kane, Song to Remember, Lady on a Train, Confidential Agent, Nobody Lives Forever, Mr. District Attorney, Sleep My Love*, and *Joan of Arc*.

JEROME COWAN *(1897–Jan. 24, 1972)*
Jerome Cowan was one of Hollywood's busiest actors in the 1930's and 1940's with his many portrayals of the urbane, suave, and sophisticated New Yorkers. He was born in New York City where he became a well-known stage actor. Cowan made his Broadway debut in support of Robert Ames in *We've Gotta Have Money*. His work in the original stage production of *Boy Meets Girl* attracted the attention of Samuel Goldwyn who brought him to Hollywood in 1936. His first picture was *Beloved Enemy*. The new medium of the film gave a wide range to his versatility, from drama to gay-lothario to playboy to city-slicker to comedy to villainous parts. His many pictures included *Shall We Dance, New Faces of 1937, Goldwyn Follies, Torrid Zone, High Sierra, The Maltese Falcon, One Foot in Heaven, Rags to Riches, Mission to Moscow, Song of Bernadette, The Fountainhead, Dallas,* and *Miracle on 34th Street*.

Jerome Cowan, in Black Zoo.

Alec Craig, right, with Robert Lowery in Dangerous Passage.

ALEC CRAIG *(1885–June 25, 1945)*
Alec Craig, a native of Scotland, won immediate recognition in the U.S. in the stage production of *Mary of Scotland*. He was brought to Hollywood by RKO for a role in *The Little Minister*, Among his other films were *Winterset, The Woman I Love, China Passage, Super Sleuth, Wise Girl, Double Danger,* and *Vivacious Lady*.

FRANK CRAVEN *(1878–Sept. 1, 1945)*
Frank Craven was famous for his expert delineation of a wide range of characters on both the stage and screen. He played the role of the narrator in the Pulitzer Prize play *Our Town* in 1938

Frank Craven, in In This Our Life.

and 1939, where his battered felt hat, briar pipe, and cracker-barrel philosophy became well known to Americans. It was as a writer that he was first brought to Hollywood in 1932, when he was signed by Fox Films to work on screenplays. He wrote for three years before he was prevailed upon to play a role in *Funny Thing Called Love*. In the years before he was featured in many motion pictures including *Barbary Coast, Small Town Girl, The Harvester, Penrod and Sam, City for Conquest, The Girl from Cheyenne,* and *The Richest Man in Town*.

Joseph Crehan, right, with Donald Woods in Case of the Stuttering Bishop.

Laura Hope Crews with Olivia de Havilland in Gone With the Wind.

JOSEPH CREHAN (1884–Apr. 15, 1966)
Joseph Crehan played General and President Ulysses S. Grant in at least a dozen films and had scores of roles as a hard-bitten newspaper editor or as a tough police chief, plainclothes detective or desk sergeant, often in movies with Edward G. Robinson. He also played the roles of kindly priest, judge, and town character. His films included *The Line-Up*, *The Case of the Lucky Legs*, *Front Page Woman*, *Frisco Kid*, *Smart Blonde*, *Night Train to Memphis*, *Falcon's Adventure*, *Louisiana*, *Dick Tracy Meets Gruesome*, *Red Desert*, *Crazylegs*, and *Roadblock*.

LAURA HOPE CREWS (1880–Nov. 13, 1942)
Laura Hope Crews came to Hollywood after a successful stage career, not as an actress but as a dramatic coach for the stars of silent pictures who were trying to make the transition to sound.

Donald Crisp with Gail Russell in The Uninvited.

She appeared in *Charming Sinners (1929)*, but her biggest break came in the role of the jealous mother in *The Silver Cord*, with Irene Dunne and Joel McCrea. Her other films included *Rafter Romance, Escapade, The Melody Lingers On, Her Master's Voice, Dr. Rhythm, The Rains Came, The Star Maker, Remember, Reno*, and *Gone with the Wind*, in which she played Aunt Pitty-Pat.

DONALD CRISP *(1882–May 25, 1974)*
Donald Crisp, one of the founders of the motion picture industry, became a top director of silent films, and then one of the most reliable character actors. Shortly before the advent of talking pictures, Crisp turned to acting exclusively. Among the important films in which he played roles were *The Little Minister, Mutiny on the Bounty, Oil for the Lamps of China, Charge of the Light Brigade, Mary of Scotland, Parnell, The Life of Emile Zola, Jezebel, Wuthering Heights, Lassie Come Home, National Velvet, Valley of Decision, and The Uninvited*. He was given the Academy Award for his performance in *How Green Was My Valley* in 1941.

FINLAY CURRIE *(1878–May. 9, 1968)*
Finlay Currie was one of the oldest living and working actors in the world. He played in many films during his career. His best friend was the late Edmund Gwenn. Fate dealt an ironic hand to both of them in 1947 when each received an Oscar nomination for best supporting actor, Gwenn for his role as St. Nick in *Miracle on 34th Street*, and Currie for the old ex-con, Provis, in *Great Expectations*. His Scottish burr, flowing gray hair, and rotundity made him a familiar figure to filmgoers the world over. Among his other films were *Edward My Son, Sleeping Car to Venice, Black Rose, Treasure Island, Mudlark, Quo Vadis, Ivanhoe, Walk East on Beacon, Stars and Stripes Forever*, and *Rob Roy*.

Finlay Currie

ESTHER DALE *(1885–July 23, 1961)*
Esther Dale was a familiar character actress who appeared in hundreds of films. No matter what the name of the character, whether it be an aunt, a grandmother, or a neighbor, Miss Dale performed the role with meticulous detail, exuding homely nobility and a warm understanding. She was the wife of Arthur Beckhard, producer and writer, who managed and directed one of the most distinguished semi-professional groups ever assembled in this country. Margaret Sullavan and Henry Fonda were among those who rose to great heights from that company. In her first screen engagement in 1934, Miss Dale performed with Noel Coward in Ben Hecht's *Crime Without Passion*. Her other films included *Dead End, Women, The Awful Truth, Back Street, Behind City Lights, Stolen Life, The Egg and I, Margie* and *A Song Is Born*.

HENRY DANIELL *(1894–Oct. 31, 1963)*
Henry Daniell, an English-born character actor, was equally at home in heroic and villainous roles, and modern or Shakespearean characterizations. After playing in many British stage productions, he came to this country to appear with Ethel Barrymore on Broadway. He made his screen debut in *Jealousy* in 1909. His screen credits included *The Awful Truth, All This and Heaven Too, Camille, Private Lives of Elizabeth and Essex, Sea Hawk, The Great Dictator, Philadelphia Story, Jane Eyre, Watch on the Rhine, The Egyptian, The Prodigal*, and *The Man in the Gray Flannel Suit*. Daniell died during the filming of *My Fair Lady* in 1963.

Henry Daniell, right, with Efram Zimbalist, Jr. in
The Chapman Report.

Esther Dale, center, with Chester Morris and
Richard Arlen in Wrecking Crew.

Jane Darwell

Harry Davenport

JANE DARWELL (1879–Aug. 13, 1967)

Jane Darwell was probably the most familiar character actress in the history of motion pictures. Born in Palmyra, Missouri, Miss Darwell entered motion pictures in the early silent days, around 1912. She appeared in many early C.B. DeMille pictures as well as with other companies. Miss Darwell appeared in over 200 films in the 1930–1955 period and was under contract with 20th Century-Fox during a 10-year span. She won the Academy Award for her brilliant performance as Ma Joad in *The Grapes of Wrath* in 1940. Miss Darwell said that "needless to say this is my favorite role." Other films included *Huckleberry Finn, Back Street, Ox-Bow Incident, Impatient Years, Sunday Dinner for a Soldier, Captain Tugboat Annie, My Darling Clementine, Three Godfathers, Wagonmaster, Caged,* and *Journey into Light.*

HARRY DAVENPORT (1866–Aug. 9, 1949)

Harry Davenport was a member of one of the theater's most illustrious families. His father was E.L. Davenport, a noted actor of his time, and on his mother's side he traced his lineage back to Jack Johnson, famous Irish actor of the 18th century. The roster of the stage plays and motion pictures in which Davenport had appeared, from

1871 up to 1934, filled two full pages of print in the 1934 Equity Magazine. Two of his most famous film portrayals were as Dr. Mead in *Gone with the Wind,* and as Colonel Skeffington in *King's Row.* His other films included *The Scoundrel, The Life of Emile Zola, Wells Fargo, The Sisters, The Cowboy and the Lady, You Can't Take It with You, Orphans of the Street, Hunchback of Notre Dame,* and *The Enchanted Forest.*

Rufe Davis, right, with Lloyd Nolan and Gladys Swarthout in Ambush.

RUFE DAVIS (1908–Dec. 13, 1974)

Born in Dinson, Oklahoma, Davis began his acting career in amateur shows. He was picked up from these shows by the Dubinsky Bros. Stock Company and subsequently appeared with the Weaver Bros. & Elviry, *The Larry Rich Show, The Radio Rubes* act and finally his own act.

Davis was brought to Hollywood in 1937 and appeared in over 49 motion pictures. In 1963 he entered television as a member of the *Petticoat Junction* cast. Among his motion picture credits were *Mountain Music, Cocoanut Grove, Big Broadcast of 1938, This Way Please, Blossoms of Broadway, Dr. Rhythm,* and *Ambush.* He also appeared in the western series *Three Mesquiteers.*

WILLIAM DEMAREST (1892–Dec. 28, 1983)

William Demarest was one of the master exponents of the characterization that includes the fish-eyed stare, crusty voice, and baleful countenance. He began his theatrical career in 1905 and was a national headliner in vaudeville. He made his first appearance on Broadway in 1914 at the famous Palace Theater. He was also with Earl Carroll's *Sketch Book Vanities Shows.* He made his film debut in *Fingerprints* in 1927. His other films include *Diamond Jim, Mr. Smith*

William Demarest

Goes to Washington, Pardon My Sarong, Hail the Conquering Hero, Miracle of Morgan's Creek, Duffy's Tavern, The Jolson Story, Red, Hot and Blue, and *Riding High.* He became well known to TV viewers as Uncle Charley on *My Three Sons.*

64

REGINALD DENNY (1891–June 16, 1967)

Reginald Denny, a native of Richmond, Surrey, England, became a screen actor with Universal in 1919. He was the star of many silent films, and with the advent of sound, became familiar

Reginald Denny with Genevieve Tobin and Marian Marsh in The Great Gambini.

as the portrayer of amiable and slightly foolish Englishmen. His sound films included *Of Human Bondage, Romeo and Juliet, Rebecca, Lost Patrol, Escape to Burma, Escape Me Never, Secret Life of Walter Mitty, Mr. Blandings Builds His Dream House,* and *Around the World in 80 Days.*

JOE DE SANTIS (1909–   )

Joe De Santis was born of Italian immigrant parents in New York. He started his career in 1931 working with various Italian companies in New York. In 1932 he joined the repertory company of Walter Hampden, touring with him for three seasons, and in 1934 he played Brutus in the C.W.A. production of *Julius Caesar.* He later worked as a W.P.A. art instructor. In 1936 he began a long radio career specializing in languages and dialects. In 1948 he did his first movie role in *Slattery's Hurricane.* He was one of radio's busiest actors in the late 1940's as well as being active on Broadway and in films and TV. His favorite roles include the part of the Italian director in *In Any Language,* the part of the father in *Cold Wind in August,* and as Big Jim Colosimo in *Al Capone.* His other film credits include *Man with a Cloak, Deadline U.S.A., The*

Joe DeSantis, right, with Frank Gorshin and Ray Danton in The George Raft Story.

Andy Devine in The Man Who Shot Liberty
Valance.

66

Last Hunt, Tension at Table Rock, The Unholy Wife, Full of Life, I Want to Live, Cry Tough, Madame X, and more recently *Beau Geste, The Professionals,* and *The Venetian Affair.*

ANDY DEVINE *(1905–Feb. 18, 1977)*

Andy Devine was a big, raspy-voiced actor who appeared in over 150 films from 1928 to 1976. He was born in Flagstaff, Arizona. Devine played football at Santa Clara College and studied briefly for the Catholic priesthood. While working as a lifeguard he was signed by a talent scout and made his first appearance in films in 1926 as an extra. He had a few leading man type roles in silents but his voice wasn't conducive to this type of role with the advent of sound. Devine was a semi-regular for five years on the Jack Benny radio show and his *"Hiya, Buck"* became a catch phrase for millions of listeners. During the 1950's he played *Jingles* on the *Wild Bill Hickok* television show. Among his films were *Spirit of Notre Dame, In Old Chicago, Yellow Jack, Stagecoach, The Fabulous Texan, Never a Dull Moment, The Man Who Shot Liberty Valance* and *How the West Was Won.*

CHARLES DINGLE *(1887–Jan. 19, 1956)*

Charles Dingle was a fifty-year veteran character actor of stage, screen, radio, and television. He was well known for his ability to play almost anything including deep-dyed villains, comedians, judges, storekeepers, or Shakespearean

Charles Dingle, with Rosalind Russell in Never Wave at a Wac.

actors and singers. He made his film debut in 1941 in *The Little Foxes* and was described by Bosley Crowther as "a perfect villain in respectable garb." His other films included *The Talk of the Town, Edge of Darkness, Unholy Partners, George Washington Slept Here, Home in Indiana, Sister Kenny, Call Me Madam, The Court Martial of Billy Mitchell,* and *Cinderella Jones.*

LUDWIG DONATH *(1900–Sept. 29, 1967)*

Ludwig Donath portrayed numerous Nazis on the American screen after arriving in Hollywood in 1940. He escaped from his native Germany and the Nazis and left behind a successful career

Ludwig Donath

as an established actor. In films, Donath also specialized in portraying sensitive, old Jewish gentlemen. His films included *Enemy Agents Meet Ellery Queen, Lady From Chung King, Tampico, The Hitler Gang* and *The Story of Dr. Wassell.*

RUTH DONNELLY *(1896–Nov. 17, 1982)*

Ruth Donnelly was one of the busiest character actresses during this period. Frequently cast in Irish-dialect parts, she made her screen debut in

1930 in *Blessed Event.* She played Sister Michael in *The Bells of St. Mary's,* and was also featured as an insane woman in *The Snake Pit.* Her other films include *Song and Dance Man, Mr. Deeds Goes to Town, Mr. Smith Goes to Washington, Model Wife, Fighting Father Dunne, Cinderella Jones, Thank Your Lucky Stars, This is the Army,* and *Wild Blue Yonder.*

Robert Douglas.

Ruth Donnelly.

ROBERT DOUGLAS (1909–   )

Robert Douglas, a native of Bletchley, Buckinghamshire, England, is an actor of considerable background and talent. From 1928 to 1930 he was a student at the Royal Academy of Dramatic Art in London, after which he became a star on the London and Broadway stage in the 1930's. In 1936 he co-starred with Merle Oberon and Rex Harrison in Alexander Korda's film *Over the Moon.* After six years in the British Navy as a naval pilot he resumed his career after World War II. Among the films in which he co-starred or was featured are *Christopher Blake, Don Juan* with Errol Flynn, *The Fountainhead, The Flame and the Arrow, Kim, Ivanhoe, Prisoner of Zenda, Flight to Tangier,* and *Helen of Troy,*

in which he appeared as Agamemmnon. In recent years he has turned to TV as producer and director. Douglas directed 18 segments of *12 O'Clock High.*

DOUGLAS DUMBRILLE (1889–Apr. 2, 1974)

Douglas Dumbrille was a long-time movie villain, who portrayed nearly everything from a mobster to mad scientists, and who frequently was cast as a corrupt politician. He was on the

Douglas Dumbrille, with Rose Hobart in The Cat Creeps.

dramatic stage before his screen debut in *His Woman* which he made with Claudette Colbert in 1931. During his first year in Hollywood he made 24 pictures and was in great demand by movie producers. His films included *Lives of a Bengal Lancer, Naughty Marietta, Cardinal Richelieu, Peter Ibbetson, Mr. Deeds Goes to Town, The Witness Chair, The Princess Comes Across, Riding High,* and *Julius Caesar.*

MARGARET DUMONT *(1889–Mar. 6, 1965)*

Margaret Dumont was the actress who played the foil to the madcap antics of the Marx Brothers. She was on the stage with the Marx Brothers, and then was a leading lady in seven of their films. She embodied the stereotype of the aristocratic grand dame of high society, elegantly dressed and handsome, and she would

Emma Dunn, with George Raft in The Glass Key.

Margaret Dumont, with Groucho Marx and Sig Ruman in A Night at the Opera.

stand statuesque and unperturbed as the Marx Brothers created low comedy around her. Her films included *Animal Crackers, Duck Soup, Gridiron Flash, A Night at the Opera, Anything Goes, A Day at the Races, The Horn Blows at Midnight,* and *Up in Arms.*

EMMA DUNN *(1875–Dec. 14, 1966)*

Emma Dunn began playing matronly parts while still a young woman. Her first starring role

on the stage was in *Old Lady 31* in 1916. Her first movie role was in 1919 and she was still active after World War II. Miss Dunn was seen in several of the Dr. Kildare films as the young doctor's mother. Her other credits included *Each Dawn I Die, Mr. Deeds Goes to Town, Mourning Becomes Electra,* and *Life with Father.*

MILDRED DUNNOCK *(1900–   )*

Mildred Dunnock made her screen debut as Miss Ronsberry in *The Corn Is Green,* a role she created on Broadway. Miss Dunnock was born in Baltimore and took her B.A. at Goucher College, after which she studied at Columbia University to earn her M.A. degree. She has had a long and successful career on Broadway. On the screen the overall impression is one of winsomeness. One of her best performances in films was as Willy Loman's wife in *Death of a Salesman* under the direction of Elia Kazan. Her other film credits include *The Kiss of Death, I Want You, Viva Zapata, Girl in White, Too Bad for You, The Jazz Singer, Bad for Each Other,* and *The Trouble with Harry.*

Mildred Dunnock

JOHN ELDREDGE *(1904–Sept. 23, 1961)*
John Eldredge was a member of the New York Civic Repertory Co. before coming to Hollywood in the 1930's. He appeared in many films including *Flirtation Walk, The White Cockatoo, Dangerous, The Woman in Red, The Holy Terror, Mr. Dodd Takes the Air,* and *King of*

John Eldredge, with Sally Blane in One Mile from Heaven.

the Underworld. He played the role of the father in television's *Meet Corliss Archer* program for several years.

DICK ELLIOTT *(1886–Dec. 22, 1961)*
Dick Elliott had a show business career that included the stage, motion picture, and television. He appeared in such plays as *Abie's Irish Rose.* His movie appearances included *We're Rich Again, It Happened in New York, Her Master's Voice, China Passage, Annie Oakley,* and *Christmas in Connecticut.* In his later years he became known for his portrayal of Santa Claus on shows with Jimmy Durante, Andy Griffith, Red Skelton, and Jack Benny.

EDWARD ELLIS *(1870–July 26, 1952)*
He was born in Coldwater, Michigan, and made his stage debut at the age of nine in *Olivia* at

Dick Elliott with Ward Bond and Walter Connolly in Penitentiary.

Hooley's Theatre, Chicago. After a number of juvenile roles, he was cast as Simon Legree in an 1890 road production of *Uncle Tom's Cabin.* Making his way to Hollywood in the early 1930's he appeared in such films as *Winterset, Return*

Edward Ellis, with Janet Beecher in Career.

of Peter Grimm, I Was a Fugitive from a Chain Gang, The Thin Man, Black Sheep, Maid of Salem, A Man to Remember, *and* A Man Betrayed. He was best known for his starring role in *Remember*, which he made for RKO in 1938.

ISOBEL ELSOM (1894–Jan. 12, 1981)

Isobel Elsom was born in Cambridge, England, and enjoyed a successful stage career in many London productions before coming to the U.S. in 1926 for the first time. She did considerable radio and stage work in the years following, and in 1939 she was in the smash hit *Ladies in Retirement*, which occupied her for two years, both in New York and on the road. In 1941 she was brought to Hollywood by MGM to repeat her role in the film version of the play. Her other films include *Seven Sweethearts, War Against Mrs. Hadley, You Were Never Lovelier, First Comes Courage, The Horn Blows at Midnight, Escape Me Never, The Ghost and Mrs. Muir,*

Isobel Elsom

The Two Mrs. Carrolls, Desiree, and Love is a Many Splendored Thing. She was also seen as Gary Cooper's prospective mother-in-law in *Casanova Brown.*

HOPE EMERSON (1897–Apr. 24, 1960)

Hope Emerson was the six-foot-two, 230-pound giant actress who was also the voice of Borden's Elsie the Cow. She made her Broadway debut playing the leader of the Amazons in *Lysistrata* with Charles Coburn. From this production she went into Fred Stone's *Smiling Faces*, in which she danced, sang, and played the piano. She also sang several summers with the St. Louis Municipal Opera's productions. After a career in vaudeville, nightclubs, and Broadway, Twentieth Century-Fox brought her to Hollywood to play the murderous masseuse who tried to choke Richard Conte to death in *Cry of the City.* Her other films included *The Bandwagon, That Wonderful Urge, Thieves' Market,* and *Roseanna McCoy* in which she portrayed the gun toting Mrs. Hatfield. In recent years she played the role of "Mother" in the *Peter Gunn* series on TV.

Hope Emerson, center, in Caged.

JOHN EMERY (1905–Nov. 16, 1964)

John Emery, featured in many important Broadway plays and Hollywood films was a handsome man with a deep resonant voice and was classified as belonging to the "profile school" of acting. His 1925 Broadway debut in *Mrs. Partridge Presents* was followed by roles with Katharine Cornell in *Barretts of Wimpole Street, St. Joan,* and *Constant Wife.* Emery went into

*John Emery, left, with James Gleason and Halli-
well Hobbes in* Here Comes Mr. Jordan.

films in 1945 in *Spellbound* with Ingrid Bergman. His other films included *Blood on the Sun*,
Frenchie, *The Voice of the Turtle*, *The Woman
in White*, and *Youngblood Hawke*. Married at
one time to Tallulah Bankhead, Emery was also
a member of the Actors Equity Council for a
number of years.

STU ERWIN *(1903–Dec. 21, 1967)*
Stu Erwin was born on a ranch in Squaw Valley,
California. While attending the University of
California he became interested in dramatics. He
appeared in several plays and had his first film

Stu Erwin

Carl Esmond, in Address Unknown.

Rex Evans, in Lord Augustus.

role in 1928. Erwin parlayed his bumbling manner into a 36-year film career. In 1936 he received the Best Supporting Actor nomination for his role in *Pigskin Parade*. In the 1950's he appeared on TV with his wife, actress June Collyer in the Stu Erwin Show. His films included *Mother Knows Best, Paramount on Parade, Make Me a Star, International House, Palooka, Ceiling Zero, Second Honeymoon, Mr. Boggs Steps Out, Our Town,* and *Son of Flubber.*

CARL ESMOND (1906-   )

Carl Esmond has given the screen some great portrayals as a villain. Born in Vienna, he first came to Hollywood in 1938 and played the wounded German aviator in *Dawn Patrol*. He also played the role of the German in Walter Wanger's *Sundown*. With the exception of *The Navy Comes Through*, in which he played the anti-Nazi violinist, and *Seven Sweethearts*, in which he played the timid lover, Esmond became thoroughly identified with Nazi roles. He played a Nazi spy in *Ministry of Fear*, but in C.B. DeMille's *The Story of Dr. Wassell* he played a Dutch officer who helps Dr. Wassell evacuate his wounded men from Java. His other pictures included *The Catman of Paris, Smash-Up, The Story of a Woman, Walk a Crooked Mile,* and *The Racers.*

REX EVANS (1903–Apr. 3, 1969)

Rex Evans, a native of England, settled in California in 1936. Prior to that he had appeared since 1926 in London vaudeville and night clubs. His Broadway stage appearances included *Three Penny Opera* and *Lady Windermere's Fan*, in which he played Lord Augustus Lorton, in support of Cornelia Otis Skinner. He also appeared for nearly two years with Carol Channing in *Gentlemen Prefer Blondes*, playing Sir Francis Beckman. Evans' screen portrayals included *Camille, The Philadelphia Story, A Woman's Face, The Thin Man Comes Home, Zaza, Frankenstein Meets the Wolfman,* and *A Star Is Born*. After Evans retired from acting he ran an art gallery, the Rex Evans Gallery, on Hollywood's famous La Cienega Blvd.

PAUL EVERTON (1869–1948)

Paul Everton was a professional actor for nearly 70 years. During his long career he appeared in a majority of the leading houses in the U.S. and Canada, and at the old Mason Opera House in Los Angeles before the turn of the century. He worked with Elsie Ferguson, Madame Janauschek, Charles Dillingham, and Eddie Cantor before starting in films in 1937. His films included *They Won't Forget, The Life of Emile Zola, The Great Garrick, Orphans of the Street, Gun Law, Topper Takes a Trip,* and *Whispering Enemies.*

Paul Everton, seated at center of table, with Claude Rains in They Won't Forget.

Tom Fadden, in Lawless Breed.

them at the age of two. Faylen attended grammar school in Chicago, and St. Joseph's Preparatory College in Kirkwood, Missouri, where he was graduated at the age of eighteen. Then he struck out for himself in show business. It was while on tour that he arrived in Los Angeles where he took a screen test. As a result he entered the ranks of free-lance film actors and during his first year and a half played in 26 pictures. In 1943 Paramount put him under contract and he appeared in over twenty pictures under this trademark with a wide diversification of roles. His big success came with the portrayal of the sadistic male nurse Bim in *The Lost Weekend*. Other films include *Grapes of Wrath, Two Years Before the Mast, The Unknown Guest, And the Angels Sing, Bring on the Girls, Race Street, Blood on the Moon*, and *Whispering Smith*.

Frank Faylen

TOM FADDEN *(1895–April 14, 1980)*

Tom Fadden started acting before the cameras in 1939, but he assumed a thespian's role first in 1915 when he joined a stock company playing in Omaha, Nebraska. From that day on he has been an actor. He played on Broadway 1923–1939 in such works as *Our Town, Nocturne, The Small Timers* and played on vaudeville's Keith Circuit, appearing at the Palace in New York in 1926. Fadden has made nearly 150 pictures working with Humphrey Bogart, Bette Davis, George Raft, Marlene Dietrich and John Wayne. A brief list of some of his film credits includes, *Destry Rides Again, The Remarkable Andrew, The Shepherd of the Hills, My Favorite Blonde, State Fair, Dragonwyck*, and *The State of the Union*.

FRANK FAYLEN *(1909–   )*

Frank Faylen began his acting career when he was a baby, carried on stage at the Orpheum Theatre in Denver by his father. His parents were the famous old headliner team of Ruf and Cusik, and Faylen went on a road tour with

FRITZ FELD *(1900–   )*

Fritz Feld, one of the most versatile men in the field of entertainment, started in motion pictures in 1919. A native of Berlin, he came to the U.S. in 1923 to play in Max Reinhardt's *The Miracle*. He was then signed by Hollywood and made a

Barry Fitzgerald

number of silent films. With Joseph Schildkraut he founded the Hollywood Playhouse, now the Hollywood Palace. Feld has been most frequently seen as a movie director, waiter, maitre d', psychiatrist, hotel clerk, and orchestra conductor in some 315 movies, 600 television programs, 30 commercials, and more than 1,000 radio programs. He has scored as a comedian, dramatic actor, pantomimist, cameraman, and director. Feld while playing in Eddie Cantor's *If You Knew Susie* hit upon the idea of a sort of trademark, his distinctive "pop"– a sound like a cork being pulled from a champagne bottle which he accomplishes by bringing the flat of him palm sharply against his rounded mouth. This device has been used to characterize his many roles in such films as *Knickerbocker Holiday, The Secret Life of Walter Mitty, Julia Misbehaves, Mexican Hayride, The Great Lover, Riding High, Little Egypt, My Favorite Spy, Call Me Madam, The French Line,* and *Barefoot in the Park.*

Frank Fenton, left, with Edmond O'Brien in Silver City.

appearing in *The Philadephia Story, Susan and God* and other bits. He toured with Katherine Cornell in *Romeo and Juliet* and other plays. He entered films in 1942 in *Lady of Burlesque,* later appearing in many motion pictures as well as many parts on television.

BARRY FITZGERALD (*1888–Jan. 4, 1961*)
Barry Fitzgerald was born in Dublin, Ireland. As a young man he was a clerk in the Irish Civil Service. He became interested in acting and joined the Abbey Theatre at night. Fitzgerald came to the United States in 1936 and his heavy Irish brogue and mischievous smile became his trademarks. As Father Fitzgibbon he won The Best Supporting Actor Award for *Going My Way* in 1944 opposite Bing Crosby. His younger brother was actor Arthur Shields. His films included *The Dawn Patrol, The Long Voyage Home, How Green Was My Valley, And Then There Were None, Welcome Stranger, Miss Tatlock's Millions,* and *The Quiet Man.*

MARY FORBES (*1883–July 22, 1974*)
The "prettiest girl in high school" in her home town of Rochester, New York, Mary Forbes became the favorite model of Harrison Fisher long before the term "cover girl" was invented. Her face became familiar in homes throughout the nation after she posed for *Anticipation* which appeared on the Christmas 1908 cover of the *Saturday Evening Post.* Her theatrical career burned brightly for 55 years and her name was to be found among such as Lillian Russell, Jane

Fritz Feld

FRANK FENTON (*1906–July 24, 1957*)
Frank Fenton, a native of Hartford, Connecticut, entered show business after his graduation from Georgetown University and played leading roles on the New York and London stages,

Cowl, and Helen Hayes. In her years on Broadway in roles large and small Miss Forbes set a record for appearing on opening night in more successes than any other performer. Inevitably Miss Forbes went to Hollywood. Motion pictures in which she played include *The Prisoner of Zenda, Abraham Lincoln,* and *Holiday.* Her last film role was in DeMille's *The Ten Commandments.*

Mary Forbes, left, with May Robson in You Can't Buy Everything.

BYRON FOULGER *(1899–Apr. 4, 1970)*

Byron Foulger was one of those fortunate actors who was constantly busy and profitably occupied in a wide variety of roles in the motion picture

Byron Foulger

and television fields for over thirty-five years. Foulger's first professional engagement (after college at University of Utah and little theatre experience) was on Broadway in the early 1920's. He appeared in such works as *Medea, Candida, Iphigenia in Aulis* and *The Idiot.* From Broadway Foulger entered a touring company, the Circuit Repertory Company of the Moroni Olsen Players, touring the principal cities of the Northwest. It was at this time he met and married Dorothy Adams. During the depression of 1929 and the early 1930's he was associated with the Pasadena Playhouse. Then came Hollywood and a career in motion pictures. A few of the titles in which Foulger appeared were *Arizona, Panther's Claw, Inspector General, Tuttles of Tahiti, Prisoner of Zenda, Human Comedy, Blood Money, Stallion Road,* and *Stand By for Action.*

DOUGLAS FOWLEY *(1911-   )*

Born and reared in Greenwich Village in New York City, Douglas Fowley aspired to the stage from childhood. He attended St. Francis Xavier Military Academy and was active in all the

Douglas Fowley, in 36 Hours to Kill.

77

school plays. Upon completion of his schooling, Fowley went into night club work and then on the stage as a singer, dancer and all-round comedian. In addition he was a barker for theatres, a Wall St. runner, an athletic coach at a summer camp and worked in the shipping department of a silk house. His first motion picture was *Mad Game* for Fox in 1933. His pictures include *Alexander's Ragtime Band, Dodge City, Slightly Dishonorable, See Here, Private Hargrove,* and *Sea of Grass.*

JOHN GALLAUDET *(1903–Nov. 5, 1983)*

John Gallaudet was born in Philadelphia, the son of an Episcopal priest. He graduated from Williams College and began an acting career on the stage which included *Coquette* with Helen Hayes, *Front Page* with Pat O'Brien, in which

John Gallaudet, right, with Jeff Donnell and Monte Hale in Outcasts of the Trail.

he played Hildy Johnson, and *The Bandwagon* with Fred Astaire and Frank Morgan. Gallaudet appeared in one silent picture, *Just Suppose,* with Richard Barthelmess in 1925. He was signed by Columbia in March, 1936, and played in his first talking picture, *Counterfeit.* His other pictures include *Shakedown, Pennies from Heaven, Little Miss Roughneck, Shady Lady, Lone Wolf in Mexico, Corpus Delicti,* and *Sing You Sinners.*

REGINALD GARDINER *(1903–July 7, 1980)*

Reginald Gardiner was an actor who proved the exception to the rule that few handsome men are amusing. A native of England, he built his

Reginald Gardiner

American film career around his comical characterization of the suave, witty, complete gentleman. His first Hollywood screen role was as a zany cop, leading an imaginary orchestra in Central Park in Eleanor Powell's first film *Born to Dance* in 1936. His other films included *Immortal Sergeant, The Horn Blows at Midnight, Sweet Rosie O'Grady, The Great Dictator, Marie Antoinette, Sweethearts, A Yank in the RAF, The Man Who Came to Dinner, Christmas in Connecticut, Cluny Brown,* and *Black Widow.*

EDWARD GARGAN *(1901–Feb. 19, 1964)*

Edward Gargan came to Hollywood in 1933, and was in demand almost immediately after his arrival, being particularly successful for his roles as frustrated, not too bright detectives and good-natured policeman. He created the role of "Bates," the dumb detective in RKO's successful *Falcon* series, and played it in more than a dozen of them. Some of his best film roles were in *While New York Sleeps, Thanks for the Memory, Cinderella Jones, Hands Across the Table, Ceiling Zero, Two Cornered Moon, My Man Godfrey, My Gal Sal, Diamond Horseshoe,* and *San Fernando Valley.* The brother of actor William Gargan, he also appeared on many network radio shows, was often heard as a narrator and actor in the popular *This Is Your FBI* show on NBC.

Edward Gargan, in Taxi, Mister.

GLADYS GEORGE (1904–Dec. 8, 1954)

Gladys George was the blonde actress who could always be termed vivacious, especially in the years when that was a popular adjective. She is perhaps most widely remembered now for her starring stage role in *Personal Appearance*. She made her Broadway debut at an early age, appearing in 1918 with Isadora Duncan in *Betrothed*. Her screen career began in 1934 in *Straight Is the Way*. Her other films included *Valiant Is the Word for Carrie, Madame X, Marie Antoinette, A Child Is Born, The Way of All Flesh, Minstrel Man, Christmas Holiday, Steppin in Society,* and *The Best Years of Our Lives.*

Gladys George, with Spencer Tracy in They Gave Him a Gun.

Alex Gerry

ALEX GERRY (1908–   )

Alex Gerry started his acting career during his undergraduate days at New York University. After graduation he joined the Washington Square Players in New York. Gerry also worked in radio in a variety of dramatic programs before World War II. After serving in the army during the war years, he decided to come to the West Coast and worked in radio including the "Lux Radio Theater." He did many plays at the Pasadena Playhouse, 1946–1949, and started in films in 1948. Among his favorite film roles are as Uncle Louis in *The Jazz Singer*, as Ben Novack in *The Bell Boy*, and as the father-in-law in *The Eddie Cantor Story*. His other films include *Panhandle, Sainted Sisters, House Across the Street, Excuse My Dust,* and *Love Is Better than Ever.*

BILLY GILBERT (1894–Sept. 23, 1971)

Billy Gilbert was the comedian who is said to have made the act of sneezing an artistic achievement. In over 200 films his big jovial face was often seen screwed in agony, followed by a spasmodic intake of breath, that awful struggle to hold it in and that final blast that blows everything down before it. So wonderful was his sneeze, so perfect in form and essence and dramatic suspense, that he was the only person to be even considered for the part of Sneezy in Walt Disney's *Snow White and the Seven Dwarfs*. Gilbert was so often cast as a foreigner in so many movies that people were frequently surprised to learn he was an American, born in Louisville, Kentucky. For many years he enjoyed

Billy Gilbert

a tremendous reputation in Hollywood as a "trouble-shooter." Whenever a director needed a comedy scene Gilbert was sent for to supply it. A few of his motion pictures were *Destry Rides Again, His Girl Friday, Tin Pan Alley, The Great Dictator, New Wine, Seven Sinners, On the Avenue, Anchors Aweigh, Three of a Kind, Fun and Fancy Free,* and *Down Among the Sheltering Palms.*

Connie Gilchrist

CONNIE GILCHRIST (1906–   )
Connie Gilchrist, a native of Brooklyn Heights, New York, has specialized in portrayals of wise-cracking Irish mothers, maids, madams, and governesses. Her pre-Hollywood stage career included *Mulatto* with Rose McLendon, *Work Is for Horses,* and *Ladies and Gentlemen* with Helen Hayes. Miss Gilchrist received excellent notices in a pre-Broadway tour on the West Coast in the latter. Leland Hayward obtained a seven-year contract with MGM for her which actually lasted ten years from 1939 to 1949. Her films include *Barnacle Bill* with Wallace Berry, *Young Dr. Kildare, Johnny Eager, Two-faced Woman,* which was Garbo's last film, *Tortilla Flats, Valley of Decision, Thin Man Returns, The Hucksters, Letter to Three Wives,* as Nora, the governess, in *Auntie Mame,* and her role singing the hit revival of *Every Little Moment,* with Judy Garland in *Presenting Lily Mars.*

James Gleason, left, with William Bendix in The Life of Riley.

JAMES GLEASON (1882–Apr. 12, 1959)
James Gleason was once described as "140 pounds of Irish dynamite." That about tells it. The vinegary, tough-talking little Irishman will long be remembered by movie fans for his dour, side of the mouth portrayals of fight managers, detectives, marine sergeants, Navy non-coms, and politicians. During his long career in the theater, movies, and TV, Gleason was actor, playwright, and producer. In 1942, he was nominated for Best Supporting Actor in Columbia's *Here Comes Mr. Jordan.* His last movie role was that of a political crony of Spencer Tracy in *The Last Hurrah.* His other films included *Arsenic and Old Lace, A Tree Grows in*

Brooklyn, Down to Earth, The Homestretch, Tycoon, Life of Riley, Riding High, Crash Dive, Keys of the Kingdom, On Your Toes, Meet John Doe, The Clock, Triple Cross, Come Fill the Cup, and *Suddenly.*

C. Henry Gordon

THOMAS GOMEZ *(1905–June 18, 1971)*

Thomas Gomez, a native of Long Island, was awarded a scholarship at the age of seventeen to the dramatic shool of which Walter Hampden was an officer. The famous Shakespearean actor was impressed with young Gomez and took him into his own company. The following year, 1924, Gomez made his professional debut, appearing in *Cyrano de Bergerac.* He was with Hampden for seven years and then with the Lunt-Fontanne troupe for seven more years. Early in 1942 he was signed by Universal and made his screen debut in *Sherlock Holmes and*

Thomas Gomez, left, with Ed Max, Mike Mazurki and Loretta Young in Come to the Stable.

the Voice of Terror. After that he appeared in a variety of characterizations, and was nominated for an Academy Award in 1947 for his portrayal of Pancho in *Ride the Pink Horse.* His other films included *Singapore, Captain from Castile, Casbah, Key Largo, Sorrowful Jones, Force of Evil, Midnight Kiss, Kim, Macao, Merry Widow,* and *Sombrero.*

C. HENRY GORDON *(1884–Dec. 3, 1940)*

C. Henry Gordon specialized in screen villainy for more than a decade. A suave, cultivated menace, Gordon achieved his scoundrelly effects with a smile, a mocking bow, a sardonic and superior twist of the underlip, the ironic dropping of an eyelid and, most important, through the purely coincidentally attributes of his features, which had a satanic cast which he never attempted to minimize. He appeared in more than fifty talking films. Some of the more prominent included *Renegades, Mata Hari* with Greta Garbo, *Night Flight, Stamboul Quest, Men in White, Louisiana Lou, Rasputin, Congo, The Crooked Circle* as Yoganda, *Miss Pinkerton* as Dr. Stewart, *Kit Carson,* and *The Crusades.* In *The Charge of the Light Brigade* he portrayed the villainous Surat Kahn, who was skewered on a spike by Errol Flynn at the fadeout in retribution for the wholesale slaughter of British soldiers and their wives.

CHARLES GRAPEWIN *(1869–Feb. 2, 1956)*

Charles Grapewin played the kind of role as a character actor in which he was called "Pop" or

Charles Grapewin, left, with Russell Simpson, Jane Darwell, Henry Fonda and O.Z. Whitehead in Grapes of Wrath.

something like it. He had a ramshackle face and Western drawl that were familiar to film goers, although, on occasion, he appeared in more clean shaven parts, such as that of Inspector Queen, father of Ellery Queen. Appearing in more than a hundred films, his two most memorable roles were as Jeeter Lester in *Tobacco Road* and Grandpa in *Grapes of Wrath*. Other pictures in which he appeared were *Shanghai, Ah! Wilderness, Artists and Models Abroad, Libeled Lady, Dust Be My Destiny, The Wizard of Oz, Johnny Apollo, They Died with Their Boots On, Crash Dive, Sand, The Petrified Forest*, and *The Good Earth*.

Sydney Greenstreet, with Ingrid Bergman in Casablanca.

SYDNEY GREENSTREET *(1879–Jan. 18, 1954)*
Sydney Greenstreet, known to millions of film-goers for his roles of mystery and villainy, was over 60 when he made his screen debut. The son of a Sandwich, England, tanner, Greenstreet spent 41 distinguished years on the stage before coming to Hollywood in 1941 to make his best-remembered picture, *The Maltese Falcon*. In his career, the 280-pound actor appeared in every Shakespearean play of record. Because he loved the theater, he had refused all previous film offers until director John Huston lured him to Hollywood to play the arch-villain's role of Kasper Gutman, dealer in curios, in *The Maltese Falcon*. The part won Greenstreet an Academy Award nomination. Another vivid role was that of the benevolent mystery man in *Casablanca*, with Humphrey Bogart and Ingrid Bergman. His

other films included *The Mask of Dimitrios, Christmas in Connecticut, Devotion, The Velvet Touch, Passage to Marseilles, The Verdict, The Hucksters, Between Two Worlds, Across the Pacific*, and *Flamingo Road*.

CHARLOTTE GREENWOOD *(1890–Jan. 18, 1978)*
Charlotte Greenwood, after several years in vaudeville, became one of Broadway's favorite comediennes, beginning with *The Passing Show of 1912*. She appeared in 1915 in the all-star production of *So Long Letty*. This was followed by a series of *Letty* shows which made her a top stage favorite throughout the country. She made her first picture in 1918, *Jane*. In 1928, after the advent of sound, she returned to films to make *Baby Mine, Girls Will Be Boys, So Long Letty, Flying High*, and *Orders Is Orders*. In 1940, she signed a contract with 20th Century-Fox. Her later films included *Star Dust, Down Argentine Way, Tall, Dark and Handsome, Moon Over Miami, The Perfect Snob, Home in Indiana, Oh, You Beautiful Doll, Peggy*, and *Oklahoma!* in which she appeared as Aunt Eller.

Charlotte Greenwood

Eddie Gribbon, center, with Frank Sully, Joe Kirkwood Jr. and Leon Errol in Joe Palooka in the Counterpunch.

EDDIE GRIBBON (1890–Sept. 28, 1965)

Eddie Gribbon was one of the original Keystone Kops. He came to Los Angeles in 1916 and after working in the Mack Sennett comedies he went to MGM in the 1920's and appeared in a number of silent pictures. After 1934 he worked at various studios including RKO, Paramount, and Warner Bros. His pictures included *Search for Beauty, Love on a Bet, The Big Shot, Maid's Night Out,* and *The Dictator.*

JAMES GRIFFITH (1916–)

Born in Los Angeles, Griffith had planned to be a professional musician until the acting bug bit him. While he was performing in a little theatre in Brentwood in 1939 a scout signed him to appear in the musical *They Can't Get You Down.* His career was interrupted by service in World War II. After the war, while writing a play, Griffith was cast in his first film, *Blonde Ice.* From that film debut Griffith has appeared in more than 50 motion pictures and 100 television shows. His film credits include *Day of Triumph, Masterson of Kansas, Eight Iron Men, Advance to the Rear, Fighting Man of the Plains, Bullwhip, The First Texan,* and *Raintree Country.*

James Griffith

PAUL GUILFOYLE (1892–Nov. 13, 1964)

Paul Guilfoyle, who was born in Jersey City, started his acting career on stage. Between 1928 and 1934 he played in such Broadway productions as *Box Seats, Zeppelin, Penny Arcade, Marathon,* and *Jayhawker.* He turned to the screen in 1935, and often appeared in the role of a villain or weakling. He had supporting parts in more than 85 films, frequently coming to an unhappy end, such as being stuffed into an automobile trunk by James Cagney playing the role of a brutal gangster in *White Heat.* Among Guilfoyle's other films were *Special Agent, Winterset, Super Sleuth, Julius Caesar, Sabotage, Thou Shalt Not Kill, The Mark of the Whistler, Follow Me Quietly,* and *The Hunted.*

Paul Guilfoyle, center, with Charles Bickford and John Litel in One Hour to Live.

EDMUND GWENN (1875–Sept. 6, 1959)

Edward Gwenn was one of the most accomplished and beloved character actors on either side of the Atlantic. Gwenn was the stocky, crinkly-eyed Englishman who played saints and villains with equal aplomb and appeal. Born into the family of a severe British civil servant, Gwenn was turned out of the house at the age of seventeen for expressing a desire to become an actor. And an actor he did become as he spent over 60 years on the stage and screen. His career was given a boost when George Bernard Shaw offered him a leading role in the play *Man and Superman* at the age of 27. He soon became a familiar figure as Shaw signed him for five subsequent productions. He found time to serve with the British Army during World War I and rose

Edmund Gwenn, in Mister 880.

from private to captain. Instead of resting on such laurels as his Academy Award performance for best supporting actor in *Miracle on 34th Street* at the age of 71, he continued to pop up on the screen at a bewildering pace. His films included *Anthony Adverse, Pride and Prejudice, The Devil and Miss Bishop, Les Miserables, Something for the Birds, Challenge to Lassie, The Trouble with Harry, Apartment for Peggy,* and *Mr. 880.*

Alan Hale

ALAN HALE SR. (1892–Jan. 22, 1950)
Alan Hale Sr. was born in Washington, D.C., the son of John MacKahn, a manufacturer of patent medicines. He attended the University of Pennsylvania, entered legit, then joined the Lubin Film Co. in Philadelphia in 1911. His movie career spanned nearly 40 years, but still

found time to be a writer, singer, actor, and director. Once he tried newspaper work and even studied to be an osteopath. His biggest off-screen success was as an inventor. Among products invented or financed were folding theatre seats, improved auto brakes, hand fire extinguishers and a formula for greaseless potato chips. He was well known for his role as "Little John" in *The Adventures of Robin Hood.* Some of his other films were *It Happened One Night, Imitation of Life, Of Human Bondage, Stella Dallas, Strawberry Blonde, Gentleman Jim, Cheyenne,* and *Whiplash.*

THURSTON HALL (1882–Feb. 20, 1958)
Thurston Hall was a character actor of note, remembered for his characterizations of bankers, businessmen and politicians. His career spanned

Thurston Hall, with Gloria Jean in Manhattan Angel.

the Broadway stage, motion pictures and television. Hall appeared on Broadway in *Mrs. Wiggs of the Cabbage Patch, Ben Hur,* and *Mourning Becomes Electra.* He also appeared on television as Cosmo Topper's boss in the *Topper* series. Appearing in motion pictures since 1915, Hall was featured in such films as *The Adventures of Mark Twain, Wilson, Brewster's Millions, Colonel Effington's Raid, The Secret Life of Walter Mitty,* and *Mourning Becomes Electra.*

SARA HADEN (1899–Sept. 15, 1981)
Sara Haden, as a character actress, appeared in over 100 films. She first appeared on the stage on tour with her mother, a well known star at

Sara Haden

Charles Halton, center, with Groucho and Chico Marx.

the time. She played a number of parts on the New York stage with such groups as Walter Hampden's Shakespearean Repertory Company, and with actors Minor Watson, Clayborne Foster and Walter Connolly. Entering films in 1934, her long list of credits included the *Andy Hardy* series, *Magnificent Obsession, Poor Little Rich Girl, Captain January, The Bishop's Wife, Rachel and the Stranger, Little Lost Angel,* and *The Fountain.*

CHARLES HALTON *(1876–Apr. 16, 1959)*

Charles Halton demonstrated an early interest in the theatre. Born in Washington, D.C., he was forced at the age of fourteen to quit school and find employment. An ascetic by nature and with a consuming desire for intellectual pursuits, he was financed by his employer through the New York Academy of Dramatic Arts. After graduation, he went directly into the long struggle in stock and finally Broadway. After closing in New York in *Dodsworth* he went with Walter Huston to Hollywood to do the film version. Here he remained, returning occasionally to the New York stage. Deft and subtle in comedy, dynamic in delivery as a villain, Halton as a character actor was a delight to critics and public alike. Among his films (over 160) were *Prisoner of Zenda, Dead End, Penrod, Jessie James,*

Dodge City, Your Mr. Lincoln, Dr. Cyclops, The Westerner, Lillian Russell, Tobacco Road, Sabotage, My Sister Eileen, Rhapsody in Blue, Wilson, A Tree Grows in Brooklyn, and *The Best Years of Our Lives.*

MARGARET HAMILTON *(1902–   )*

Margaret Hamilton was born in Cleveland, Ohio. She graduated from Miss Wheelock's Kindergarten Training School in Boston, Massachusetts. Throughout her schooling she appeared in various plays and theatrical productions. Before entering the theatre professionally she taught kindergarten and nursery school for a number of years. Her theatrical career included community playhouses, Broadway stage, off-Broadway, summer stock, radio, television, and motion pictures. Throughout her career she has continued her interest in children and education by organizing a therapy program for boys and girls, a story-telling group for Los Angeles Children's Hospital and serving on the Beverly Hills Board of Education and on the P.T.A. Board. Her many film credits include *Another Language, Farmer Takes a Wife, Little Chickadee, State of the Union, Wizard of Oz, Guest in the House, Moon's Our Home,* and *Life of Hans Christian Anderson.*

Margaret Hamilton, left, with Sara Haden in Way Down East.

SIR CEDRIC HARDWICKE (1893–Aug. 6, 1964)

Sir Cedric Hardwicke was born in Stourbridge, England. He began his stage career in that country in 1912 and appeared in his first film one year later. It was 1926 before he made his second film, but his career didn't really blossom until the 1930's. In a long film career in the USA the distinguished character actor was always properly British. He was still active in films when he died in 1964. His films included *Les Miserables, King Solomon's Mines, On Borrowed Time, Stanley and Livingstone, The Hunchback of Notre Dame, Tom Brown's School Days, Suspicion, Wilson, The Keys of the Kingdom,* and *Salome.*

PERCY HELTON (1894–Sept. 11, 1971)

Born in New York into a theatrical family, Percy Helton started acting at two years of age with his father at Tony Pastor's. He spent five years with David Belasco as a child actor and three years with George M. Cohan. During World War I, Helton served in France, returning to

Sid Cedric Hardwicke in Salome.

Percy Helton

86

Broadway to renew his acting career when it was over. His Broadway career included such work as *Young America, The Five Million, To the Ladies,* and *One Sunday Afternoon.* His distinctive voice and characterizations subsequently earned him character parts in numerous films including *Miracle on 34th Street, Call Northside 777, Hazard, Chicken Every Sunday, My Friend Irma, Fancy Pants, The Robe, Call Me Madam, A Star Is Born,* and *How to Marry a Millionaire.*

HUGH HERBERT *(1885–Mar. 12, 1952)*
Hugh Herbert as a film comedian was known for his fidgety hands and giggling "woo-woo." Born in Binghamton, New York, he attended Cornell University. He was a stage headliner for nearly 25 years but also well known as a playwright. During his career, he wrote 150 vaudeville sketches, and plays. Herbert arrived in Hollywood with Will Morrissey's *Exposures of*

Hugh Herbert, left, with Allen Jenkins in Sh! The Octopus

1926. In the early film days he acted, wrote, and directed. He was co-author of the first full-length talking picture *The Lights of New York.* His motion picture appearances included *Good Time Charley, She Had to Say Yes, The Lost Squadron, Million Dollar Legs, Gold Diggers of 1935, Midsummer Night's Dream, Traveling Saleslady, Ever Since Eve, Beauty for Sale, Kismet, A Miracle Can Happen,* and *Beautiful Blonde from Bashful Bend.*

JUANO HERNANDEZ *(1898–July 17, 1970)*
Born in Puerto Rico and immigrating to New York, Hernandez had a lifetime in all branches of show business before entering films. Moving, over the years, from carnival to carnival and cir-

Juano Hernandez, in Something of Value.

cus to minstrel show, he worked over into comedy and dramatic sketches, and finally settled down in New York as an actor. He appeared in many successful productions and also appeared on radio. His Hollywood engagements grew out of his stage appearances. Beckoned from New York, he made his film debut in *Intruder in the Dust.* Other credits included *Stars in My Crown, Young Man with a Horn, The Breaking Point, Kiss Me Deadly,* and *Trail Ransom.*

JEAN HERSHOLT *(1886–June 2, 1956)*
Jean Hersholt was born in Copenhagen, Denmark. His parents were actors and he too became interested in acting while attending Copenhagen Art School. After becoming an actor himself, he emigrated in 1914 to the United States. In 1915 he appeared in his first film. Hersholt was one of the great character actors of the silent screen. In contrast to his later image, he played villain-

Jean Hersholt in Reunion.

88

ous roles. He became well known as the kindly Dr. Christian on radio as well as in films and he appeared as Dr. Dafoe in the Dionne quintuplet series. Throughout his career Hersholt was interested in working for various charitable organizations and was the founder of the Motion Picture Relief Fund. His many films included *Hell's Hinges, Greed, Grand Hotel, Dinner at Eight, The Country Doctor, Reunion, Seventh Heaven, Alexander's Ragtime Band, Meet Dr. Christian*, and *Dr. Christian Meets the Women*.

LOUIS JEAN HEYDT (1905–Jan. 29, 1960)

Louis Jean Heydt, a native of Montclair, New Jersey, attended Worcester Academy and Dartmouth College. He started a career in journalism but turned to the stage. Before going to Hollywood in 1937, where he played in more

Louis Jean Heydt

than 150 movies, he appeared in a number of important Broadway productions. Throughout his career he alternated between stage and screen roles and later television. His screen credits included *Test Pilot, Each Day I Die, Gone with the Wind, Tortilla Flat, Thirty Seconds Over Tokyo, Abe Lincoln in Illinois, Come to the Stable, Rawhide*, and *Dive Bomber*.

HERBERT HEYES (1889–May 31, 1958)

Born in Vader, Washington, Heyes made his acting debut at age ten in 1906 with the Baker Stock Company in Portland, Oregon. In 1910 he was engaged by James K. Hackett playing a

Herbert Heyes

variety of roles. He became a leading man in stock, moved on to Broadway, and began to divide his time between the legitimate stage and silent screen. His debut in silent pictures was in 1916 as leading man to Theda Bara in *Under Two Flags*. Starring roles followed in many silent productions and then radio. His return to motion pictures as a featured character actor came after *State of the Union* on the New York stage. His character roles included *A Place in the Sun* (his favorite), *The Court Martial of Billy Mitchell, The Far Horizons, Miracle on 34th Street, Ever Since Eve, Only the Valiant, Kiss Tomorrow Goodby, Park Row, The Ten Commandments, Ruby Gentry*, and *Sincerely Yours*.

RUSSELL HICKS (1895–June 1, 1957)

Russell Hicks, long a character actor on screen, stage and television, was born in Baltimore. After his graduation from prep school in Maryland he entered the business world. Later, over his parents' objections to a theatrical career, he entered motion pictures. He played bit parts in

Birth of a Nation and *Intolerance*. His first stage role was in *It Pays to Smile*. For many years he was one of Hollywood's busiest character actors, appearing in such films as *The Bandit of Sherwood Forest, Gay Blades, The Pilgrim Lady, The Hunted, Samson and Delilah, Overland Telegraph, As You Were, The Maverick, Man of Conflict,* and *Seventh Cavalry*.

Samuel S. Hinds, in The Road Back.

Russell Hicks

HALLIWELL HOBBES *(1877–Feb. 20, 1962)*
Halliwell Hobbes was born, appropriately, in Stratford-on-Avon. After a career on the British stage, where he appeared with such greats as

Halliwell Hobbes

SAMUEL S. HINDS *(1875–Oct. 13, 1948)*
Samuel S. Hinds, one of the busiest character actors in the history of Hollywood, began his career after the 1929 depression had wiped out his fortune. Born in Brooklyn of wealthy parents, Hinds attended Phillips Academy, Harvard, and New York Universities. He entered the field of law in New York and later moved to Pasadena in 1905. A drama enthusiast and a founder of the Pasadena Playhouse, Hinds caught on in pictures, playing in more than 150. Some of his outstanding features were *Little Women, You Can't Take It with You,* the *Dr. Kildare* series, *Destry Rides Again, The Boys from Syracuse, Call Northside 777, Zanzibar, Escape in the Desert, Uncle Harry,* and *The Runaround.*

Mrs. Patrick Cambell and Ellen Terry, he came to the United States in 1923, appearing on Broadway in *The Swan*. Hobbes made his screen debut in 1929 and occasionally returned to Broadway. Though he never considered himself a "film actor," and his favorite and most successful roles were on the stage, he appeared in over 150 films.

These included *Dr. Jekyll and Mr. Hyde, Mandalay, Gaslight, Mr. Skeffington, Casanova Brown, You Can't Take It with You, Here Comes Mr. Jordan*, and *Miracle in the Rain.*

FAY HOLDEN *(1893–June 23, 1973)*
Fay Holden, born in England, began acting at the age of nine. She subsequently appeared in several dramas and musical comedies in London. She came to America with her husband to work

Fay Holden, as Mother Hardy with Mickey Rooney.

for William Patrick Campbell in New York, later appearing in Boston and Canada. Upon entering films she changed her stage name, Gaby Fay, to Fay Holden. Her film credits included *Polo Joe, Double or Nothing, Sweethearts, Bitter Sweet, Ziegfeld Girl*, and her favorite, the *Andy Hardy* series.

TAYLOR HOLMES *(1878–Sept. 30, 1959)*
Born in Newark, New Jersey, he first appeared professionally in vaudeville on the Keith vaude-

ville circuit. But he quickly transferred to the legitimate stage and made a Broadway debut, playing utility parts of all kinds. His climb was rapid and he appeared in more than 100 successful plays. He went to California first in 1920, starring in a series of silent comedies. Then he returned to the New York stage. There were two more returns to California and films and finally, in 1947, Holmes returned to Hollywood and took

Taylor Holmes, left, with Marie Windsor and Richard Denning in Double Deal.

up permanent residence. His many movies included *The Return of Sherlock Holmes, Only the Brave, An American Tragedy, Dinner at Eight, Nana, Great Expectations, Joan of Arc, Kiss of Death*, and *Mr. Belvedere Goes to College.*

OSCAR HOMOLKA *(1898–Jan. 27, 1978)*
An able architect was lost when Oscar Homolka decided to become an actor. Born in Vienna and after attending college for one year, despite parental objections, he steered a straight dramatic course. Following service in World War I he picked up experience by joining a theatrical circuit and then a stock company. Later he became a member of the noted Raimund Theater in Vienna and in 1923 joined Max Reinhardt's company. After leaving Reinhardt he went to England where he made his film debut in *Rhodes of Africa*. In 1937 he was brought to Hollywood for his first film. He returned to England after this initial chore and did not see Hollywood again until 1939. Alternating between Hollywood and the New York

Oscar Homolka, left, with Valli and Sir Cedric Hardwicke in The White Tower.

scores of pictures to follow were *Alice in Wonderland, Your Uncle Dudley, Top Hat, Lost Horizon, The Merry Widow, Sunny, Here Comes Mr. Jordan, I Married an Angel, Arsenic and Old Lace, Brazil, Cinderella Jones,* and *All My Sons.*

stage kept the actor busy. He established himself in films with roles in *Ebb Tide, Rage in Heaven, Seven Sinners, War and Peace, Mission to Moscow, Hostages,* and *I Remember Mama.*

EDWARD EVERETT HORTON *(1886–Sept. 29, 1970)*
Edward Everett Horton was born in Brooklyn, New York. He attended school in Brooklyn, Oberlin Academy, Oberlin College, Polytechnic Institute (Brooklyn) and Columbia University. In college he wrote and produced plays and, wanting to act, made his debut with a traveling

BILLY HOUSE *(1890–Sept. 23, 1961)*
Billy House started his career as a trumpet player in his native Mankato, Minnesota, joined a minstrel show, and then became a tent-show performer in Texas and Oklahoma. Winning a fat man contest resulted in an engagement to ap-

Billy House

Edward Everett Horton, right, with Eric Blore in Top Hat.

company in *The Mikado,* in 1910. Subsequently he played many stock engagements and made several road tours. Horton made his screen debut in 1921 in *Too Much Business.* Among the many

pear in vaudeville, which brought him to the Palace in New York in 1925. He went on to star and appear in various Broadway productions. His career alternated between the Broadway stage and films and eventually television. His many film roles included appearances in *Smart Money, Merry-Go-Round, Bedlam, The Stranger, Trail Street, The Egg and I, Where Danger Lives, Santa Fe,* and *People Will Talk.*

JOHN HOYT *(1905–   )*
Born John Hoysradt in New York City, Hoyt evidenced a hankering for a stage career early in life. An interest in drama continued while he attended Yale University, but a brief career in teaching came first. He became a history instruc-

tor at Groton, where his pupils included Elliot Roosevelt and Franklin Jr. Convinced that teaching was too narrow a life, Hoyt joined the Summer Theatre at Southampton, Long Island, under Monty Wooley's direction. Between summer seasons he appeared with Stuart Walker's repertory company in Cincinnati. His Broadway debut came in 1931. Later, in 1935, he turned to musical shows, scoring with Bob Hope and Fanny Brice in the *Ziegfeld Follies*. In 1938 he deserted the stage for the cabaret spotlight. He made his film debut in 1945 in Paramount's *O.S.S.* Other film roles have included *Sealed Verdict, Lawless, Outside the Wall, The Great Dan Patch, Brute Force, Winter Meeting, To the Ends of the Earth, The Bribe,* and *Everybody Does It.*

John Hoyt, in Riot in Juvenile Prison.

HAROLD HUBER *(1910–Sept. 29, 1959)*
Harold Huber was born in New York City and received a law degree from Columbia University, however, he turned to acting instead. His first major Broadway role was in *Farewell to Arms*. In 1933 he went to Hollywood for films. At the height of his film career, he was seldom idle. When not making gangster pictures, he was appearing in other sadistic type parts such as an Arab or Mongolian. Some of Huber's movie roles included *The Bowery, The Thin Man, Naughty Marietta, G-Men, San Francisco, The Good Earth,* and *The Adventures of Marco Polo.*

Harold Huber, in Charlie Chan on Broadway.

HENRY HULL *(1890 Mar. 8, 1977)*
Although known mainly as one of the great names in the theatre, Henry Hull also had a long record of almost 40 years in motion pictures. Hull made his first theatrical appearance in New York in 1909. In 1916, the year of his first Broadway triumph, he also made his film debut at Fort Lee, New Jersey. After that he was kept busy in both media and later in television. The theatre was a family institution. Born in Louisville, Kentucky, when his father was a dramatic critic, he started out as a mining engineer. But the call of the theatre was too strong so he joined a repertory company, playing every type of part. Hull made his first trip to Hollywood in 1924 to recreate for film his role in *The Man Who Came Back*. He shuttled between New York and Hollywood after that as well as playing with

Henry Hull, in My Son, My Son!

Arthur Hunnicutt

touring companies throughout America. His long film record includes *Lifeboat, Jesse James, Mourning Becomes Electra, The Great Gatsby, Yellow Jack, High Sierra, Now and Forever, Kentucky Rifle,* and *The Deadly Peacemaker.*

ARTHUR HUNNICUTT (1911–Sept. 26, 1979)
Arthur Hunnicutt was born in Gravelly, Arkansas, receiving his early education in the local schools. He was forced to leave college in his junior year due to a lack of funds, and determined to become an actor, went to Martha's Vineyard, Massachusetts. Bit roles followed and then a jump to New York and the Theatre Guild's production of *Love's Old Sweet Song.* Other successful Broadway appearances included *Green Grow the Lilacs* and *Tobacco Road.* In 1942 he went to Hollywood to make *Wildcat.* Returning to New York, Hunnicutt continued his Broadway career until summoned to films again in 1948. His picture credits included *Dan Patch, Pinky, Stars in My Crown, Broken Arrow, Two Flags West, Red Badge of Courage, Lust for Gold, The Big Sky,* and *This Man Is Mine.*

PAUL HURST (1888–Feb. 27, 1953)
Paul Hurst was born and reared on the Miller and Lux Ranch in Tulare County, California. He started his theatre career as a scene painter, playing his first stage role in 1907 in San Fran-

Paul Hurst, left, with Gloria Stuart and Michael Whalen in Island in the Sky.

cisco. For the next few years he played character roles in various Pacific coast stage productions. He entered pictures in 1911 as writer, actor and director of westerns. He worked at all the studios and appeared first as a heavy, and then a comedian. For several years he was comedy relief in

94

the *Monte Hale* western series at Republic. His many screen appearances included *Robin Hood of El Dorado, In Old Chicago, Alexander's Ragtime Band, Super Sleuth, Cafe Society, Hold That Co-Ed, Topper Takes a Trip,* and *The Sun Shines Bright.*

Warren Hymer, with Marie Wilson.

WARREN HYMER *(1906–Mar. 25, 1948)*
Hymer was born in New York City. After studying play writing at Yale University for a year, he went to London, where he appeared in a stage production. He returned to New York in 1928 and went to Hollywood the following year to enter films. His first film was *Up the River.* His screen bow introduced him as a comedian, and his career thereafter was devoted to comic and heavy roles, for both of which he became well known.

Rex Ingram and Georgia Burke in Anna Lucasta.

REX INGRAM *(1895–Sept. 19, 1969)*
Rex Ingram was educated at Northwestern University and appeared in many stage roles in addition to his work in films. His stage roles included *Emperor Jones, Lulubelle, Porgy,* and *Green Pastures.* He appeared in the first Tarzan picture in support of Elmo Lincoln. His better roles in films included De Lawd in *Green Pastures,* Lucifer Jr. in *Cabin in the Sky,* and the giant Genii in *Thief of Bagdad.* Ingram also appeared in *Salome, The Ten Commandments, King of Kings, The Sign of the Cross, Dark Waters,* and *A Thousand and One Nights.*

GEORGE IRVING *(1874–Sept. 11, 1961)*
George Irving was born in New York City and played as leading man to Maude Adams in his early stage days. He entered the infant motion picture industry in 1913, directing many films before returning to acting in character roles. His films included *The Goose Hangs High, Craig's Wife, Morgan of the Marines, Godless Girl, The Dance of Life, Thunderbolt, Paris Bound, Son of Dracula, Christmas Holiday,* and *Lady in the Death House.*

George Irving with Robert Sterling in Yesterday's Heroes.

THOMAS E. JACKSON *(1886–Sept. 7, 1967)*
Jackson was born in New York City and began acting in school plays. In 1912 he got a small part in the original *Yellow Jacket* and later the *Property Man* in which he also toured. There

followed a number of years of stock and Broadway through 1928, when he went to Hollywood. Jackson made his film debut in 1928 and subsequently appeared in over 100 pictures, making the transition in later years to television. Among his film credits were *Good News, Broadway, Little Caesar, Call of the Wild, It Had to Happen, Little Miss Nobody, Grand Jury, Crime Takes a Holiday,* the *Torchy Blaine* series, the *Thin Man* series, and *Nancy Drew*.

roles in *The Gunfighter* and Leo McCarey's *My Son John*. His most remembered role was probably that of Turk in the film version of *Come Back Little Sheba*. His other films include *Sea Hornet, Big Leaguer, Sea of Lost Ships, Violent Men, Shanghai Story,* and *The Dirty Dozen*.

Thomas E. Jackson, in Broadway.

Allen Jenkins, in Sins of Man.

RICHARD JAECKEL (1926–)
Richard Jaeckel won a role as a young Marine in *Guadalcanal Diary* within weeks of finishing at Hollywood High School in 1943. He played in many action pictures following that film including *The Sands of Iwo Jima, Jungle Patrol,* and *Battleground*. He had small but impressive

Richard Jaeckel

ALLEN JENKINS (1900–July 20, 1974)
Allen Jenkins built a whole career in films around his type-cast part of the doltish, quasi-humorous gangster. A native of New York, he appeared in over 125 pictures after making his motion picture debut in 1932 by repeating his Broadway role in the film version of *Blessed Event*. His other films included *Three on a Match, I Am a Fugitive from a Chain Gang, 42nd Street, Twenty Million Sweethearts, Whirlpool, Tortilla Flat, The Senator Was Indiscreet, Inside Story, Behave Yourself,* and *Let's Go Navy*.

FRANK JENKS (1902–May 13, 1967)
Frank Jenks started his show business career as a musician in vaudeville from 1922–1934. He entered pictures in 1934 and was a contract player at Universal, where his first prominent

part was in *100 Men and a Girl.* Jenks was in over 100 films during his career, including *Letter of Introduction, Follow the Fleet, Back Street, Petty Girl, The Storm, His Girl Friday,*

Isabel Jewel with H. B. Warner, Edward Everett Horton, Ronald Colman, and Thomas Mitchell in Lost Horizon.

Frank Jenks, in The Last Warning.

To Please a Lady, Lucky Losers, Woman on the Run, Mother Didn't Tell Me and *White Lightning.* During 1953–1954 he was in the *Colonel Flack* teleseries live, and from 1956–1959 in the filmed version.

Ben Johnson in The Train Robbers.

ISABEL JEWEL *(1913–   )*

Isabel Jewel was born in the little cowtown of Shoshoni, Wyoming. Her family lived on a horse ranch, which accounts for the fact that she is probably the most accomplished horsewoman ever to appear in films. Miss Jewel appeared in college dramatics at Hamilton College in Kentucky. She went into a stock company in Chicago and later wound up in the hit Broadway show *Blessed Event.* It was her work in this which sent her to Hollywood to appear in the film version of the production. From 1933 until 1946 she appeared in 80 films. Among some of the films in which she has appeared are *Bondage, Bombshell, Manhattan Melodrama, A Tale of Two Cities, The Lost Horizon, Career Woman, Marked Woman, Northwest Passage, Irene, High Sierra,* and *Dancing Feet.*

BEN JOHNSON (1918–)

Ben Johnson was born in Foracre, Oklahoma, the son of a cowboy and world champion steer roper. He started his film career as a stuntman and soon became a favorite of director John Ford. Johnson made his first film as an actor in 1948 and was the world's champion steer roper in 1953. He won the Best Supporting Actor Award for *The Last Picture Show* in 1971. His films include *Three Godfathers, Mighty Joe Young, Wagonmaster, Shane, The Rare Breed, The Wild Bunch, Chisum, The Train Robbers, Dillinger,* and *Bite the Bullet.*

I. STANFORD JOLLEY (1900–Dec. 6, 1978)

I. Stanford Jolley was in show business for nearly 45 years, participating in stock, Broadway stage shows, B.B. Keith and Loew Inc. vaudeville circuits, radio, TV, and motion pictures. He arrived in Hollywood in 1935 and did considerable radio work in "Lux Theatre" and "Matinee Play-

I. Stanford Jolley

house." He soon started doing gangster parts in *Dead End Kids* films, and did thirteen episode serials, several *Charlie Chan* stories, and similar productions. Toward the end of the 1930's he began doing "top heavies" in westerns, and found this such a lucrative field that this is where he remained. As a freelance character actor he played close to 500 screen credit parts of wide variety.

98

GORDON JONES (1912–June 20, 1963)

Gordon Jones was a former UCLA football player who became a popular character actor in films and television, specializing in comic roles. Prior to World War II he played varied roles in many movies produced by MGM, RKO, Repub-

Gordon Jones

lic, United Artists, and Columbia. Among his leading roles were as the "Ramblin' Wreck from Georgia Tech" in *My Sister Eileen*, and a comedy pilot lead in *Flying Tigers*. After returning from the army after the war he entered the television field and appeared in *Private Secretary* and the *Abbott and Costello Show*, in which he was cast as the much-maligned policeman. One of his last screen credits was *The Secret Life of Walter Mitty*. Other films in which he appeared were *Wistful Widow of Wagon Gap, Sound Off, China Passage, Out West with the Hardys, Pride of the Navy, Disputed Passage, They All Kissed the Bride, Gobs and Gals,* and *Foreign Affair.*

VICTOR JORY (1902–Feb. 11, 1982)

Victor Jory started his acting career at the Pasadena Playhouse in 1918 under Gilmor Brown while still a high school student. He left the University of California after one semester and began a roving theatrical career which lasted twelve years. He went to New York in 1930 and

Victor Jory

made his Broadway bow in *Berkeley Square*, and did featured roles in *Tonight or Never* and *Command to Love*. While visiting friends in California in 1932, Jory was persuaded to play the lead in *Louder, Please*, the Norman Krasna comedy which brought him a screen contract at Fox. Jory appeared in over 125 films and listed his favorite roles as Oberon in *A Midsummer Night's Dream*, as Injun Joe in the *Adventures of Tom Sawyer*, as Jed in *The Fugitive Kind*, as Barker in *State Fair*, as Carpetbagger in *Gone with the Wind*, and as Father in *The Miracle Worker*.

ALLYN JOSLYN *(1905–Jan. 21, 1981)*

Allyn Joslyn was one of Hollywood's most versatile character actors. After a successful radio career in more than 3500 shows, he entered films

Allyn Joslyn, right, with Red Skelton in Public Pigeon No. 1.

in the Warner Brothers picture *They Won't Forget*. This was the picture that introduced Lana Turner to moviegoers. Joslyn was usually cast as a cold-blooded newspaperman or as a suave, but bored member of the society set. His pictures included *They Won't Forget, Hollywood Hotel, Sweethearts, Cafe Society, My Sister Eileen, The Immortal Sergeant, The Affairs of Martha, The Great McGinty, Only Angels Have Wings, The Horn Blows at Midnight, Shocking Miss Pilgrim, If You Knew Susie,* and *The Lady Takes a Sailor.*

MARVIN KAPLAN *(1927–)*

Marvin Kaplan has stolen many scenes from other movie actors with his thick horn-rimmed glasses and an owlish expression that is somewhere between wistful and perplexed. He was born in Brooklyn and was educated at New York University and Brooklyn College and became an English teacher. After World War II he studied playwriting at the University of Southern California. While performing in a theater group there he was discovered by

Marvin Kaplan, right with June Allyson and David Wayne in The Reformer and the Redhead.

Katharine Hepburn, who got him a part in *Adam's Rib*. His other films include *Key to the City, The Reformer and the Redhead, I Can Get It for You Wholesale, Criminal Lawyer, Angels in the Outfield, Behave Yourself, An Old Spanish Custom,* and *The Fat Man.*

KURT KATCH *(1893–Aug. 14, 1958)*

Kurt Katch was a Lithuanian-born actor who came to the U.S. in 1937 and moved to Hollywood in 1941. A student of Max Reinhardt, Katch had lead roles in German productions. He organized the Kulturbund Deutscher Juden Theater in Berlin, and later established a

Kurt Katch, second from left, with Ricardo Cortez in Make Your Own Bed.

Yiddish-speaking theater in Warsaw, Poland. He spoke German, Yiddish, Polish and English. Katch appeared in about fifty motion pictures, the last one being *The Young Lions.* He played Uncle Chris in the *I Remember Mama* television plays and appeared in more than 200 TV shows.

Larry Keating, left, with Robert Wagner in Stopover Tokyo.

His films included *Wife Takes a Flyer, Berlin Correspondent, Background to Danger, Mission to Moscow, Watch on the Rhine, The Mask of Dimitrios, The Conspirators, The Seventh Cross, Salome,* and *Song of Love.*

LARRY KEATING *(1899–Aug. 26, 1963)*

Larry Keating, trim and hearty, with receding hair and a neat mustache, played many film roles as a lawyer, doctor, editor or businessman. He was born in St. Paul, Minnesota, and was a nephew of Tommy Burns, heavyweight boxing champion of the world from 1906 to 1908. He spent seven years with radio's *This Is Your F.B.I.,* and for six years, beginning in 1953, he played Harry Morton in the *George Burns and Gracie Allen Show* on TV. From 1960 until his death he played Alan Young's irascible neighbor, Roger Addison, in the *Mister Ed* series. He had featured roles in more than 40 movies including *Come Fill the Cup, Carson City, When Worlds Collide, Inferno, Above and Beyond, A Lion Is in the Street, The Mating Season, Mister 880, Monkey Business,* and *Daddy Long Legs.*

ROBERT KEITH *(1898–Dec. 23, 1966)*

Robert Keith came to Hollywood after more than 30 years as a stage actor. Born in Fowler, Indiana, he started his career as a youth in silent movie houses, where he sang illustrated songs to piano accompaniment. In 1927 he wrote a play called *The Tightwad* that was produced on Broadway by Lee Shubert. The show did not have a long run, but was well liked by the critics. In 1930 Universal called him to Hollywood, not as an actor, but to write dialogue for the new "talkies." Keith stayed in Hollywood for two years writing for such films as *Peace on Earth* starring Lew Ayres and Andy Devine, and the original *Destry Rides Again* starring Tom Mix. Keith then returned to Broadway as an actor. He appeared in such plays as *The Great God Brown, The Children's Hour,* and *Mr. Roberts.* In 1949 Sam Goldwyn called him to Hollywood to portray Susan Hayward's father in *My Foolish Heart.* His other films include *Edge of Doom,*

Robert Keith, with John Hamilton, desk sergeant,
June Allyson and Frank Sully in The Reformer and
the Redhead.

Fourteen Hours, I Want You, Somebody Loves Me, Small Town Girl, Battle Circus, The Wild One, Young at Heart, Guys and Dolls, Love Me or Leave Me, and *Written on the Wind*. He was the father of actor Brian Keith.

CECIL KELLAWAY (1890–Feb. 28, 1973)

Cecil Kellaway, a native of Capetown, South Africa, was an actor, author, and director for the Australian cinema for seventeen years before coming to Hollywood. He came to the U.S. in the 1930's and was given some gangster bit parts by RKO. He became discouraged and returned to Australia. Director William Wyler, even though he had seen Kellaway in "B" pictures, wanted him for *Wuthering Heights*. Kellaway returned, signed a contract with Paramount, and remained in Hollywood thereafter. His other films included *Intermezzo, The Invisible Man Returns, Bahama Passage, My Heart Belongs to Daddy, I Married a Witch, Frenchman's Creek, Love Letters, Mrs. Parkington, The Postman Always Rings Twice, Luck of the Irish, Kim, Harvey, Kitty,* and *Guess Who's Coming to Dinner.* He and Edmund Gwenn were cousins.

JOHN KELLOGG (1916–   )

John Kellogg became a member of the South Shore Players in Cohasset. A scout for the Shuberts saw him and brought him to New York for the leading role in *Honor Bright*. That show was a flop, but he was given the male lead in the road show of *Brother Rat*. He was next accepted for a role in *The Zero Hour*, a production of the Hollywood Theater Alliance. After serving from 1942 to 1944 in the Marine Corps he went back to Hollywood and signed a contract with Columbia. His first film was *Johnny O'Clock*. Among his other films were included *Thirty Seconds Over Tokyo, A Walk in the Sun, The Strange Love of Martha Ivers,* and *Twelve O'Clock High*.

Cecil Kellaway in Tammy Tell Me True.

John Kellogg

Cy Kendall, left, with Wendell Heyburn, Humphrey Bogart and Billy Hallop in Crime School.

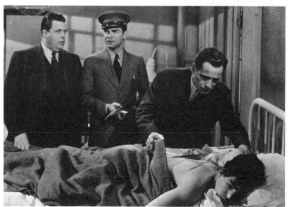

CY KENDALL *(1898–July 22, 1953)*

Cy Kendall began his professional career in 1906 at the Pasadena Playhouse, and he was a charter member of the Playhouse's 18 Actors, Inc. He appeared in more than 100 pictures during his screen career and in more than 100 productions at the Pasadena theater. Among his films were *Man Hunt, Hot Money, Dancing Feet, Men Without Souls, Andy Hardy Meets a Debutante, Wilson, The Tiger Woman, Power of the Whistler, Fighting Mad,* and *Perilous Waters.*

EDGAR KENNEDY *(1890–Nov. 9, 1948)*

Edgar Kennedy was the originator of the "slow burn" in movies which was, along with his almost completely bald head, his trademark for many years. In films since 1911, he was one of the original Keystone Cops. Mack Sennett gave him his start after spotting him as a boxer on the Pacific Coast. When sound came in, he deserted Hollywood for vaudeville for several years. He returned after a few years, and in 1930 signed with RKO to star in a series of two-reelers entitled the *Average Man* series. During his career Kennedy appeared in more than 500 films, nearly all of them comedies, which is considered to be a record both for longevity and for the number of pictures involved. Some of the sound films in which he appeared included 106 *Average Man* two-reel comedies, *Son of the Border, All of Me, San Francisco, A Star Is Born, Hollywood Hotel, Three Men on a Horse, The Black Doll, Scandal Street, Crazy House, Anchors Aweigh,* and *The Sin of Harold Diddlebock.*

TOM KENNEDY *(1885–Oct. 6, 1965)*

Tom Kennedy's hulking form and honest Irish face with the smashed nose made him familiar to generations of film fans as a portrayer of big, dumb cops, bartenders, taxi drivers and the like. He was born in New York City and despite his "dumb" comedy roles he was an honor student in mathematics in college. He was also a football star and boxing champ and won the national amateur heavyweight title in 1908. He was accepted into the police force, but turned instead to professional boxing. His first job connected with the movies was as a trainer for Douglas Fairbanks Sr. He made his film debut in 1915 in *One Round Hogan.* His screen credits include *Pack Up Your Troubles, She Done Him Wrong, Down to Their Last Yacht, Marry the Girl, She Had to Eat, Mexican Spitfire Out West, Rosie the Riveter,* and *Gold Fever.*

Tom Kennedy, left, in Armored Car.

Guy Kibbee, in Babbitt.

Edgar Kennedy, right, with Harold Lloyd and Jimmy Conlin in Mad Wednesday.

GUY KIBBEE (1882–May 24, 1956)

Guy Kibbee was typed throughout his stage and screen career as the round-domed, cracker-barrel, foxy grandpa character. He appeared in half a dozen Broadway shows before *Torch Song* in 1930 brought him a chance at Hollywood. Kibbee, born in El Paso, Texas, the son of a newspaperman, left home at thirteen to begin his theatrical career on Mississippi showboats. He appeared in picture after picture during the 1930's, played in several Shirley Temple movies and made a series of *Scattergood Baines* films. Among the other pictures in which he appeared were *42nd Street, Lilly Turner, Gold Diggers of 1933, Easy to Love, Rain, Captain Blood, Babbitt, Three Men on a Horse, Girl Crazy, The Horn Blows at Midnight,* and *Dixie Jamboree.* His last movie was *Three Godfathers,* made with John Wayne in 1949.

PERCY KILBRIDE (1888–Dec. 11, 1964)

Percy Kilbride scored his greatest success as an actor in the role of a drawling, salty, slow-grinning farmer, Pa Kettle. Teamed with Marjorie Main as Ma Kettle, Kilbride first played Kettle in a 1947 film, *The Egg and I,* starring Claudette Colbert and Fred MacMurray. Kilbride and Miss Main went on to become the stars of seven *Ma and Pa Kettle* movies, the last one filmed in 1953. Universal-International Studios reportedly grossed 10 million from the series, regarded as virtually saving the studio's fiscal life at its low point in the late 1940's and early 1950's. Born in San Francisco, the son of a machinery installer, Kilbride played more than 800 roles on the stage after his Broadway debut in 1928 in a play, *Those We Love.* He became one of Hollywood's busiest character actors after his first film role as the garrulous undertaker in *George Washington Slept Here* in 1942. He appeared in eighteen pictures from 1942 to 1946. A bachelor, his mild and reflective nature in 1949 earned him the title of "Hollywood's Most Marriageable Actor" from the Midwestern Association of Practical Nurses. His other screen appearances included *State Fair, Welcome Stranger, Black Bart, You Gotta Stay Happy, You Were Meant for Me, Mr. Soft Touch, Sun Comes Up,* and *Free for All.*

Percy Kilbride, left, with Claudette Colbert in The Egg and I.

Victor Kilian, in Atlantic Convoy.

VICTOR KILIAN (1898–Mar. 11, 1979)

Victor Kilian had his first experience in acting with a "rep" company in New England in 1909. A native of Jersey City, New Jersey, his real start in the theater came in 1924 when he joined the *Desire Under the Elms* company with Walter Huston and Mary Morris. After a long stage career he went to Hollywood in 1936 although he had made a few movies in New York before that. Kilian played in about 140 pictures and his favorite role was in a "short" called *The Happiest Man on Earth* with Paul Kelly and written by Albert Maltz. Other favorite parts were in *Seventh Heaven, Huckleberry Finn, Ramona,* and *Only Angels Have Wings.* His other films included *Road to Glory, Banjo on My Knee, Tom Sawyer, Dr. Cyclops, Chad Hanna, Reap the Wild Wind, Boys' Town, Riff Raff, Gentlemen's Agreement, Oxbow Incident, Atlantic Convoy, Young Tom Edison, Dangerous Passage,* and *Spellbound.*

Leonid Kinskey, in Down Argentine Way.

Walter Kingsford, in Experiment Alcatraz.

WALTER KINGSFORD *(1881–Feb. 7, 1958)*
Walter Kingsford appeared in supporting stage, film, and TV roles for over 40 years. He was born in Redhill, England, and began his career on the London stage. Kingsford appeared with John Drew, Ethel Barrymore, Mary Nash, and Fay Bainter in New York and London stage plays. He began making films in the U.S. in 1934. Among the films in which he appeared included *Pursuit of Happiness, The President Vanishes, Three Men in White, Hi Diddle Diddle, Mr. Skeffington, Between Two Women, Hitler Gang, The Brigand, The Pathfinder,* and *Walking My Baby Back Home.*

LEONID KINSKEY *(1903–)*
Leonid Kinskey started his theatrical career as a "mime" at the Alexandrinski Theater in St. Petersburg (Leningrad), Russia, as part of a group of students. This experience led to his being given the opportunity to perform in two other Imperial Theaters. After the Russian Revolution he played in many different European countries, then toured with the newly organized "Firebird Theater" through South America as the youthful star of this successful company. Kinskey came to the U.S. as a part of this group. Al Jolson's Viennese musical *Wunder Bar* brought him to Hollywood where he had his first part in a talking picture, *Trouble- in Paradise,* directed by Ernst Lubitsch. He went on to play in approximately a hundred pictures, including favorite roles in such pictures as *Les Miserables, Rhythm on the Range,* in which he introduced, together with Bing Crosby, Martha Raye, and Bob Burns, the hit song *I'm an Old Cowhand;* the role of the frightened peasant murderer, Simon, in Tolstoy's story *Resurrection,* the screen title being *We Live Again;* the youthful informer in *Algiers;* the role of the "chicken" in *So Ends Our Night;* the "gigolo galore," Tito, in *Down Argentine Way;* and the Russian would-be composer in *On Your Toes.*

FUZZY KNIGHT *(1901–Feb. 23, 1976)*
Fuzzy Knight was probably the king of the cowboy comedians during the golden age of the talking film. He was born in Fairmont, West Virginia, and made his first appearance as an

105

"Fuzzy" Knight, with Maria Montez in Boss of Bullion City.

Clarence Kolb, center, with Frank M. Thomas and Joe E. Brown in Beware Spooks!

entertainer at the age of fifteen when he played an end man in a tent-show minstrel troupe. After graduating in law from the University of West Virginia, where he had played in a dance band, he decided upon a career on the stage. Singing and playing in vaudeville, Broadway shows and night clubs from 1924 to 1930, he became a top-flight entertainer. He appeared in Earl Carroll's *Vanities* in 1927, the musical comedy hit, *Here's How* in 1928, Ned Wayburn's *Gambols* in 1929 and toured the Keith vaudeville circuit. His films included *She Done Him Wrong, Bodyguard, This Day and Age, George White's Scandals, The Trail of the Lonesome Pine, The Plainsman, Apache Trail, Deep in the Heart of Texas*, and many other westerns.

CLARENCE KOLB *(1874–Nov. 25, 1964)*
Clarence Kolb developed the figure of the greying, irascible, aggressive, sentimental, slave-driving tycoon into one of the most popular comedy characterizations in films and TV. In recent years he was best known as Mr. Honeywell, the boss on the *My Little Margie* TV series. A native of Cleveland, Ohio, Kolb and Max Dill became vaudeville favorites on the West Coast as the Dutch dialect team of Kolb and Dill. They last appeared together in a popular musical, *The High Cost of Living*, in 1947. Among the scores of movies in which Kolb appeared were *The Toast of New York, Wells Fargo, Gold Is Where You Find It, Merrily We Live, Carefree, The Sky's the Limit, Standing Room Only, Irish Eyes Are Smiling, Three Is a Family, Fun on a Weekend*, and *Christmas Eve*.

Otto Kruger

OTTO KRUGER *(1885–Sept. 6, 1974)*
Otto Kruger was truly "an actor who needed no introduction." For more than five decades his name in the cast of a stage play or motion picture was an assurance of a topnotch performance. Born in Toledo, Ohio, he was educated at the University of Michigan and Columbia University. He made his Broadway debut in *The Natural Law*. Among his many Broadway successes were *Easy Come, Easy Go, The Royal Family, Private Lives, Accent on Youth*, and *Parnell*. In 1920 in New York, Kruger made his screen debut in the silent film, *Under the Red*

Robe, for Cosmopolitan. He continued to appear in pictures along with his stage work until 1932, when he was brought to Hollywood and placed under contract by MGM, where he made his first "talkie," *Turn Back the Clock*. Among his more than 100 screen roles included appearances in *Gallant Lady, Treasure Island, Men in White, Dr. Ehrlich's Magic Bullet, Saboteur, Corregidor, Cover Girl, Murder, My Sweet, 711 Ocean Drive, High Noon, Magnificent Obsession, Black Widow*, and *The Last Command*. In later years Kruger returned occasionally to the stage, both in New York and on the road, and flavored his screen career with frequent radio and TV appearances.

JACK LAMBERT *(1920-   )*
Jack Lambert, a native of Yonkers, New York, had stage experience on Broadway when he arrived in Hollywood, in 1943. His first film was *Swing Fever*. His other films include *Lost Angel, Right About Face, Hostages, Stage Door Canteen, The Cross of Lorraine, Tomorrow's Harvest, Duffy's Tavern, The Killers*, and *Dick Tracy vs. the Claw*.

Jack Lambert

ELSA LANCHESTER *(1902-   )*
Elsa Lanchester is the well-known writer and actress wife of the late Charles Laughton. Born in England, she began her career at sixteen in the

Elsa Lanchester

Children's Theater in London. Her first role in films was in England in the silent version of *The Constant Nymph*. She and her husband came to this country after they both had appeared in *The Private Life of Henry VIII*. Miss Lanchester has appeared in some of Hollywood's finest films since 1935 in addition to acting on the New York and London stage. Some of her film credits include *David Copperfield, Bride of Frankenstein, Tales of Manhattan, The Spiral Staircase, The Razor's Edge, The Big Clock, Come to the Stable, Secret Garden, Les Miserables, The Bishop's Wife, Lassie Come Home*, and *Forever and a Day*.

Charles Lane in The Invisible Woman.

CHARLES LANE (1899–)

Charles Lane has been in more than 200 movies and scores of TV shows during a Hollywood career of more than 40 years. His earnest and lean-faced physiognomy, framed in rimless spectacles, has usually been seen as a tax collector, a grouchy millionaire or an acerbic banker. Some of the pictures in which he has appeared include *42nd Street, Gold Diggers of 1933, Broadway Melody, Nothing Sacred, Mr Smith Goes to Washington, The Milky Way,* and *You Can't Take It with You.* Lane made his Hollywood debut, fresh from the Pasadena Playhouse, in 1930, and appeared in twenty-three pictures in 1933 alone. In recent years he has frequently appeared on many TV series, and was a semi-regular on *Petticoat Junction* in the part of the Scrooge-like railroad trouble-shooter, Homer Bedloe.

RICHARD LANE (1900–Sept 5, 1982)

Richard Lane left George White's *Scandals* in 1937 to come to Hollywood under contract to RKO. A veteran of more than 165 feature films, he was also in recent years a very popular sports announcer in the Los Angeles area. Among his movie credits were *The Outcasts of Poker Flat, Wise Girl, This Marriage Business, Exposed, Union Pacific, Here Come the Coeds, Boston Blackie's Rendezvous, I Can Get It for You Wholesale, Take Me Out to the Ballgame,* and *Quicksand.*

Richard Lane, right, with Preston Foster and Lynn Bari in News is Made at Night.

Charles LaTorre

CHARLES A. (DOTTORE) LA TORRE (1895–)

Charles La Torre started his acting career as a teenager at the Greenwich Settlement house in Greenwich Village. He later appeared in Moss Hart's first Broadway play, *The Love Bandit,* produced under the title of *The Hold-up Man,* as the leading "heavy." La Torre appeared in about fifty or more Broadway productions including *Twelve Miles Out, Gentlemen Prefer Blondes, Tampico, Hot Cha,* and *Louisina Purchase.* He also appeared in many stock companies in the 1920's and 1930's. La Torre's first screen appearance was in D.W. Griffith's *America* in 1923, many other silent pictures. In 1936 he appeared in *Camille* starring Greta Garbo. He was brought back to Hollywood in 1941 by Paramount to recreate his original role in *Louisiana Purchase* and has appeared in over 100 films since. In addition to this role, his favorite performances came in *Passage to Marseilles, Sunset in the West,* and *Hidden City.* Among his other screen credits are *Blue Skies, My Sister Eileen, Brothers Ricco, Omar Khayam, Aladdin's Lamp, 711 Ocean Drive, A Double Life, The Tiajuana Story, The Hairy Ape, Diplomatic Courier, Kismet, Mission to Moscow* and *Enter Arsene Lupin.* In recent years, La Torre has also been active in hotel management in the Los Angeles area.

Marc Lawrence

MARC LAWRENCE (1909–   )

Marc Lawrence has been identified as "the guy with the scarred-up mug who plays in all those gangster parts." There is a great deal of truth in this sort of recognition. Born in the Bronx, he was educated at CCNY and studied with Eva Le Gallienne. He was on the New York stage in *Sour Mountain* and *Waiting for Lefty* before coming to Hollywood in 1932 under contract to Columbia. Since 1939 he has free-lanced, studied and was a close friend of Michael Chekov. His more than 100 film credits include parts in *White Woman*, *Dr. Socrates*, *Ox-Bow Incident*, *Shepherd of the Hills*, *Asphalt Jungle*, *Key Largo*, *Cloak and Dagger*, *The Virginian*, *Captain for Castile*, *Helen of Troy*, and *Custer of the West*.

CANADA LEE (1907–May 9, 1952)

Canada Lee was a onetime boxer who quit the prize ring and turned to acting after losing an eye as a result of a boxing accident. His most notable stage triumph was in Richard Wright's *Native Son*. He also won praise for his portrayal of Calaban in Shakespeare's *The Tempest*, and in the lead role in *Othello*. He was in several Hollywood films including *Lifeboat* and *Body and Soul*, in which he played a boxer. His last film was *Cry the Beloved Country*, which was released in January, 1951.

Canada Lee, right, with Richard Hylton in Lost Boundaries.

FRITZ LEIBER (1882–Oct. 14, 1949)

Fritz Leiber was a noted Shakespearean actor who was one of the early venturers from the stage into films. He made his motion picture debut in

Fritz Leiber

1917. Born in Chicago, Leiber joined the Ben Greet company at the age of twenty. With George Ford he organized the Shakespearean Repertory Company, with which they toured from 1920 to 1929. He played in many silent pictures including *If I Were King*, *Anthony and Cleopatra*, and *The Queen of Sheba*. *A Tale of Two Cities*, *The Story of Louis Pasteur*, *Hearts in Bondage*, *Champagne Waltz*, *The Prince and the Pauper*, *The Great Garrick*, *Down Under the Sea*, *They Made Her a Spy*, *Adventures of Casanova*, *Anthony Adverse*, *Another Part of the Forest*, and *Bride of Vengeance*. Leiber died shortly after completing a role in MGM's *Devil's Doorway*.

Sheldon Leonard, left, with James Gleason in Take One False Step.

SHELDON LEONARD (1907–)

Sheldon Leonard was on the Broadway stage for ten years before coming to Hollywood in the late 1930's. He had appeared in a score of plays including *Kiss the Boys Goodbye*, *Having Wonderful Time*, and *Margin of Error*. A native New Yorker, his first screen role started with *Another Thin Man* in 1939. He has played in more than 100 pictures during his career, mainly cast as a gangster. His other films include *Tall, Dark and Handsome*, *Tortilla Flat*, *Rise and Shine*, *Lucky Jordan*, *Somewhere in the Night*, *Her Kind of Man*, *It's a Wonderful Life*, *The Gangster*, *If You Knew Susie*, *Sinbad the Sailor*, and *Guys and Dolls*. In recent years Leonard has become a highly successful TV director and producer of the *Make Room for Daddy* and *I Spy* series.

MITCHELL LEWIS (1880–Aug. 24, 1956)

Mitchell Lewis attended the U.S Naval Academy at Annapolis and later graduated from Syracuse University. He began his stage career in New York shortly after the turn of the century, touring with Willie Collier in 1902. He later appeared with such stage luminaries as William Faversham, Dustin Farnum, Holbrook Blinn, and Nazimova. He began his screen career in 1914 and was under contract to MGM after 1937, appearing in dozens of that company's films. Lewis was on the original board of the Motion Picture Relief Fund in 1925, and was always active in charity work throughout his career. His film credits included: *A Tale of Two Cities*, *Sutter's Gold*, *Espionage*, *Meet John Doe*, *Cairo* and *Count of Monte Cristo*.

Mitchell Lewis, with Steffi Duna in Red Morning.

JOHN LITEL (1892–Feb. 3, 1972)

John Litel was a sturdy, handsome man of vigorous, authoritative bearing, one of the most recognizable and accomplished character actors of the period. Born in Albany, Wisconsin, he graduated from the University of Pennsylvania. His first picture was *The Sleeping Porch* in 1929. His many other films included *The Black Legion*, *The Life of Emile Zola*, *The Trial of Mary*

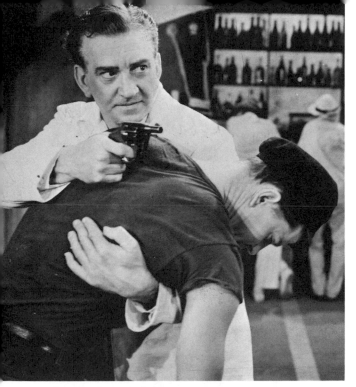

John Litel, in Submarine Base.

more than four decades. In the 1920's he appeared with all of the great stars. In Hollywood he was considered among the cleverest with make-up. At least once, he appeared as six different characters in a single picture. In 1925 he appeared as a barber in *The Torrent*, the picture in which Greta Garbo made her debut in this country. Littlefield was born in San Antonio, Texas, and attended Staunton Military Academy. He went on the stage in stock shows before going to Hollywood for his first picture, *Rose on the Range*. Among the talking films in which he appeared were *Seven Keys to Baldpate, Saturday's Children, Mother Knows Best, Clear the Deck, Big Money, Johnny Come Lately, Whistling in Dixie, Goodnight Sweetheart, Scared Stiff, Casanova in Burlesque, and Susanna Pass.*

Dugan, the *Henry Aldrich* series, *The Enchanted Forest, Salome, Where She Danced, San Antonio, Cass Timberlane, Crimson Canary,* and *Heaven Only Knows.*

Norman Lloyd, in The Southerner.

Lucien Littlefield, second from left, with Andrew Toombes, Dorothy Stickney and Jackie Cooper in What a Life.

LUCIEN LITTLEFIELD *(1895–June 4, 1960)*
Lucien Littlefield was a gifted character actor whose characterizations of the balding, wizened, meek, little man brought him a wide variety of roles in his long career. He entered motion pictures in 1913 and was in constant demand for

NORMAN LLOYD *(1914–)*
Norman Lloyd started his acting career as an apprentice with Eva Le Gallienne at the Civic Repertory Theater in the early 1930's. He appeared on Broadway in *Noah* with Pierre Frenay in 1935, and later became a leading actor in the Federal Theater's *Living Newspaper*, as well as being a member of the original company of The Mercury Theater. Lloyd was once described as the world's lightest "heavy" at 125 lbs. He made his screen debut as Fry in Alfred Hitchcock's *Saboteur* in 1941. This villainous role as well as his performances in *The Southerner* and *Walk in the Sun* remain his favorite screen accomplish-

111

Richard Loo, left, with Dana Andrews in The
Purple Heart.

ment. His other screen credits include *The Unseen*, *Spellbound*, *The Green Years*, *Letter for Evie*, *Beginning or the End*, *Scene of the Crime*, *No Minor Vices*, *Calamity Jane and Sam Bass*, *Buccaneer's Girl*, *The Black Book*, and *Limelight*. As of 1984, Lloyd can be seen as a regular in *St. Elsewhere* on TV.

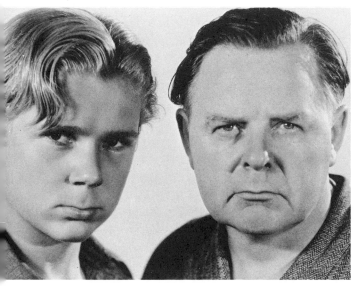

Gene Lockhart, right, with Jackie Cooper in The Devil Is a Sissy.

GENE LOCKHART *(1891–Mar. 31, 1957)*

Gene Lockhart was born in London, Ontario, of English-Scotch-Irish parents and was educated in Canadian and English schools. Displaying an early interest in dramatics and music, he appeared professionally at the age of six as a Scottish dancer with the Kilties Band, a Scotch Highlander band attached to the 48th Canadian Regiment. Later he sang in concert in Canada, frequently appearing on the same program with Bea Lillie. He came to the U.S. as a young man and appeared in stage shows including Gilbert and Sullivan's *Ruddigore*, *Handy Man*, *Sure Fire*, *Sun Up*, *Bunk of 1926* (a revue of which he was the author) and *Ah, Wilderness*, the Theater Guild production starring George M. Cohan, 1933-1934, in which Lockhart played the inebriate Uncle Sid. This was his favorite stage role and his deft portrayal of that character resulted in his coming to Hollywood, with an RKO contract. His first picture was *By Your*

Leave, in 1934. He appeared in more than 125 pictures in his career, including several years as a contract player for Warner Bros. Among some of the roles he performed on the screen were Lushin in *Crime and Punishment*, Bob Cratchit in *A Christmas Carol*, and Stephen Douglas in *Abe Lincoln in Illinois*. In Walter Wanger's *Algiers* in 1938, his role as the scoundrel Regis won as Academy Award nomination as best supporting actor. His other pictures included *The House on 92nd Street*, *Leave Her to Heaven*, *Meet Me on Broadway*, *That's the Spirit*, *The Shocking Miss Pilgrim*, *Miracle on 34th Street*, *Foxes of Harrow*, *Joan of Arc*. His daughter, June Lockhart, has been a successful actress in her own right in recent years in films and TV.

TOM LONDON *(1889–Dec. 5, 1963)*

Tom London began his motion picture career in *The Great Train Robbery* and went on to become famous for his roles as a sheriff in movies and TV westerns. A native of Louisville, Kentucky, he came to Hollywood in 1917. His many other films included *King of Kings*, *Cowboy and the Lady*, *East of Borneo*, *Secret Six*, *Hell Divers*, *Dr. Jekyll and Mr. Hyde*, *Dishonored*, *Earl Carroll's Vanities*, *Three's a Crowd*, *Behind City Lights*, and *The Undercover Woman*.

Tom London, right, with Wild Bill Elliott in Vigilantes of Dodge City.

RICHARD LOO *(1903–Dec. 8, 1983)*

Richard Loo, although he often portrayed Japanese "heavies" in the 1940's, was Chinese. He was born in Hawaii, but came to the U.S.

as a teenager, and was graduated from the University of California. He drifted into work in theatrical companies on the West Coast and in 1931 made his first movie for Columbia, *Dirigible*, starring Jack Holt and Fay Wray. Among his more than 100 film credits included *The Bitter Tea of General Yen, The Good Earth, Submarine Raider, The Road to Morocco, Wake Island, Jack London, Keys of the Kingdom, The Purple Heart, God Is My Co-Pilot, China Sky, Tokyo Rose, First Yank into Tokyo, Back to Bataan, The Cobra Strikes, The Shanghai Story,* and *Love Is a Many Splendored Thing.*

PETER LORRE *(1904–Mar. 23, 1964)*

Peter Lorre portrayed his film roles of villain, sleuth and maniac with suave understatement in tones tinged with the accents of his native Hungary. "He was the vilest of villains on the screen; he was the little man of gigantic crimes." Lorre grew up in Vienna, and as a stage-struck teenager he ran away from home. For a decade he played bit parts in small productions. In 1931, he obtained his first film role as the psychopathic child killer in the German film classic *M.* This portrayal made him internationally famous. He continued portraying sleepy-voiced psychopaths in his Hollywood career until John Huston cast him in a quasi-comic role in *The Maltese Falcon* with Humphrey Bogart and Sidney Greenstreet. Lorre and Greenstreet later appeared in numerous films together. He was not always the villain, however. For years he portrayed "Mr. Moto," the inscrutable, an invincible Japanese detective. His other screen credits included *The Constant Nymph, The Cross of Lorraine, Passage to Marseille, The Mask of Dimitrios, Confidential Agent, Three Strangers, Beast with Five Fingers, The Verdict,* and *Rope of Sand.*

MONTAGU LOVE *(1877–May 17, 1943)*

Montagu Love was a native of Portsmouth, England, whose first job was as an illustrator for a London weekly newspaper. He was sent on assignment to South Africa at the end of the Boer War and in later years sold many of his military drawings. After a career on the London stage he came to the U.S in 1914 with Cyril Maude in

Montagu Love

a road show production of *Grumpy.* He became a star with the old World Film Co. in Ft. Lee, New Jersey, about 1916. His talking films included *His Double Life, Clive of India, The Crusades, Lloyd's of London, Sutter's Gold, The White Angel, The Prince and the Pauper, The Life of Emile Zola, Tovarich, Parnell, The Prisoner of Zenda, The Buccaneer, Adventures of Robin Hood,* and *Gunga Din.* His last film was Warner Brothers' *The Constant Nymph.*

KEYE LUKE *(1904–)*

Keye Luke is probably most famous for his portrayals as Charlie Chan's No. 1 son and as a rival doctor's assistant to Van Johnson in MGM's *Dr. Gillespie* series. He studied architecture at the University of Washington after attending high school in Seattle. He became a commercial artist for West Coast Theaters in Hollywood and also worked for RKO's publicity department. When the studio needed a Chinese player who spoke perfect English for a short subject, he turned actor. His first feature film was his role of the Chinese doctor with Garbo in *The Painted Veil.* His other films include *Oil for the Lamps of China, The Good Earth, Disputed Passage, Dragon Seed, Three Men in White, First Yank in Tokyo, Tokyo Rose, Bamboo Prison, Love Is a Many Splendored Thing,* and *Around the World in 80 Days.*

Keye Luke

Russell Stock Co. in Redlands, California, in the summer of 1927. After a long career in stock and in radio as an actor and announcer, Lummis went to the Broadway stage in 1943. Among his Broadway plays were *Peepshow, Catherine Was Great, Antony and Cleopatra, Edward, My Son,* and *As You Like it.* He went west in 1951 and began his career in TV and films. Among the motion pictures in which he appeared were *The Winning Team, Les Miserables, Bloodhounds of Broadway, Port Sinister, Ruby Gentry, Mississippi Gambler, My Sister, Eileen, Trial of Billy Mitchell, The Cobweb, Julius Caesar,* and *How to Marry a Millionaire.* In addition, Lummis has appeared in more than 400 filmed and live TV shows.

DAYTON LUMMIS *(1903–   )*

Dayton Lummis, after studying for the theater at the Martha Oatman School in Los Angeles, received his first professional engagement in the

Dayton Lummis, from the TV series Cavalcade of America.

DONALD MacBRIDE *(1893–June 21, 1957)*

Donald MacBride's stage career dated back to his appearance as a teenage singer. A native of Brooklyn, he made his first film appearances in a series of Sidney Drew comedies at the old Vitagraph studio in his native city. Twenty-five

Donald MacBride

years elapsed before he again entered films. MacBride kept busy in stock and vaudeville and in long-run Broadway shows like *George White's Scandals.* It was the Broadway production of *Room Service* that took him to Hollywood in 1938 for the film version. He remained to play in scores of movies and television shows. Among his film credits are *The Story of Irene and Vernon Castle, The Great Man Votes, Blondie Takes a Vacation, The Incredible Mr. Williams, Time of Their Lives, Egg and I, Good News, Dark Horse, Northwest Passage,* and *Beat the Band.*

BARTON MacLANE *(1902–Jan. 1, 1969)*
Born in Columbia, South Carolina, MacLane went to Wesleyan University in Middletown, Connecticut, majoring in English with plans to be a writer. In his senior year he developed into a football star and as a result crashed the movies. He did bit parts and extra work at the Astoria

Barton MacLane, with Glenda Farrell in Torchy Blane, The Adventurous Blonde.

studios and studied a little at the Academy of Dramatic Arts in New York. Gradually he gained acting experience as a Broadway actor. Subsequently he made it to Hollywood and films again, making nearly 150 films as well as a television series *The Outlaws.* His many film credits included *Frisco Kid, San Quentin, Prince and the Pauper, Treasure of the Sierra Madre, You Only Live Once, Jungle Flight,* and *Cheyenne.*

ALINE MacMAHON *(1899–)*
Miss MacMahon first journeyed to Hollywood to appear in the stage version and later screen production of *Once in a Lifetime.* The daughter of William MacMahon, she was born in McKees-

port, Pennsylvania. While still a small child she moved to New York, later graduating from Erasmus Hall and Barnard College. From childhood her ambition was to become an actress. Her first professional role after leaving college was in *The Madras House,* at the Neighborhood Playhouse in New York City. She remained with this group for three years, and then was signed to a contract by Lee Shubert. Returning to the screen from time to time, she has appeared in such films as *Roseanna McCoy, The Search, Five Star Final, Silver Dollar, Ah, Wilderness, One Way Passage, Tish, The Great Mouthpiece,* and *Dragon Seed.*

Aline MacMahon, left, with Jean Simmons and Thomas Chalmers in All the Way Home.

GEORGE MACREADY *(1899–July 2, 1973)*
Macready was born in Providence, Rhode Island, and educated at Brown University. After attending dramatic school and appearing in more than 175 plays both in stock and Broadway, he went to Hollywood for a screen career. In his film career he followed the path of a double-dyed villain of treachery, deceit, and doublecross. Macready's initial film role was in *The Commandos Strike at Dawn.* After that he appeared in numerous pictures, among them *The Story of*

George Macready, in Seven Days in May.

Dr. Wassell, The Big Clock, Knock on Any Door, Wilson, A Song to Remember, Gilda, Johnny Allegro, Alias Nick Beal, The Seventh Cross, Lawless, and *Tarzan's Peril.* In later years he was featured as Martin Peyton on the TV series *Peyton Place.*

MARJORIE MAIN *(1890–Apr. 10, 1975)*

Miss Main was born Mary Tomlinson in Acton, Indiana. She received her education in the Elkhart, Indiana public schools, Knickerbocker Hall, Franklin College, and Hamilton College, Kentucky. Throughout her schooling she was active in amateur dramatics and against her parents' wishes joined a Shakespearean company playing the Chautauqua circuit. She played the Orpheum Theatre circuit, played stock, and teamed with W.C. Fields on Broadway. Then followed a series of hits including *Salvation* and *Burlesque.* At this peak of her career, she retired to be with her husband where she remained until his death in 1934. Seeking solace she returned to the stage in *Dead End* and repeated her role for the film version. After her role in *Dead End* she appeared in over 90 pictures including the famous *Ma and Pa Kettle* series. These many films included *The Women, Meet Me in St. Louis, Harvey Girls, The Egg and I, Heaven Can Wait, Wistful Widow of Wagon Gap, Shepherd of the Hills,* and *Friendly Persuasion.*

Marjorie Main, in Meet Me in St. Louis.

MILES MANDER *(1888–Feb. 8, 1946)*

Born in Wolverhampton, England, the son of an English manufacturer, Mander became an extra in a London motion-picture studio in 1928 after going through a large inheritance. His early adventures included experiences as a prize-fight promoter, horse racer, sheep rancher, automobile racer, and aviation enthusiast. After entering the theatrical business he was to become not only an actor but also playwright, director, and author. His Hollywood film career included over 70 pictures including *Three Musketeers, Lloyd's of London, Kidnapped, Suez, Here's to Romance,* and *Slave Ship.*

Miles Mander, in Babies for Sale.

CHRIS-PIN MARTIN *(1893–June 27, 1953)*

Born Ysabel Ponciana Chris-Pin Martin Piaz, he was known as a youngster in Tucson, Arizona, as "El Comico"—the funny one. He began his

Chris-Pin Martin

film career in 1911 with a troupe of Indians. After numerous years of working as an extra, he was elevated to feature billing. He was known primarily for his characterization of Pancho in the *Cisco Kid* series. In these he played opposite Warner Baxter, Duncan Renaldo, Gilbert Roland and Cesar Romero. Other pics include *In Old Arizona, The Gay Desperado, Stagecoach, Rimfire, Frontier Marshall,* and *The Beautiful Blonde from Bashful Bend.*

LeROY MASON (1903–Oct. 13, 1947)
LeRoy Mason started his screen career at the old William Fox studios in 1919, and appeared with such western stars as Tom Mix, William Farnum, and Buck Jones. Usually associated with badman characterizations, he appeared in such

films as *Climax, Smoky* serial, *Rainbow Valley, Western Gold, The Spy Ring, The Painted Trail, Rhythm of the Saddle, Gold Mine in the Sky,* and *Santa Fe Stampede.*

Aubrey Mather, center, in The Importance of Being Earnest.

AUBREY MATHER (1885–Jan. 15, 1958)
Born in Minchinhampton, England, Mather made his first stage appearance in the provinces in 1905 and his London debut in *Brewster's Millions* at Wyndham's Theatre in 1909. His first New York appearance was in 1919 in *Luck of the Navy* and there followed later Broadway productions. Aubrey appeared in both British and American films including *The Wife Takes a Flyer, Mighty McGurk, The Hucksters, It Happended in Brooklyn, Night Must Fall, Life Begins with Love,* and *Jamaica Inn.*

Leroy Mason, right, with Bud Geary, Hal Taliaferro and Kenne Duncan in Vigilantes of Dodge City.

Edwin Max, right, with Raymond Burr.

EDWIN MAX *(1909–Oct. 17, 1980)*
Edwin Max was born in Savannah, Georgia, moving with his family to San Francisco where they remained until 1938. He had intended to study civil engineering, but financial reverses stopped his plans. After working as a waiter aboard ship he returned to San Francisco and took up radio work and participation in Little Theatre groups. Max moved to Los Angeles where he worked intensively in radio. Radio led to his screen debut in RKO Radio's *Follow Me Quietly* in 1948. Other film credits included *Here Come the Nelsons, Bloodhounds of Broadway, Love That Brute* and *Francis Goes to the Races.*

MIKE MAZURKI *(1909–   )*
Born in Lwow, Ukraine, Mazurki was brought to Cohoes, upper New York State when he was six. He won academic and athletic honors in high school and a scholarship to Manhattan College

Mike Mazurki, right, with Dick Powell in Murder My Sweet.

from which he graduated. He was lured by professional basketball, football and then into wrestling. While wrestling in Los Angeles, Mazurki was signed to portray a Chinese wrestler in *The Shanghai Gesture*, his first film. Since his debut in 1942 he has appeared in over 125 motion pictures, more than 200 television shows and on the legitimate stage. Among his credits are *Moon and Sixpence, Mission to Moscow, Canter-*

ville *Ghost, Unconquered, Nightmare Alley, Samson and Delilah, Rope of Sand,* and his two favorite roles in *Murder My Sweet,* and *Farewell My Lovely.*

HATTIE McDANIEL *(1895–Oct. 26, 1952)*
Miss McDaniel began her film career in 1931 and appeared in over 300 films, winning an Academy Award in 1940 for her portrayal of "Mammy" in *Gone with the Wind.* Her fame rested on her ability as a comedienne but her versatility made her much in demand for other roles. She was born in Wichita, Kansas, where at the age of fifteen she decided to become an actress. Her first professional job was as a vocalist with an or-

Hattie McDaniel, right, with Vivien Leigh in Gone with the Wind.

chestra. While on the road she arrived in Hollywood where she was cast for the role of "Queenie" in a screen version of *Show Boat.* Some of her films included *Great Lie, Maryland, George Washington Slept Here, Since You Went Away, The Little Colonel, Song of the South, Saratoga, Margie,* and *Never Say Goodby.*

FRANCIS McDONALD *(1891–Sept. 18, 1968)*
Francis McDonald was born in Bowling Green, Kentucky and began his career in films in 1912. The talented actor played a wide range of roles in a long film career including Indians, south sea islanders, French Canadians, gangsters, chauffeurs, stagecoach drivers, sheriffs, apache dancers, aviators, prize fighters, riverboat

Francis McDonald.

in *The Gold Bug* at the Casino Theatre, New York. After several seasons on Broadway and touring with Charles Froham's companies he went to Hollywood. He appeared in many films playing Lincoln in *The Littlest Rebel, Union Pacific* and *The Prisoner of Shark Island.* Among his other film roles were *Min and Bill, Good News, Wells Fargo, Boom Town, Little Miss Marker,* and *The Mad Empress.*

FRANK McHUGH *(1899–Sept. 11, 1981)*
Born in Homestead, Pennsylvania, McHugh made his debut in his parents' traveling stock company at the age of ten. Other stock engagements followed and at seventeen he graduated into juvenile roles with the Marguerite Bryant players. Later he joined the Sherman Kelly Stock Co. from which he went into vaudeville play-

gamblers, and biblical characters. He held a college degree and was one of the first members of the Hollywood Masquers Club. His films included *The Last Trail, Count of Monte Cristo, Prisoner of Shark Island, Geronimo, Northwest Mounted Police, The Girl From Alaska, My Pal Trigger, Rancho Notorious* and *The Saga of Hemp Brown.*

FRANK McGLYNN *(1867–May 18, 1951)*
Frank McGlynn was best known for his portrayal of Abraham Lincoln in the John Drinkwater play. He appeared in the title role in 1919 and continued to portray Lincoln in various motion pictures. McGlynn made his stage debut in 1896

Frank McGlynn, right, in The Trail of the Lonesome Pine.

Frank McHugh

ing the Orpheum and Keith circuits. Resident stock and Broadway then followed. In 1930, McHugh went to Hollywood working under contract to Warner Bros. and later free lancing. His many films included *Top Speed, Dawn Patrol, The Front Page, One Way Passage, The Velvet Touch, The Tougher They Come, Mighty Joe Young, My Son John, Going My Way, Bowery to Broadway, Medal for Benny,* and *State Fair.*

DONALD MEEK (1878–Nov. 18, 1946)

Meek, a comedian and character actor, played more than eight hundred roles in his stage and screen career which covered 58 years. A slight, bald, quavering-voiced character, Meek as an actor became the favorite milquetoast type of character. Born in Glasgow, Scotland, he began his theatrical career at the age of eight. When

Donald Meek, left, with Bing Crosby in Pennies from Heaven.

he was fourteen he came to the U.S with an acrobatic troupe, but a fall turned him to acting. Meek was forced to become a character actor at eighteen when a tropical fever contracted in the Spanish American War made him bald. He made his screen debut in 1928., but motion pictures did not become full-time until 1933. In the succeeding years he made over 100 films including *You Can't Take It with You, Adventures of Tom Sawyer, Barbary Coast, The Informer, Captain Blood, Pennies from Heaven, Little Miss Broadway,* and *State Fair.*

Sid Melton

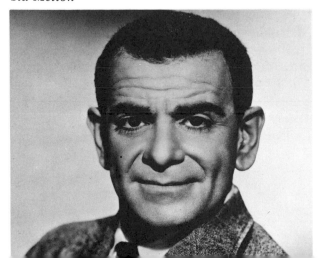

SID MELTON (   )

Sid Melton was born in Brooklyn, New York. His early career was spent on the stage touring with such productions as *See My Lawyer, The Man Who Came to Dinner* and *Three Men on a Horse.* In 1945 Melton went to Hollywood where he made his film debut in *Motel Wives.* Since entering films he has appeared in such pictures as *Doctor Broadway, Tough Assignment, Steel Helmet* (favorite role), *The Lost Continent, Lemon Drop Kid,* and *Savage Drums.*

UNA MERKEL (1903–   )

Miss Merkel was born in Covington, Kentucky. Following schooling in her home town and, later, Philadelphia, she moved to New York to study acting. Her first stage experience came in *Montmarte* as a cigarette girl. A number of Broadway productions followed and one *Coquette* brought her to the attention of Hollywood and a role in the film *Abraham Lincoln.* During long term contracts at Twentieth Century-

Una Merkel, with Lynne Overman in Once Over Lightly.

Fox and MGM, along with countless free-lance castings, Miss Merkel became an outstanding character actress, notably as a comedienne. Among her many film credits are *Daddy Long Legs, Private Lives, Reunion in Vienna, The Merry Widow, Saratoga, This Is the Army, The Kentuckian, Bundle of Joy, I Love Melvin,* and *Rich, Young and Pretty.*

CHARLES B. MIDDLETON (1879–Apr. 22, 1949)

A show business veteran of almost 50 years, he was born in Elizabethtown, Kentucky. He started his career with carnivals and circuses at an early age. He later appeared in stock companies—vaudeville and legit. He entered pictures in 1927. His sinister appearance made him ideally

Charles B. Middleton, left, with James Blaine and Charles Stevens, right.

suited for the role of "Ming the Merciless" in the *Flash Gordon* serials. Although he will be remembered most for this portrayal, he made over 100 features which include *Alexander Hamilton, Duck Soup, David Harum, Mrs. Wiggs of the Cabbage Patch, The Oklahoma Kid, Chad Hanna, Grapes of Wrath,* and *Virginia City.*

Robert Middleton, as Sam Jordan in Friendly Persuasion.

ROBERT MIDDLETON (1911–June 14, 1977)

Robert Middleton was born Samuel Messu in Cincinnati, Ohio. From 1928-1933 he attended the Cincinnati College of Music, the Cincinnati Conservatory of Music and Carnegie Institute of Technology. His early career was spent in radio as an announcer and actor and later, Middleton made the transfer to television. Following performances on Broadway in *Ondine,* he moved into films. Middleton's pictures included *Friendly Persuasion, Big Combo, Court Jester, Desperate Hours, Trial, The Silver Chalice, Proud Ones,* and *Red Sundown.*

JAMES MILLICAN (1910–Nov. 24, 1955)

James Millican was born in Pallisades, New York, attended the University of Southern California and later MGM's dramatic school. His first start in pictures came in 1933 when he appeared in *Mills of the Gods.* With over 100 screen credits Millican played more western roles than

James Millican, right, with Richard Denning and Trudy Marshall in Disaster.

any other type. He also staged several rodeos in association with Wild Bill Elliott. Among his many film credits are *Command Decision, Born to Kill, Rogues Regiment, High Noon, Gunfighters, 14 Hours, I Was a Communist for the FBI,* and *Warpath.*

123

Esther Minciotti, right, in Marty, *with Augusta Ciolli.*

ESTHER MINCIOTTI *(1888–Apr. 15, 1962)*
Born in Italy, Esther Minciotti appeared as leading lady in a repertory troupe that also starred her husband. She first came to the U.S. in 1908 to present Italian versions of Shakespeare. Here in the U.S. she became a character actress of stage, film, and television. One of her best known performances was as the mother in the film *Marty*. She also acted in television on such showns as *Studio One* and *Armstrong Circle Theatre*. Among her screen credits are *House of Strangers*, *Strictly Dishonorable*, and *The Wrong Man*.

GRANT MITCHELL *(1874–May 1, 1957)*
Mitchell, a native of Columbus, Ohio, attended Yale College and Harvard Law School and practiced law before turning to acting. He made his stage debut in 1902 and for the next 25 years was

Grant Mitchell and Louise Fazenda

constantly on the stage. He entered motion pictures in 1933. In motion pictures he was known for his portrayals of comic fathers, meek bank clerks and similar roles. His film career included roles in scores of pictures such as *Arsenic and Old Lace*, *See Here, Private Hargrove*, *Laura*, *A Medal for Benny*, the *Blondie* series, *Easy to Wed*, *Cinderella Jones*, *It Happened on Fifth Avenue*, *Dinner at Eight*, and *Who Killed Doc Robbin*.

Thomas Mitchell, and Barbara O'Neil in Gone with the Wind.

THOMAS MITCHELL *(1892–Dec. 17, 1962)*
Thomas Mitchell was born in Elizabeth, New Jersey, of Irish immigrant parents. His father was in the newspaper business and his older brother was a newspaperman. After graduating from high school, Mitchell also became a newspaper reporter. He moved to show business by writing skits in his spare time. From writing he moved into acting, traveling the United States with various stock companies. He was also active on television. His first Hollywood appearance was in the movie *Cloudy with Showers* in 1934. His best known pictures were *Stagecoach*, for which he won an Oscar in 1939 for his portrayal of a whiskey-soaked doctor, *Lost Horizon*, *Mr. Smith Goes to Washington*, *Gone with the Wind*, *The Long Voyage*, *The Outlaw*, *Wilson*, *Keys of the Kingdom*, and *High Noon*.

GERALD MOHR *(1914–1968)*
Born in New York, Mohr grew up in an environment dominated by music and science. Relatives

Gerald Mohr

Juanita Moore, right, in Imitation of Life.

in New York, London and Paris. Her first appearance as an actress came with a part in Sartre's *No Exit*, an Ebony Showcase production in Los Angeles. She then made the transition to films and television. Her featured film roles have included *Lydia Bailey, A Band of Angels, Affair in Trinidad, The Girl Can't Help It, Something of Value*, and *Imitation of Life*, for which she received an Oscar nomination.

steered him into music at an early age and later, medicine claimed his interest in planning a career. While in medical school at Columbia University, he was invited to make an audition as a radio announcer. He was immediately hired by CBS and shortly was made the network's youngest special events reporter. After being urged to try for the Broadway stage, Mohr did and made his debut in *The Petrified Forest*. In 1937 he joined the Mercury Theater Company from which he went into films. His first film role was in *Lady in Burlesque*. World War II interrupted his screen career, but he returned after being honorably discharged to continue in such films as *Gilda, The Magnificent Rogue, Heaven Only Knows, The Lone Wolf* series, *Two Guys from Texas*, and *Seven Witnesses*.

JUANITA MOORE (1922–)
Juanita Moore was born in Los Angeles. As a child she worked in her parents' ice cream parlor. She attended Los Angeles City College where she studied drama and took part in college theatricals. Branching into night club work, Miss Moore gained rapid success, appearing in famous clubs

VICTOR MOORE (1876–July 23, 1962)
Victor Moore made a lengthy and successful stage and motion picture career out of a shy, gentle impersonation of the little man. He entered

Victor Moore, in Meet the Missus.

125

the theatre in 1893 as a super, going on to play in many major Broadway shows and vaudeville. In 1916 Moore entered silent pictures, doing a number of pictures until his return to the New York stage in 1925. After creating a number of roles, including Vice President Alexander Throttelbottom in Gershwin's *Of Thee I Sing*, he returned to films in 1934. Among his major film credits are *Louisiana Purchase, Make Way for Tomorrow, Radio City Revels, Star Spangled Rhythm, Ziegfeld Follies, It Happened on Fifth Avenue, This Marriage Business*, and *We're Not Married*. In 1955 he made his last film, *The Seven Year Itch*.

AGNES MOOREHEAD (1906–Apr. 30, 1974)

Born in Clinton, Massachusetts, Miss Moorehead moved with her family to Reedsbury, Wisconsin. She received a Master's Degree from the University of Wisconsin and then attended the American Academy of Dramatic Arts in New York, where she was an honor student. Miss Moorehead made her professional debut on the New York stage with appearances in *Marco's Millions, Courage, Candlelight* and other productions. She then became one of the most ac-

Agnes Moorehead

tive performers on early daytime radio. During one of her radio shows she met Orson Welles and was signed to the Mercury Players. When he made the film *Citizen Kane* in 1941, Miss Moorehead was cast as Kane's mother for her film debut. She followed with *The Magnificent Ambersons* which won her the first of her

Academy nominations. Miss Moorehead then divided her time among screen, theatre and television roles. Among her numerous screen credits were *Our Vines Have Tender Grapes, Mrs. Parkington, Since You Went Away, Jane Eyre, The Seventh Cross, Journey into Fear, Dragon Seed, Johnny Belinda, Show Boat*, and *Magnificent Obsession*.

POLLY MORAN (1883–Jan. 25, 1952)

Born in Chicago, Miss Moran became one of the screen's most rollicking low comics. She started her career on the stage at the age of twelve in Chicago. While appearing on the Orpheum stage in Los Angeles in 1915, Mack Sennett discovered her and launched her film career in his comedies where she gained fame portraying the comic Western character *Sheriff Nell*. She achieved her

Polly Moran, left, with Katharine Hepburn in Adam's Rib.

greatest fame in a series of films with Marie Dressler. Miss Moran continued in films actively until 1940, when she retired. After emerging in 1949 for a brief role in *Adam's Rib*, she retired permanently. Her best-known roles were in *The Road to Mandalay, The Black Bird, The Unknown, Bringing up Father, The Callahans and Murphys*, and *The Green Ghost*.

HARRY MORGAN (1915–)

Harry Morgan was born Harry Bratsbury in Detroit, Michigan. Although he is best known to television viewers as Colonel Sherman Potter on "M*A*S*H" he has appeared in more than

Harry Morgan, center, with Fredric March and Donna Anderson in Inherit the Wind.

85 films in a career that started in 1942. Very adept at comedy, he appeared in several "heavy" roles in his early film career. On television he was also a regular in "December Bride," "Pete and Gladys" and "Dragnet" where he played officer Bill Gannon. His films include *The Omaha Trail, The Ox-Bow Incident, Wing and a Prayer, The Big Clock, The Blue Veil, Bend of the River, The Far Country, Inherit the Wind, Support Your Local Sheriff* and *The Shootist.*

RALPH MORGAN (1883–June 11, 1956)
Ralph Morgan appeared in more than sixty films and a score of movies during a long and distinguished career. He was the brother of Frank Morgan, stage and screen comedy star. One of Morgan's best remembered roles was that of Charles Marsden in Eugene O'Neill's *Strange Interlude* in 1929-1932 on the New York stage, on

Ralph Morgan, left, with William Henry in Geronimo.

tour, in London and in the Hollywood film. Morgan was educated at Trinity School and Columbia University, graduating with a law degree in 1904, but he decided on a career on the stage. He went to Hollywood in 1931 and devoted his talents to movies for the next decade or more.

Among his pictures were *The Magnificent Obsession, Anthony Adverse, Life of Emile Zola,* and *Wells Fargo.* Probably his most famous screen role was that of Czar Nicholas II in the film *Rasputin* with Ethel, John and Lionel Barrymore. Morgan was a founder and once president of the Screen Actors Guild.

ALBERTO MORIN (1912–   )
Born in Puerto Rico and educated in France, Alberto Morin came from a family with no connection to the dramatic arts. He worked in

Alberto Morin

France for Pathé Frères, studied drama in Spain and later in Mexico at the Escuela de Mimica, after which he gained practical experience in Mexico, both in the theatre and in motion pictures. Morin was brought to Hollywood to make Spanish language pictures for Fox Studios and remained to build a solid career as a character actor, leaving occasionally to make stage appearances. In Hollywood he was kept busy in films, radio and later television. His many film credits include *The Charge of the Light Brigade, The Good Earth, Suez, Stanley and Livingstone, Lloyd's of London, For Whom the Bell Tolls, Gone with the Wind, Asphalt Jungle, Casablanca,* and *Key Largo,* the last two of which provided him with favorite roles.

ROBERT MORLEY (1908–   )

The only son of an Army officer, Morley was born in Wiltshire, England. He first appeared at the Strand Theatre in 1929, as a pirate in *Treasure Island*. A tour followed and life became so depressing that Morley retired from the stage for six months to sell vacuum cleaners. He resumed his acting and also tried playwriting, doing a comedy entitled *Short Story* which had a West End run. He then went to Cornwall and

Robert Morley, center, with Sandra Dee and James Stewart in Take Her, She's Mine.

opened a small summer theatre, where he remained until asked to appear at the Gate Theatre in a play about Oscar Wilde. His next appearance was in *The Great Romances*, a part which brought him to Hollywood for his first film, *Marie Antoinette*, with Norma Shearer. Morley returned to England and the stage with performances in such successes as *The Man Who Came to Dinner* and *The First Gentleman*, and *Edward My Son*. He did not return to Hollywood for 22 years. He has divided his time between stage, TV and films. Among his film credits are *Major Barbara, Beau Brummel, Oscar Wilde, The Great Gilbert and Sullivan, Nine Hours to Rama, The Alphabet Murders, Topkapi,* and *The Loved One.*

ARNOLD MOSS (1911–   )

Born in Brooklyn, New York, Moss did not begin his acting career until after completing his master's degree at New York University. Wanting something more than a teaching career

offered, he joined the LeGallienne Civic Repertory Theater, appearing in *Peter Pan.* He branched out into radio. When not acting he wrote and produced such radio shows as *Dick Tracy* and *Inner Sanctum.* In 1946, Moss made his film debut in *Temptation.* Moss continued his career in films as well as on the stage and television. Among his film roles are *The Loves of Carmen, Reign of Terror, Quebec, Border Incident, Kim,* and *My Favorite Spy.*

Arnold Moss, center, with Dean Stockwell in Kim.

ALAN MOWBRAY (1896–Mar. 25, 1969)

Born in London of a non-theatrical family, Mowbray came to America after World War I and went into acting as a desperation measure when he went broke in 1923. Mowbray went on

Alan Mowbray, left, with Hugh Herbert, Mary Boland, Mischa Auer, Frank McHugh and Carol Hughes in Marry the Girl.

tour with the Theatre Guild, winding up in Hollywood where he entered films. Mowbray counts some thirteen Shaw productions, plus a number of Noel Coward hits, among his legitimate comedy castings. His film record covers a quarter of a century, during which time he played everything from custard-pie comedies to George Washington. Versatility has been his trademark in some 150 featured roles in motion pictures. His many film credits include *Alexander Hamilton, Panama Hattie, Powers Girl, Captain from Castile, Androcles and the Lion, King and I, Prince of Thieves, Sunbonnet Sue,* and *Jackpot.*

LEONARD MUDIE *(1883–Apr. 14, 1965)* Born Leonard Mudie Cheetham in England, Mudie began his career at the Gaiety Theatre, Manchester, in 1908 as a member of Miss Horn-

Leonard Mudie with Lee Patrick in The Nurse's Secret.

130

Herbert Mundin, right, with Maureen O'Sullivan and Johnny Weissmuller in Tarzan Escapes.

iman's Company. Mudie came to the United States in 1914 and made his New York debut at the Comedy Theatre in *Consequences*. Numerous stage productions followed as well as a tour of the United States. In 1933, Mudie went to Hollywood where he appeared in *Voltaire*. Following this screen debut he appeared in many films including *Cardinal Richelieu, Captain*

Blood, Magnificent Obsession, Anthony Adverse, Adventures of Robin Hood, Suez, Devil's Island, and *Song of My Heart.*

HERBERT MUNDIN (1898–Mar. 4, 1939)
He was a farmboy born in Lancashire, England. He emerged from a wireless operator's post on a World War I mine sweeper to join an itinerant

group of music hall players in England. His work attracted the attention of Andre Charlot, who signed him for *Charlot's Revue*. He came to New York in 1924 and then a tour of Australia followed in 1928 in *The Desert Song*. He migrated to Hollywood in 1931 where he became a leading character actor in films until his death in an automobile accident. His films include *Almost Married, Cavalcade, David Copperfield, Black Sheep, Mutiny on the Bounty, Tarzan Escapes, Another Dawn, Adventures of Robin Hood*, and *Lord Jeff*.

ONA MUNSON (1906–Feb. 11, 1955)

Ona Munson in her entertainment career has been a ballet dancer, a musical comedy star, stage tragedienne, and "bad woman" in motion pictures. Born in Portland, Oregon. In school she majored in English literature. Following a successful career on the Broadway musical comedy stage she went to Hollywood in 1933 with the intention of playing in musical comedies but was pegged for dramatic roles. One of the highlights

Ona Munson, with Joseph Schildkraut in The Castaway.

132

of her career was her portrayal of "Belle Watling" in *Gone with the Wind*. Other films have included *Five Star Final, Lady from Louisiana, Wild Geese Calling, Shanghai Gesture, The Cheaters, Dakota*, and *Red House*.

CLARENCE MUSE (1889–Oct. 13, 1979)

Clarence Muse had a long and varied career in the entertainment field. He was a minstrel singer, vaudeville actor, producer, concert singer, composer, musical stage star, radio and television entertainer, and motion picture actor. Born in Baltimore, Maryland, he was educated at Dickinson College, studying law, but leaving it for a career in music. His career as a singing entertainer led him into broader fields. Muse made his debut as a screen actor in *Hearts in*

Clarence Muse, right, with Leo Gorcey in That Gang of Mine.

Dixie in 1928 and then was to become one of the leading black actors in Hollywood. Among his film credits were *Riding High, The Great Dan Patch, Unconquered, Show Boat, Zanzibar, Night and Day, My Favorite Brunette, Spirit of Youth*, and *Follow Your Heart*.

J. CARROL NAISH (1897–Jan. 24, 1973)

J. Carroll Naish, though he was a native New Yorker of Irish ancestry, his dark eyes, swarthy skin and gift for accents made him one of the busiest actors playing Latin types. He also appeared as an Englishman, an ape, an old woman, a Swede, a Negro, an Indian, a Japanese, a Malayan, a Chinese, and a Pole. Seldom

J. Carrol Naish

on either the stage or screen did he play an Irishman. After several years on the Broadway stage, he settled down in the movies in the 1930's. Naish was twice nominated for an Academy Award. He was first nominated for his role as the bewildered Italian prisoner in *Sahara* in 1943, and was again nominated for his portrayal of the Mexican father in 1945's *A Medal for Benny*. His other films included *Cheer Up and Smile, Scotland Yard, The Southerner, House of Frankenstein, Beast with Five Fingers*, and *Humoresque*. He appeared on many TV shows and also in the series *Life with Luigi* and *Charlie Chan*.

ALAN NAPIER *(1903–   )*

Alan Napier was born in Birmingham, England, and was the first member of his family to go into the theater. He was educated at Clifton College and trained for the theater at the Royal Academy of Dramatic Art in London. His first engagement was with the famous Oxford Players who also gave a start to other unknowns at the time—John Gielgud, Flora Robson, Margaret Webster, Robert Morley, and Tyrone Guthrie. Napier graduated to the West End and the Old Vic in 1929, where for ten years he played featured roles with all the great stars of the time. He was brought to New York in 1940 to play opposite Gladys George in *Lady in Waiting* by Brock Pemberton. He first went to Hollywood in 1941, although he had previously made some pictures in England. His films include *The Uninvited, Song of Bernadette, Action in Arabia, House of the Seven Gables, The Hairy Ape, Dark Waters, Hangover Square, Forever Amber, Macbeth, Joan of Arc, Hills of Home, Across the Wide Missouri, Julius Caesar*, and *Desiree*. He has appeared in many TV dramatic shows, and was the familiar figure of Alfred the butler on the *Batman* series.

Alan Napier, as Captain Kidd in Double Crossbones.

MILDRED NATWICK *(1908–   )*

Mildred Natwick has spent much of her career portraying women older than her actual years. She was born in Baltimore, Maryland, where her father was in the lumber business, and was educated in Baltimore schools and at Bryn Mawr. She made her professional stage debut in *Carrie Nation* in 1932. Her screen debut came in 1940 with her portrayal of the Cockney prostitute for John Ford's *Long Voyage Home*. Her first major film role, and perhaps best remembered, was that of Mrs. Minnett in *The Enchanted Cottage* which starred Robert Young, Dorothy McGuire, and Herbert Marshall. Among her other films are *The Late George Apley, Woman's Vengeance, Three Godfathers, She Wore a Yellow Ribbon, Cheaper by the Dozen, The Quiet Man, The Trouble with Harry,* and *Barefoot in the Park.*

Mildred Natwick

PAUL "TINY" NEWLAN *(1903–Nov. 23, 1973)*
Paul Newlan was born in Plattsmouth, Nebraska. He moved to Kansas City, Missouri, when he was nine months old, attended grade schools in Kansas City and high school in St. Joseph, Missouri. He broke into show business at the Garden Theatre, Kansas City, working for $18 a week and appearing in ten shows a day. Newlan attended the University of Missouri for two years before playing professional basketball and football. Deciding to go back into show business, he was playing in stock in St. Joseph when offered a two year contract by Paramount. Later he appeared in countless films and TV productions including *Ballad of Furnace Creek, Southern Yankee, Never a Dull Moment, Come Share My Love, Against All Flags, Pirates of Tripoli, To Catch a Thief, The Buccaneers,* and *The Tijuana Story.* Two of his favorite roles were in the TV series *Twelve O'Clock High,* and *M-Squad* in which Newlan was featured as the Captain.

Paul "Tiny" Newlan, in Lonely Man.

Robert Newton, right, with Bobby Driscoll in Treasure Island.

ROBERT NEWTON *(1905–Mar. 25, 1956)*
Robert Newton was an actor with the tremendous capability of portraying such obviously contradictory qualities as shrewd cunning and incredible stupidity, and making them believable. His role as the bumbling Inspector Fix in *Around the World in Eighty Days* was of this type. He was born in Shaftesbury, Dorset, and was educated at Newbury Grammar School and in Switzerland. He made his first appearance on

134

the stage in 1920 in *Henry VI*. His first London appearance was in *London Life* at the Theatre Royal, Drury Lane, in June, 1924. In 1931, he made his New York debut in Noel Coward's *Private Lives*, taking over the part from Laurence Olivier. He made his screen debut in 1937 in *Fire Over England*. His other pictures included *Dark Journey, Farewell Again, The Beachcomber, Jamaica Inn, Gaslight, Hell's Cargo, Major Barbara, Henry V, Odd Man Out, Oliver Twist, Obsession, Blackbeard the Pirate,* and *Treasure Island*, in which he played Long John Silver.

JACK NORTON *(1889–Oct. 15, 1958)*
Jack Norton was the "lovable drunk" in vaudeville shows, films, and television for many years. In tophat, tails and mustache, hanging onto a lamppost, he played the drunk in such shows as *The Ziegfeld Follies, Earl Carroll's*

Jack Norton, with Bette Davis in Marked Woman.

Vanities, Five O'Clock Girl, Flo-Flo, and *The Florida Girl*. After 1934 he was typed as a film drunk, and was obliged to drink stage highballs, usually consisting of ginger ale spiked with bicarbonate of soda. Norton, although in real life a teetotaler himself, would follow drunks for blocks, studying their mannerisms. He appeared in over 100 films which included *Cockeyed Cavaliers, Calling All Cars, His Night Out, Captain Tugboat Annie, The Great Mystic, Strange Confession, The Spoilers, The Fleet's In, Taxi, Mister, Bringing Up Father,* and *Linda Be Good*.

PHILLIP OBER *(1902–Sept. 13, 1982)*
Phillip Ober was an actor who was as familiar to Broadway theater goers as to movie fans. Born in Fort Payne, Alabama, he was on the Broadway stage for over twenty years before Mel Ferrer brought him to Hollywood for *The Secret*

Phillip Ober

Fury. His list of film roles include parts in *Never a Dull Moment, The Magnificent Yankee, The Dull Knife, Come Back, Little Sheba, From Here to Eternity, Broken Lance,* and *10 North Frederick*. In his sixties Ober switched from acting to the diplomatic service. For the last fifteen years of his life he served as a consular agent in Puerto Vallarta, Mexico. Ober was once married to actress Vivian Vance.

UNA O'CONNOR *(1880–Feb. 4, 1959)*
Una O'Connor was at the beginning of her career a member of the Abbey Players in Ireland and later appeared on the London and Broadway stages. She was cast in the housekeeper role in Noel Coward's *Cavalcade* in London, and when Fox Films produced the film version in 1933, Miss O'Connor was brought to Hollywood to repeat her role. She appeared in scores of plays and films in the years following, but achieved

Una O'Connor, in The Bells of St. Mary's.

her greatest fame for her portrayals of waspish Irish, Cockney and Scottish servants, whose icy glances expressed the utmost in contempt. Her films included *Pleasure Cruise, The Invisible Man, David Copperfield, The Informer, Rose Marie, Little Lord Fauntleroy, Lloyd's of London, Christmas in Connecticut, The Bells of St. Mary's, Cluny Brown,* and *Of Human Bondage.* Her last film was *Witness for the Prosecution,* in which she played an acidulous Scottish maid.

EDNA MAY OLIVER *(1883–Nov. 9, 1942)*
Edna May Oliver was born in Boston and was on the stage for twenty years before entering films with Famous Players Paramount at Astoria, Long Island, in 1923. She arrived in Hollywood

Edna May Oliver, left, and Madge Evans in David Copperfield.

in 1930 to begin her career in talking films. She played in *Half-Shot at Sunrise,* and *Cimarron* with Richard Dix and Irene Dunne. Her other films included *Alice in Wonderland, The Poor Rich, David Copperfield, A Tale of Two Cities, Romeo and Juliet, Parnell, Little Miss Broadway,* and *The Story of Vernon and Irene Castle.*

MORONI OLSEN *(1889–Nov. 22, 1954)*
Moroni Olsen was born in Ogden, Utah, and was educated at the University of Utah. He started acting in Chautauqua plays, and in the 1920's he organized his own repertory company, the Moroni Olsen Players, which traveled through the West. In the early 1930's he was on Broadway in such plays as *Medea, Romeo and Juliet,* and *Joan of Arc.* He made his screen debut in

Moroni Olsen

The Three Musketeers in the role of Porthos in 1935. Concurrent with his film career he was active in Pasadena Playhouse productions, and directed many top plays himself. For several years he was director of Hollywood's famed Pilgrimage Play. His screen roles included parts in such pictures as *Annie Oakley, Mary of Scotland, Grand Jury, The Farmer in the Dell, Kentucky, Air Force, Buffalo Bill, Mildred Pierce, Possessed, Life with Father, Call Northside 777,* and *The Fountainhead.*

HENRY O'NEILL *(1891–May 18, 1961)*
Henry O'Neill appeared in more than 150 films. He came to Hollywood in 1933 after several years on Broadway. Born in Orange, New Jersey, he abandoned his formal education after a year of college to join a traveling stock company. In

Henry O'Neill, in Anthony Adverse.

World War I O'Neill served as a chief petty officer in the Navy. He returned to acting in 1919, and his first major role on Broadway was that of Paddy in Eugene O'Neill's *The Hairy Ape.* The two men, who were not related, became good friends, and the actor later appeared in many other O'Neill plays. Aristocratic-looking, with keen blue eyes, gray hair, aquiline features and kindly manner, O'Neill was typed by nature for patrician parts. He appeared in such movies as *Oil for the Lamps of China, The Story of Louis Pasteur, Marked Woman, The Life of Emile Zola, Wells Fargo, Jezebel, Amazing Dr. Clitterhouse, Dodge City, Juarez, 'Til We Meet Again, Billy the Kid, Tortilla Flat, Brother Rat,* and *The Green Years.*

Frank Orth, in Mother Wore Tights.

FRANK ORTH *(1880–Mar. 17, 1962)*
Frank Orth, who portrayed Inspector Farraday in the *Boston Blackie* television series, spent a lifetime in show business. He began his career in vaudeville in 1897 and retired in 1959 after undergoing throat surgery. His wife of 50 years, Ann Codee, who was his vaudeville partner, died in 1961. During his long film career Orth made the first foreign language film shorts in sound for Warner Bros. in 1928. He also appeared in both the *Nancy Drew* and *Dr. Kildare* series of films. His other film credits included *The Dolly Sisters, The Lost Weekend, Doll Face, It Had to Be You, Cheaper by the Dozen, Father of the Bride, Houdini,* and *Here Come the Girls.*

"BLACK" JACK O'SHEA *(1906–Oct. 1, 1967)*
"Black" Jack O'Shea was born in San Francisco two weeks prior to the great earthquake of 1906. He entered motion pictures in the early 1930's and became one of the top heavies, billed as "the man you love to hate." In addition to his acting chores he did stuntwork for Lou Costello and doubled for Leo Carrillo and Orson Welles. He appeared in numerous TV series and made many personal appearance tours with Bob Steele, Sunset Carson, Lash LaRue and Tim Holt. In his last years he operated an antique shop in

"Black" Jack O'Shea

Paradise, California and was an honorary sheriff of that community. His films included *Law of the Lash, Wyoming, Rio Grande Raiders, The San Antonio Kid,* and *Sons of the Pioneers.*

MARIA OUSPENSKAYA *(1887–Dec. 3, 1949)*
Maria Ouspenskaya first came to this country in 1924 with the Moscow Art Theater. She stayed in the United States and during the next twenty-five years became, for American theater and movie fans, one of the most familiar and pleasing character actresses. Her accent, luminous eyes, Tartar features and finished performances were far more impressive than more widely advertised portrayals by more beautiful film stars. In movies, she was not perturbed if she was cast repeatedly in the role of gracious grand-

her Broadway role as the Baroness von Obersdorf. Miss Ouspenskaya received an Academy Award nomination for her performance. Her other films included *Conquest* with Greta Garbo, *Love Affair, The Rains Came, Dr. Ehrlich's Magic Bullet, Waterloo Bridge, Kings Row, I've Always Loved You, Wyoming,* and *A Kiss in the Dark.*

GARRY OWEN *(1897–June 1, 1951)*
Garry Owen went on the vaudeville stage with his mother and later on the Broadway stage in *Square Crooks, Miss Manhattan,* and others. His film credits included *Bombay Mail, Little Miss Marker, No Ransom, Arsenic and Old Lace, Tiger Woman, The Phantom Speaks, Dark Mirror,* and *Swell Guy.*

Maria Ouspenskaya, in Phantom of Paris.

Garry Owen, with Joan Crawford in Mildred Pierce.

REGINALD OWEN *(1887–Nov. 5, 1972)*
Reginald Owen was a native of Hartfordshire, England, and studied for a theatrical career in Sir Herbert Tree's Academy of Dramatic Arts. He became a great favorite on the English stage and first came to the U.S. in 1924 in a play called *The Swan.* He appeared in silent pictures here

mother or villainous harridan. A skillful actress, she was equally at ease in *Frankenstein Meets the Wolf Man,* and *Kings Row.* She made her movie debut in 1936 in *Dodsworth,* recreating

138

Reginald Owen

and his first talking film was *The Letter*, in which he played the husband. His other pictures included *Nana, The House of Rothschild, Of Human Bondage, A Tale of Two Cities, Madame X, Mrs. Miniver, Voltaire, White Cargo, Random Harvest, Kitty, Cluny Brown,* and *Green Dolphin Street.*

MABEL PAIGE (1880–Feb. 8, 1954)
Mabel Paige made her debut at the age of four in *Van the Virginian*. When she was eleven she

Mabel Paige, left, and Dorothy Morris in Gallant Thoroughbred.

began starring in plays written for her and headed her own stock company. She bore the tag of "Idol of the South." Miss Paige appeared in a number of silent films. After retirement for eleven years she returned to the stage in the 1930's appearing in several plays on Broadway. She also returned to films again usually in the role of a dowager. She reached eminence in *Lucky Jordan* in the role of the panhandling grandmother. Among the films in which she appeared were *Young and Willing, True to Life, The Crystal Ball, Happy-Go-Lucky, Murder He Says, She Wouldn't Say Yes, Out of This World,* and *Dangerous Partners.*

NESTOR PAIVA (1905–Sept. 9, 1966)
A flair for dialects and mimicry made Nestor Paiva decide to become an actor. He attended St. John's School in Fresno, the University of San Francisco and later the University of California at Berkeley where he graduated with an A.B. degree. One of his principal college activities was drama. Paiva made his stage debut in the Greek Theatre in Berkeley in *Antigone*. He set a record at the university by appearing in a total of 80 plays. Following graduation in 1932, Paiva did a series of plays in Oakland and San Francisco and continued his regular appearances at the Berkeley Community Playhouse. In 1934, Paiva

Nestor Paiva, with Dorothy Patrick in Follow Me Quietly.

joined the Los Angeles company staging *The Drunkard*. He continued in the play for eleven years and combined this work with picture roles. Finally the film work became so heavy that he was forced to drop out of *The Drunkard*. From 1938 to 1967 Paiva appeared in 132 motion pictures playing every type of role. A few of his many pictures were *The Road to Utopia, Humoresque, A Thousand and One Nights, Mr. Reckless, Mr. Blandings Builds His Dream House, A Likely Story,* and *Follow Me Quietly.*

EUGENE PALLETTE *(1889–Sept. 3, 1954)*
Frog-voiced, pot-bellied Eugene Pallette, an ex-streetcar conductor and ex-jockey, was one of Hollywood's most popular character actors. Born in Winfield, Kansas, to a theatrical couple touring the country in *East Lynne*, Pallette grew up to follow in their footsteps.. He made his film debut in 1910 as an extra and within a week was

Franklin Pangborn

Eugene Pallette, in Steamboat Round the Bend.

starring in one-reelers. By 1917 he was starring with Norma Talmadge as a leading man. Enlisting in the Air Corps in World War I, he returned to Hollywood in 1919 to find himself virtually forgotten. He then turned to the roly-poly character roles that made him famous. Gaining weight steadily, he once tipped the scales at over 300 pounds. He was a veteran of dozens of films at all major studios including *Slightly Dangerous, The Male Animal, Suspense, Robin Hood, The Kansan, Manhattan Serenade, Step Lively, The Cheaters,* and *In Old Sacramento.*

FRANKLIN PANGBORN *(1889–July 20, 1958)*
Franklin Pangborn had a distinguished career in serious drama before he became an outstanding success as a comedian. He worked for nearly every studio and with most of the stars in the film

world. A native of Newark, New Jersey, he started on the New York stage and toured with Mme. Alla Nazimova, managing the company. He also toured with Jessie Bonstelle before World War I. Pangborn did not become a full-time comedian until 1936, when his hilarious bit as a frantic tabulator of a society scavenger hunt in *My Man Godfrey* led him into 27 other films within the following year. Pangborn made a fortune with his endless appearances as hotel clerk, floorwalker, ribbon clerk, dress designer, or store manager. He specialized in a state of trembling dishevelment, outrage, confusion, harrassment or coyness brought on by the antics of customers and guests. His Hollywood work included parts in *The Horn Blows at Midnight, The Bank Dick, Never Give a Sucker an Even Break, George Washington Slept Here, See My Lawyer, You Came Along, Calendar Girl, Rebecca of Sunnybrook Farm, A Star Is Born, My Man Godfrey,* and *Stage Door.*

EMORY PARNELL *(1892–June 22, 1979)*
Born in St. Paul, Minnesota, Emory Parnell started his career as a concert violinist. He majored in vocal music and instrumental music at Morningside College in Sioux City, Iowa, leaving college in 1912 to earn his living. Parnell toured the Chautauqua and Lyceum circuits and their affiliated bureaus for thirteen years. In 1926 he settled in Columbus, Ohio, to become head booking agent for the bureaus he had served as an entertainer. He quit the booking business in 1930 to become an actor and narrator in commercial films in Detroit. In 1937, Parnell took

Emory Parnell, second from left, with Lloyd Bridges in Hideout.

the plunge and moved to the Pacific Coast where he was signed by RKO for his first film role, a part in *Dr. Rhythm* which landed on the cutting room floor. Other films included *Louisiana Purchase, Pride of the Yankees, Mr. Lucky, My Client, Curly, Colonel Effingham's Raid, Calendar Girl, Beautiful Blonde from Bashful Bend, Hellfire, Violence,* and *Young Ideas.*

LEE PATRICK (1911–Nov. 25, 1982)

Lee Patrick was born in New York, grew up and went to school in Chicago. She had no thought of becoming an actress, but following the death of her father and on the advice of George Arliss, went directly on the stage to get practical experience. Miss Patrick learned the trade with various stock companies making her debut in

Lee Patrick, as Mrs. Topper in TV series.

Punch and Judy. Broadway plays followed and subsequently films. Her first motion picture was *Strange Cargo.* Many films were to follow, among them *The Maltese Falcon* in which she played Effie, her favorite role, *Mildred Pierce, George Washington Slept Here, Mrs. Parkington, The Snake Pit, Mother Wore Tights, South of Suez.* After 1955 she was seen in *Pillow Talk, Auntie Mame, Summer Smoke, Vertigo,* to mention only a few.

ELIZABETH PATTERSON (1875–Jan. 31, 1966)

Miss Patterson, the daughter of a Savannah judge, outraged family tradition by going on the stage. Her first roles were with the old Ben Greet Players in Chicago and through the Middle West in 1907 when she played Shakespeare. Follow-

Elizabeth Patterson, right, with Walter Connolly, Randolph Scott, Janet Beecher, Margaret Sullavan, and Dickie Moore in So Red the Rose.

ing several seasons with Greet, Miss Patterson joined the Stewart-Walker Company. The Washington Square Players claimed her next and her Broadway debut came soon afterward when Booth Tarkington recommended her for a role in his play *Intimate Strangers.* Her first appearance in films came in 1926 in the silent picture *The Book of Charm.* Miss Patterson had a deep aversion for films and did not return to Hollywood until 1929. Her film credits number over 100 and include *A Bill of Divorcement, Tom*

Sawyer, Daddy Long Legs, High, Wide and Handsome, Alexander Graham Bell, Tobacco Road, So Red the Rose, Remember the Night, and *Pal Joey.*

NAT PENDLETON (1895–Oct. 11, 1967)

Nat Pendleton, businessman, professional wrestler and screen comedian, was born near Davenport, Iowa. He grew up in Ohio and New York and as a schoolboy first displayed a talent for acting. After a successful career as a wrestler,

Nat Pendleton, with Joan Davis in Life Begins in College.

he represented the U.S. in the 1920 Olympic games, also became the World's Champion in 1924. He traveled to Hollywood in 1927 and began to work steadily in films. He made appearances in *Big House Blues, The Laughing Lady, The Sea Wolf, Spirit of Notre Dame, Secret Witness, Deception, Dr. Gillespie's Criminal Case, Swing Fever, Buck Privates Come Home, Scared to Death, The Great Ziegfeld,* and *The Crowd Roars.*

BILL PHILLIPS (1908–June 27, 1957)

Bill Phillips was born in Washington, D.C., where he received a college degree at the George Washington University. In school he gained

142

celebrity as an athlete in football, track and wrestling as well as boxing. His physique and acting ability enabled him to win the role of the New Jersey Toughie in *See Here, Private Hargrove,* and an MGM contract. Prior to his screen career, Phillips was a member of Eva LeGallienne's Civic Repertory Theater group. His film roles included *Music for Millions, Ziegfeld Follies, Action in the North Atlantic, Thirty Seconds Over Tokyo, Harvey Girls, Sea of Grass, Johnny Allegro,* and *New York Confidential.*

Bill Phillips, right, with George Raft and George Macready in Johnny Allegro.

SLIM PICKENS (1919–Nov. 20, 1983)

Born Louis Lindley in Kingsburg, California, Slim sat on his first horse at two, rode well at four and at fifteen quit school to sign for his first rodeo. He became the country's top clown, the

Slim Pickens

highest paid bull buffoon in history. He fought over 3,000 bulls. Pickens made his screen debut in *Rocky Mountain* and appeared in many films, including the *Rex Allen* westerns, *Boy from Oklahoma*, *The Outcast*, *Last Command*, *Stranger at My Door*, *Great Locomotive Chase*, *One-eyed Jacks*, and *Dr. Strangelove*.

ZASU PITTS (1898–June 7, 1963)

Miss Pitts' trademark of the "fluid, fluttering hands" and "Oh dear me" were to be seen in over 200 films. Her first role, in 1917, was with Mary Pickford in *The Little American* and her last, as a telephone operator in *It's a Mad, Mad, Mad, Mad, World*. Miss Pitts was born in Parsons, Kansas, and moved with her family to Santa Cruz, California, as a child. She received her unusual first name as a result of her mother's desire not to anger her two sisters. Their names were Susan and Eliza and not being able to decide after which to name the child she compromised by taking the first syllable of one name and the last syllable of the other. With a gift of mimicry she went to Hollywood to look for work. She was signed and was cast in ingenue roles in

Zasu Pitts

silent films. When sound revolutionized the industry, Miss Pitts found herself in a new career as a comedienne. She made her Broadway debut in 1944 in *Ramshackle Inn* and appeared in 1953 in a short-lived revival of *The Bat*. She also made many television appearances in the 1950's. Among her many film credits are *No, No Nanette*, *The Guardsman*, *Mrs. Wiggs of the Cabbage Patch*, *Ruggles of Red Gap*, *Nurse Edith Cavell*, *Miss Polly*, *Life with Father*, *Francis*, *Tish*, and *52nd Street*.

TOM POWERS (1890–Nov. 9, 1955)

Tom Powers appeared on Broadway for 35 years and in scores of films and TV shows. He made his screen debut with the old Vitagraph Company in New York in 1910. He appeared with the Theater Guild on stage for ten years and had a role in the original stage production *Strange Interlude*. Powers went to Hollywood in 1943 to appear in Paramount's *Double Indemnity* and

Tom Powers

subsequently appeared in a number of films. Some of his better known pictures were *Julius Caesar*, *The Farmer's Daughter*, and *Two Years Before the Mast*. On TV, he was familiar for his parts in "Climax" and "Fireside Theater". He also wrote several books, among them the best-selling *He Knew Them All*.

Jed Prouty, in one of the family pictures, Borrowing Trouble.

Frank Puglia

JED PROUTY *(1879–May 10, 1956)*

Prouty was born in Boston of non-professional parents and went on the stage while still in his teens, in famous old Austen Stone's Museum in Boston. After getting experience in stock he went into variety as a singer and then into a song and dance act on the Keith circuit. He was headlined a number of years in vaudeville and then joined Klaw and Erlanger. He remained with these producers for 17 years. Until 1921 he alternated between Broadway and headlining on vaudeville tours in the east. Then he went to Hollywood and played in a number of silent films at various studios. Then came his stuttering role in MGM's first *Broadway Melody* in 1929. The simulated speech defect almost "shelved" him for pictures. When 20th Century-Fox began production of *Every Saturday Night*, Prouty was cast as the father. It marked the beginning of his fifty-first year in the theater and a number of films including *Broadway Melody, Music in the Air, Private Scandal, Under Your Spell, The Texas Rangers, Happy-Go-Lucky, One Hundred Men and a Girl, Duke of West Point,* and *Goodbye Broadway.*

FRANK PUGLIA *(1892–Oct. 25, 1975)*

Opera conductor, villain, padre, chief of police, doctor, diplomat, Frank Puglia played every type of role on the stage and in films. Born in Italy, Puglia began his career at the age of thirteen in a traveling operetta company. Brought to America in 1907 by his father, he worked in a laundry until he joined an Italian theatrical group performing drama, comedy, operetta and opera. In 1921, Puglia entered stock at the Olympic Theatre in New York. While appearing here in *The Two Orphans,* D.W. Griffith signed him to appear in the epic *Orphans of the Storm.* That was his first picture and the beginning of a film career which included *Viva Villa, Charlie Chan in Panama, Torrid Zone, Arise My Love, Now Voyager, Phantom of the Opera, Jungle Book, Yellow Jack, Billy the Kid, Balalaika, May Time,* and *Blood on the Sun.*

JOHN QUALEN *(1899–   )*

John Qualen is one of the most active and versatile actors in motion pictures. He was born in Vancouver, B.C., the son of a Norwegian pastor. His family moved to the United States and eventually settled in Elgin, Illinois. In Elgin, he won an oratorical contest and was awarded a year's scholarship to Northwestern University. He played the Lyceum-Chautauqua circuit and in 1929 he moved to New York where he was cast in the now famous role of the Swedish janitor in Elmer Rice's *Street Scene.* When Sam Goldwyn brought *Street Scene* to the screen Qualen repeated his role, after making his screen debut in *Arrowsmith* with Ronald Colman and Helen Hayes. He moved permanently to Los Angeles in 1933 and has done 174 pictures in 40 years in Hollywood. One of his best known roles

John Qualen

Eddie Quillan

was that of Papa Dionne in *The Country Doctor*, the story of the Dionne quintuplets. He has played a wide variety of roles including his memorable homesick sailor in *The Long Voyage Home*. Among his other films are *Casablanca*, *The Fugitive*, *Grapes of Wrath*, *Hans Christian Andersen*, *His Girl Friday*, *The Searchers*, *Unchained*, *High and the Mighty*, *Two Rode Together*, *American Romance*, and *Whipsaw*. His versatility extends to TV as well, having appeared on many shows. He is treasurer of the Authors Club, founded in 1940 by Rupert Hughes, and he is historian of the Masquers.

EDDIE QUILLAN (1907–)
Eddie Quillan, from the time that he was able to walk and recite, was part of the Quillan act, which included his Scotch-Irish father and various other members of the family. In 1925, Eddie, three brothers and a sister played at the Orpheum Theater in Los Angeles. Mack Sennett saw them and signed Eddie to a contract, after which he made eighteen comedies for the great comedy director. Quillan's first feature film was

C.B. DeMille's *The Godless Girl*. Among his other films are *Up and at 'Em*, *The Big Shot*, *Dark Mountain*, *This Is the Life*, *Moonlight and Cactus*, *A Guy Could Change*, *Sideshow*, and *Brigadoon*.

RAGS RAGLAND (1906– Aug. 20, 1946)
John Morgan (Rags) Ragland, personable comedian who described his rise from burlesque to Broadway and then to films as a "transition from rags to breeches," was born in Louisville, Kentucky. As a youngster he was truck driver, preliminary boxer and assistant projectionist in a theatre. His first try at show business was with Minsky's burlesque in New York. He rose to the ranks of topflight comedians during the following 12 years. In 1938 he appeared on Broadway in *Who's Who*. He came to stardom as the rollicking sailor in Ethel Merman's *Panama Hattie*. In 1941 he was summoned to Hollywood to play his original role in the screen version of *Panama Hattie*. During his brief screen career he appeared in *Girl Crazy*, *DuBarry Was a Lady*, *Whistling in Brooklyn*, *The Canterville Ghost*, *Three Men in White*, *Meet the People*, *Anchors Aweigh*, *Abbott and Costello in Hollywood*, *Her Highness and the Bellboy*, and *The Hoodlum Saint*.

Rags Ragland in Sunday Punch.

JESSIE RALPH *(1865– May 30, 1944)*
Miss Ralph, a character actress of stage and
screen, made her debut at sixteen with a stock
company in Providence, Rhode Island. She later
went on Broadway, appearing in support of Jane
Cowl in *Romeo and Juliet*. In 1927 she appeared
in *The Road to Rome* both on Broadway and
later in Paris when an American season was inaugurated there. She appeared in many other
Broadway plays including many George M.
Cohan productions, both musical and non-

Jessie Ralph, in Camille.

146

musical before going to Hollywood. In the long list of her motion pictures are *David Copperfield, San Francisco, Les Miserables, One Night of Love, The Bluebird, Drums Along the Mohawk, Cafe Society, Four Girls in White, Cocktail Hour,* and *Walking on Air.*

Mikhail Rasumny, with Franchot Tone in Her Husband's Affairs.

MIKHAIL RASUMNY (1890– Feb. 17, 1956)
Mikhail Rasumny, once an illustrious member of the Moscow Art Theatre troupe, also dishwasher, bill collector, and pilot of a hearse, came to America in 1935 with the famed Moscow troupe. He toured America for three months and remained when his colleagues departed. A native of Odessa, Russia, and the son of a famous Jewish cantor, he knew the legitimate theatre by the age of 14. He toured the Crimea with a small cooperative theatre group and later joined a company headed by Paul Orlenev, star of the Russian theatre. He toured the provinces and eventually reached Moscow and then the United States. Rasumny made his way to Hollywood in 1940 and after a job as dishwasher and tour after tour of the studios landed a part in *Comrade X.* After his debut in motion pictures he played a variety of dialect roles in such films as *Hold Back the Dawn, Wake Island, This Gun for Hire, Bring on the Girls, For Whom the Bell Tolls,* and *Anything Can Happen.*

GREGORY RATOFF (1897– Dec. 14, 1960)
Gregory Ratoff, known for his heavily accented speech which was sprinkled with illogical but amusing grammatical construction and the misuse of words, was born in St. Petersburg,

Gregory Ratoff, in Sing, Baby, Sing.

Russia. He was educated at the Imperial School of Commerce in St. Petersburg and immigrated to the U.S. in 1922. Ratoff, besides acting, turned to directing, producing and writing many movies in his long career. In his acting he became typed as a producer and throughout his career he played producers and managers in pictures like *Once in a Lifetime, What Price Hollywood, Sitting Pretty,* and *All About Eve.* Other film acting credits included *Thirteen Women, Professional Sweetheart, Let's Fall in Love, Top of the Town,* and *George White's Scandals.*

ALAN REED (1907– June 14, 1977)
Radio audiences knew him as poet Falstaff Openshaw of the *Fred Allen Show,* Solom Levy of the *Abie's Irish Rose* serial, Clancy the Cop in *Duffy's Tavern,* Pasquale on *Life with Luigi,* Mr. Clyde on *My Friend Irma,* etc. At his peak in radio he was doing 35 shows a week stooging for such greats as Fanny Brice, Fred Allen, Ed-

Alan Reed, seated, with Doug Evans, Paul Guilfoyle and Eddie Albert in Actors and Sin.

die Cantor, Bert Lahr, Milton Berle and Burns and Allen. Born in New York City, Reed went from George Washington High School to Columbia University where he completed a course in journalism. Soon after graduation he turned to acting with the Provincetown Playhouse. Mastering some 22 dialects led to his steady success in radio and a return to the stage. He played the title role in *The Pirate* with the Lunts on Broadway and that led to other roles for the Theatre Guild. Eventually, movie bids came in. His first picture was *Days of Glory*.

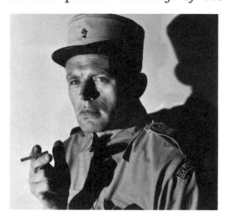

Otto Reichow

OTTO REICHOW (1904-   )

Considered the "perfect type" as a German soldier or a Nazi, Otto Reichow has been cast in the part over 100 times. Born in Tempelburg, Pomerania, Germany, Mr. Reichow first acted in Berlin in 1928 in *Testament of Dr. Mabuse*. In 1936 he went to France for Jean Renoir's *La Grande Illusion*. In 1937 he journeyed to the United States and commenced his film career in Hollywood in 1941. Reichow has always tried to portray Nazis as convincingly as he saw them–savagely and realistically–because his brother was killed by them in Berlin in 1933. This led to his typecasting in Hollywood and also for the pictures made for the Army Air Force Motion Picture Unit during World War II. Since 1941 he has appeared in over 200 pictures which included *A Yank in the RAF, Paris Calling, Desperate Journey, Berlin Correspondent, The Moon Is Down, Five Graves to Cairo, The Hitler Gang, Paris Underground, Dangerous Millions, Secret Life of Walter Mitty, Rogues Regiment* (favorite role), *I Was a Male War Bride, Desert Rats,* and *The Student Prince*.

Carl Benton Reid

CARL BENTON REID (1893–Mar. 15, 1973)

Born in Lansing, Michigan, Reid developed a love for poetry and literature at an early age which later led him to the theatre. A graduate in Dramatic Arts from the Carnegie Institute of Technology he joined the Cleveland Playhouse where he did a number of roles from 1922–1939. From 1939–1950 he played on Broadway and with various stock companies and road productions. In 1950 Reid became "a permanent fixture" in Hollywood. Important to Reid's work in motion pictures was the experience gained during the years 1934–36 with the "Old Globe Theatre Co." doing short versions of Shakespearian plays at the Century of Progress Exposition in Chicago and the San Diego Exposition. Beginning in 1950 Reid's work was in films and television. A few of his principal motion picture credits included his two favorites *The Great Caruso*, as Ann Blyth's father and Clem Rogers in *The Will Rogers Story* as well as *The Admiral Halsey Story, The Little Foxes, The North Star, The Egyptian, Broken Lance, Time Limit,* and *The Left Hand of God*.

ANN REVERE (1903-   )

Miss Revere, a descendant of Paul Revere, was born in New York City. She attended grammar and high school in Westfield, New Jersey, and was graduated from Wellesley College. While at Wellesley she played a number of dramatic roles. Two years were then spent at the American Laboratory Theatre and two years training

Ann Revere, in The Song of Bernadette.

(1928–30) at the Stuart Walker Stock Company. Miss Revere did a great deal of summer stock which led to her first success in the Broadway production of *Double Door*, which in turn was purchased by Paramount Pictures and led to her first picture in Hollywood in 1934. In 1940, Miss Revere took up residence in Hollywood where she completed forty motion pictures during the next ten years. The roles ranged over a wide area of characterization. Her career as a "mother" began with *The Song of Bernadette*, for which she was nominated for an Oscar, and included *National Velvet* for which she received an Oscar, and *Gentleman's Agreement* which resulted in another nomination. Other credits include *The Howards of Virginia, H. M. Pulham, Esq., Remember the Day, Rainbow Island, Keys of the Kingdom, Dragonwyck, Forever Amber,* and *Scudda Hoo, Scudda Hay* and *A Place in the Sun.*

ADELINE DE WALT REYNOLDS (1862–Aug. 13, 1961)

Mrs. Reynolds started acting at the age of 70, two years after receiving a degree from the University of California at Berkeley. Mrs. Reynolds appeared in her first picture in 1941, *Come Live with Me*. Subsequently, and apparently as frequently as she liked, she latched onto a succession of top roles in such productions as *Going My Way, Tales of Manhattan, A Tree Grows in Brooklyn, The Corn Is Green, Lydia Bailey,* and *Pony Soldier*. At the time of her death at 98 she was the oldest active member on the roster of the Screen Actors Guild.

Adeline Dewalt Reynolds, left, with Anne Francis in Lydia Bailey.

Renie Riano, with Willie Best and Joe Yule in Jiggs and Maggie in Jackpot Jitters.

RENIE RIANO (1899–July 3, 1971)

Renie Riano appeared in over 120 films during more than 60 years in show business. Miss Riano, London-born, was the third generation of a theatrical family. She made her debut in her parents' act when she was just over two years old. By the time she was four she was doing a single in vaudeville as Baby Renie. She performed in a variety of Broadway shows, including Irving Berlin's *Music Box Revue*. Her biggest thrills included her four command performances for King George V and Queen Mary. Her films included *Tovarich, Outside of Paradise, Spring Madness, Thanks for Everything, Four's a Crowd, The Man Who Wouldn't Talk, Kit Carson, You're the One,* and *Blondie for Victory*.

Addison Richards, in The Black Doll.

ADDISON RICHARDS (1902–Mar. 22, 1964)

A native of Zanesville, Ohio, Richards was graduated by Washington State University and did graduate work at Pomona College. He launched his acting career in the Pilgrimage Play in 1926. In 1930 he became associate director of the fledgling Pasadena Community Playhouse. He turned to films in 1933 and quickly made a mark as a solid character actor. During his 31 years in films, which also included considerable TV work, he worked for the majority of major studios and many independents as a free-lance. Among his many credits were such films as *Spellbound, Anna and the King of Siam, Don't Gamble with Strangers, Call Northside 777, Lulu Belle, Fort Yuma,* and *The Andy Hardy* series.

STANLEY RIDGES *(1892–Apr. 22, 1951)*

Stanley Ridges, best known for his portrayals of typically American doctors and lawyers, was born in England. It was through the efforts of Beatrice Lillie that he made his stage debut in London in *O' Boy.* His success in this musical led to his coming to New York where he starred in *Rose of China.* The actor's first movie was made in New York. This was *Crime Without Passion.* He also worked in Noel Coward's *The Scoundrel* before going to Hollywood where he was cast in many films including *Yellow Jack, If I Were King, This Is the Army, Wilson, The Master Race, Story of Dr. Wassell, The Suspect, God Is My Co-Pilot, Captain Eddie, Possessed,* and *You're My Everything.*

Stanley Ridges in Black Friday.

Elizabeth Risdon with Brandon Tynan and the children, Peter Holden and Virginia Weidler, in The Great Man Votes.

ELIZABETH RISDON *(1888–Dec. 20, 1958)*

Elizabeth Risdon was born in London, where she became affiliated with the Academy of Dramatic Art, first as a pupil and later as a student instructor. In 1912 Miss Risdon came to America to make a successful Broadway debut in *Fanny's First Play* for the Schuberts. She returned to England for more theatrical experience and returned to the United States in 1917 where she remained. Besides her performances for Shaw, she was leading lady for such stellar artists as George Arliss, Otis Skinner, and William Faversham. She was also under contract to the Theatre Guild for many years, after which she went to Hollywood for motion picture work. Her talking picture debut was in 1935 in Columbia's *Guard That Girl.* Alternating between comedy and tragedy parts, she appeared in such films as *The Unseen, Shocking Miss Pilgrim, Romance of Rosy Ridge, Life with Father, Crime and Punishment, The Final Hour,* and *Mourning Becomes Electra.*

THELMA RITTER *(1905–Feb. 5, 1969)*

Born in Brooklyn, Miss Ritter was introduced to theatricals in grammar school at the age of eight and was playing bits with stock companies while attending high school. Working at various jobs summers she raised tuition and attended the American Academy for a year. She played repertory at the Poli Theatre in Elizabeth, New Jersey, and up and down New England. During the

Thelma Ritter

depression, when work could not be found, she started making the rounds of radio where she became a regular on the top programs. Miss Ritter began her film career with a bit part in *Miracle on 34th Street.* She read her one line so wonderfully that Darryl Zanuck ordered her part built up, signed her to an exclusive contract and built her into an outstanding character actress. During her career she was nominated for the Oscar, won an Emmy Award, and won the Antoinette Perry Award, the Achievement Award of the American Academy of Dramatic Arts. Among her motion picture credits are *Letter to*

Julian Rivero, right, with Gilbert Roland in Robin Hood of Monterey.

Three Wives, All About Eve, The Mating Season, With a Song in My Heart, Pillow Talk, Titanic, Rear Window, Daddy Long Legs, and *How the West Was Won.*

JULIAN RIVERO (1890–Feb. 24, 1976)

Julian Rivero was a native Californian who spent his early years in San Francisco. He apprenticed under the great Shakespearean actor Robert B. Mantell. In the early years of movies he became adept as a cameraman and in 1922 he married a Welsh girl named Isabel Thomas. In 1923 he was one of the stars of the silent film block-buster *The Bright Shawl.* His wife became one of the Mack Sennett bathing beauties. Mrs. Rivero retired when their daughter Lorraine was born. Rivero worked for such great silent directors as John Ford ("The Iron Horse"), Raoul Walsh, Frank Borzage, etc. He also potboiled in educational comedies, Hal Roach comedies and westerns. In the 1930's Rivero appeared in countless westerns with Bob Steele, Buck Jones, Tim McCoy, Hoot Gibson, Harry Carey, and Tom Tyler, often playing the heavy. His favorite film roles were as Chico's father in *The Adventures of Chico,* one of the first real life animal adventure films, and as the Barber who gives Humphrey Bogart that awful haircut in *Treasure of the Sierra Madre.* Rivero was a longtime close friend of Leo Carrillo.

Flora Robson

FLORA ROBSON (1902–   )

Born in South Shields, England, Miss Robson found her father a willing second in her dreams of a theatrical career and he gladly financed her studies at the Royal Academy of Dramatic Arts. A large girl, with the staunch physical characteristics of the stony land in which she was born, Miss Robson specialized in character portrayals. Her most outstanding success on the stage was *Autumn.* She played the Empress Elizabeth in Bergner's *Catherine the Great,* and followed with Queen Elizabeth in *Fire Over England,* a portrayal which eventually netted her the opportunity of playing Ellen in Samuel Goldwyn's production of *Wuthering Heights,* which marked her debut in American films. Since then she has appeared in such films as *We Are Not Alone, Bahama Passage, Caesar and Cleopatra,* and *Saratoga Trunk* which won for her an Academy nomination as best supporting actress of 1946.

May Robson, with Franchot Tone.

MAY ROBSON (1858–Oct. 20, 1942)

For 58 years, Miss Robson was famous in England and America for both her stage and screen characterizations She was known in Hollywood as an "indefatigable trouper." She was born in Melbourne, Australia, and educated in Brussels, Paris, and London. Shortly after her early marriage at the age of sixteen to E.H. Gore, British inventor, Miss Robson came to New York. Her first successful starring role on Broadway was *The Rejuvenation of Aunt Mary,* in 1907. She invariably played character parts, so many that it was said of her that no one really knew what May Robson looked like. She made her motion picture debut in 1924. After her first film ventures she returned to the stage for a few seasons but went back to pictures in 1930. Her better known pictures include *If I Had a Million,*

Reunion in Vienna, Dinner at Eight, Lady for a Day, Anna Karenina, A Star Is Born, Million Dollar Baby, Grand Old Girl, The Texan, and *Strange Interlude.*

BENNY RUBIN *(1899–)*

Born in Boston, Benny Rubin started his professional career as a singer and dancer in that city in 1915. His first apearances were in "tab" shows and then on show boats on the Ohio and Mississippi Rivers. In 1918–19 he appeared as a Jewish and Dutch comic in burlesque, and from 1919–27 in big time vaudeville, night clubs and radio. In 1927 Rubin was signed by MGM for films and from 1932 on has been a free-lance player in all media of show business. A featured player in 165 feature pictures and some 55 two reelers, Rubin has played every conceivable character, doing each dialect proficiently. His films include *Traveling Saleslady, Molly and Me, Alibi Ike, George White's Scandals, On Again, Off Again, High Flyers,* and *The Headleys at Home.*

Herbert Rudley

taken into the professional theatre where he did a number of plays in repertory over a three year period. Rudley made his Broadway debut in Elmer Rice's *We, the People,* and followed this with some 25 other plays with featured and leading roles. Among his many film credits are *Rhapsody in Blue* (favorite role), *A Walk in the Sun, The Seventh Cross, The Master Race, Joan of Arc, Brewster's Millions, Casbah, The Silver Chalice, That Certain Feeling, Raw Edge,* and *Beloved Infidel.*

Benny Rubin, with Jack Benny.

HERBERT RUDLEY *(1911–)*

With no previous family connections with the theatre, Herbert Rudley won a scholarship to Eve LeGallienne's Repertory Theatre Studio in New York. After three months study he was

CHARLIE RUGGLES *(1886–Dec. 23, 1970)*

In over 60 years of show business Charlie Ruggles managed to hit everything from stock to Broadway, motion pictures, radio and TV. It was in 1905 that he made his acting debut portraying a schoolboy in a San Francisco stock company production of the play *Nathan Hale.* Rug-

Charlie Ruggles, with Mary Boland in Early to Bed.

gles first appeared on the New York stage at the Lincoln Square Theatre in 1907. A year later, he returned to Los Angeles, where for the next six years he played with the Morosco Stock Company. From 1914 to 1929, he traveled the country, appearing on virtually every stage in the nation. In 1930, he entered motion pictures at the Paramount Long Island Studios. He was sent to Hollywood and for the next 11 years appeared in countless films. He left Paramount in 1941 to free-lance. Throughout the 1940's he also devoted much time to radio. The war years found him one of Hollywood's most active entertainers on the service camp circuit. In recent years he enjoyed touring in summer stock as well as motion pictures and TV appearances. Among his motion pictures were *Charley's Aunt, Smiling Lieutenant, This Reckless Age, If I Had a Million, Alice in Wonderland, Ruggles of Red Gap, Anything Goes, Exclusive, Balalaika, The Farmer's Daughter, Maryland, No Time for Comedy, Our Hearts Were Young and Gay*, and *It Happened on Fifth Avenue*, playing the part of Michael O'Connor, his favorite role.

SIG RUMAN (1884–Feb. 14, 1967)

Sig Ruman made over 120 movies, played parts in Broadway shows and frequently appeared in television productions. He was born in Hamburg, Germany, attended college in Ilmenau in Thuringia. After a year's study of electro-technology he returned to Hamburg and studied for the stage. He made his debut in minor roles in Bielefeld, Germany. Next he went to Stettin and after that to the Kaiser's own theatre in Kiel.

Sig Ruman

Following service in World War I, Ruman journeyed to New York in 1924. While doing German language plays at the Irving Place Theatre, Georgie Jessel discovered him and then so did George S. Kaufman and Alexander Wollcott. Later he co-starred with Katharine Cornell and Ethel Barrymore. In 1934, 20th Century-Fox lured him to Hollywood and he was kept almost constantly busy appearing in pictures. Regardless of the size of his role, he never failed to turn in a first rate characterization. The many pictures in which he appeared are too numerous to list, but a few of the principal ones are *A Night at the Opera, Seventh Heaven, Maytime, Heidi, The Great Waltz, Dr. Ehrlich's Magic Bullet, Casablanca, Emperor's Waltz, Song of Bernadette*, and *Stalag 17*.

S.Z. (CUDDLES) SAKALL (1883–Feb. 12, 1955)

In addition to the more than 22 American films in which he played, S.Z. Sakall appeared in many European films before he fled from Nazi Germany in 1939 to come to the United States. Known to many film fans as Cuddles, Sakall, born in Budapest, became a stage and screen principal in Vienna and Berlin before his arrival in the United States. Remembered for his chubby cheeks and fractured English he appeared in such films as *Casablanca, Look for the Silver Lining, Lullaby of Broadway, Tea for Two, Sugarfoot*, and *Whiplash*.

WALTER SANDE (1906–Feb. 22, 1972)

Walter Sande always planned a musical career and followed one until he was 32 years of age. Born in Denver, Colorado, he went with his family to Portland, Oregon, where he attended school. He began the study of music when only six and by the time he was 30 he could play any known musical instrument. He quit college dur-

Walter Sande, right, with Humphrey Bogart in To Have and Have Not.

S. Z. Sakall in The Man Who Lost Himself.

ing his junior year to take an engagement with a band. For several years he was musical director for Fox West Coast Theaters. In 1937 he arrived in Hollywood. A friend suggested he turn his talents to the screen. His first picture was the *Goldwyn Follies* and from then on he continued as a film actor. His many picture credits included *Life of the Party, Ladies in Distress, You Can't Fool Your Wife, Timber, What Next, Corporal Hargrove, Killer McCoy, Prince of Thieves, Canadian Pacific,* and *Tucson.*

JOSEPH SCHILDKRAUT *(1895–Jan. 21, 1964)*
Joseph Schildkraut was born in Vienna, Austria. The son of actor Rudolf Schildkraut, he became a star in the Austrian theater and made his first film in 1914. Schildkraut came to the United States where he appeared on the New York stage. He was a leading man in silents and then drifted into character roles. In 1937 he won an Oscar for Best Supporting Actor for his role of Captain Dreyfuss in *The Life of Emile Zola.* Schildkraut is probably best remembered for his portrayal of Otto Frank in *The Diary of Anne Frank.* His

other films included *The King of Kings, Show Boat, Cleopatra, Viva Villa!, The Crusades, Slave Ship, Lancer Spy, Suez, The Rains Came, Flame of the Barbary Coast* and *The Greatest Story Ever Told.*

GUS SCHILLING *(1908-June 16, 1957)*
Gus Schilling's early career was in musical comedy and burlesque. He appeared in such shows as *Hold Everything, Flying High,* and in the Earl Carroll Vanities. After two seasons of radio work with Mercury Productions he went into motion pictures, establishing himself as a character actor and comedian. He appeared in such films as *Stork Bites Man, Return of October, Macbeth, Lady from Shanghai, Our Very Own, On Dangerous Ground, One Big Affair,* and *She Couldn't Say No.*

ROLFE SEDAN *(1896–Sept. 15, 1982)*
Born in New York City, Sedan had plans for entering the field of scientific agriculture. As a boy he began acting with a few of the early film companies in New York. This led to vaudeville

Joseph Schildkraut with Millie Perkins in The Diary of Anne Frank.

Gus Schilling, in Stork Bites Man.

Rolfe Sedan

and later society dancing. Sedan migrated into stock and eventually Broadway, appearing for the Shuberts as principal comedian in comic operas and musical comedies. His many legitimate appearances eventually led to motion pictures and then radio and television. Among the many films in which Sedan appeared were *The Iron Mask, Ruggles of Red Gap, April in Paris, Mississippi Gambler, The Spy, Merry Widow, Blue Beard's 8th Wife,* and *That Forsyte Woman.*

DAN SEYMOUR *(1915–)*

Dan Seymour spent his early theatrical days becoming a comedian. After success in eastern nightclubs he moved to Hollywood to try the movies. He made the grade at the first studio he tried, Paramount. Originally cast as a villain, he has played nothing but heavies in a total of more than 40 films. He has appeared in such films as *Casablanca, Young Man with a Horn, Intrigue, Johnny Belinda, Key Largo, The Blue Veil, Mara Maru, Glory Alley,* and *The Bride Comes to Yellow Sky.*

Dan Seymour, second from left, with Humphrey Bogart in To Have and Have Not.

HARRY SHANNON *(1890–July 27, 1964)*

Harry Shannon was born and educated in the public schools and political wards of Saginaw, Michigan. He loved to dance and sing and when, at the age of fifteen, a traveling repertoire found a need for a juvenile, Shannon stepped into the breach. This path led to New York and from one role to another. When things got bad on Broadway he turned to tent shows, Chautauquas and other forms of theatrical entertainment. Success in vaudeville followed and by 1910 Shannon was well established in musical comedy and dramatic stock. While appearing in Joseph Schildkraut's Hollywood Theater Guild venture, he attracted the attention of film makers and became featured in a number of sound shorts. After a return to Broadway he cast his lot permanently with films and was featured in *Hold Back the Dawn, The Lady Is Willing, Citizen Kane, In Old California, Mrs. Wiggs of the Cabbage Patch, This Gun for Hire, Random Harvest, Executive Suite, High Noon,* and *Young Tom Edison.*

Harry Shannon, right, with Richard Martin and Tim Holt in Rustlers.

Arthur Shields

ARTHUR SHIELDS (1896–Apr. 27, 1970)
Like the majority of the noted Abbey Players, Arthur Shields was a Dubliner by birth. Educated in the schools of his native city, developing acting ambitions at an early age, he started his professional career at the Abbey Theatre in 1914. He appeared in some 200 plays and directed about 20 more for this group. He appeared in a few silent pictures in England and Ireland as early as 1910, but his part in *The Plough and the Stars* for RKO was his first role in a talking picture. Other film credits included *Drums Along the Mohawk, The Long Voyage Home, The Keys of the Kingdom, National*

Velvet, The Corn Is Green, The Shocking Miss Pilgrim, She Wore a Yellow Ribbon, People Against O'Hara, and *Quiet Man.* He was a brother of Barry Fitzgerald.

RUSSELL SIMPSON (1880–Dec. 12, 1959)
Russell Simpson's acting assignments during his lifetime ran the gamut from romantic leads to character parts. He was born and raised near San Francisco. At 18 he participated in the Alaska goldrush. When he returned to Seattle he enrolled in acting school. Gaining Broadway via roles with touring companies he became associated with David Belasco. He first arrived in Hollywood in 1917 to make a silent picture and returned the next year to stay. While in Hollywood Simpson appeared in more than 200 motion pictures and a number of television films. His motion picture credits included *Grapes of Wrath, Girl of the Golden West, My Darling Clementine, Romance of Rosy Ridge, Beautiful Blonde from Bashful Bend, Saddle Tramp, 7 Brides for 7 Brothers, Last Command,* and *Friendly Persuasion.*

Russell Simpson

WALTER SLEZAK (1902–April 22, 1983)
Walter Slezak was born in Vienna, Austria, the son of opera star Leo Slezak. He came to America first in 1909, and stayed five years, while his father starred at the Metropolitan Opera, then, returning to Vienna, he completed his schooling at a private seminary and the University of Vienna. Despite his heritage, he did not delib-

Walter Slezak, in Come September.

erately set out to be an actor. He became one by accident. Spotted by director Michael Curtiz in 1922, Slezak was put into Curtiz' film spectacle, *Sodom and Gomorrah.* In 1929 Lee Shubert saw him in a Viennese musical comedy and brought him to America to appear in *Meet My Sister.* On Broadway he scored in such long-run hits as *May Wine, Ode to Liberty,* and *Music in the Air.* While appearing as a guest star in a Spring Festival at the University of Texas, Leo McCarey offered Slezak the role as the Baron in *Once Upon a Honeymoon.* His picture credits included *This Land Is Mine, The Fallen Sparrow, Lifeboat, Till We Meet Again, Salome, Where She Danced, The Spanish Main, Cornered,* and *Sinbad the Sailor.*

EVERETT SLOANE (1909–Aug. 6, 1965)
Everett Sloane, a top character in motion pictures and television, made his stage debut at the age of seven. A native New Yorker, Sloane entered the University of Pennsylvania but left in 1927 to join a stock company. When roles be-

Everett Sloane

came scarce, he took a job as a stockbroker's runner. When the 1929 stock market crash hurt his job, he turned to radio acting, appearing in a number of radio dramas. In some fifteen years in radio he played 15,000 roles. Sloane made his Broadway debut in 1935 in *Boy Meets Girl.* He joined the Orson Welles Mercury Theatre group and was to go with Welles into motion pictures. His motion picture credits included *Citizen Kane, Lady from Shanghai, Prince of Foxes, The Men, Bird of Paradise, The Enforcer, Sirocco, Blue Veil, Desert Fox, The Big Knife,* and *Home from the Hill.*

C. Aubrey Smith

C. AUBREY SMITH (1863–Dec. 20, 1948)
Sir Charles Aubrey Smith with his towering form and jutty eyebrows became the screen's typification of the aristocratic Englishman. Sir Aubrey made his screen debut in this country in 1915, but even then he had behind him an impressive list of honors in acting and athletics. Born in London he attended Charterhouse School and Cambridge. His original aim was medicine but drama and cricket sidetracked him. While establishing a theatrical reputation he found time to tour South Africa and Australia with championship teams. He made his stage debut in 1892 touring the provinces, appearing later with the leading actors of his time. He made his first American tour in 1896. From then on he made periodic visits to the U.S. until 1915 when he entered movie work here. Following his original screen debut he made films in England and continued on the stage. Beginning in 1930 and with few exceptions his time was spent in Hollywood. He is best remembered for his characterizations in such films as *The Crusades, Cleopatra,*

159

Prisoner of Zenda, Lloyd's of London, Clive of India, Madame Curie, Romeo and Juliet, Lives of a Bengal Lancer, The Four Feathers, Kidnapped, Waterloo Bridge, and *Rebecca.*

HOWARD I. SMITH *(1894–Jan. 10, 1968)*

Born in Attleboro, Massachusetts, later moving to Montreal, Smith began his entertainment career entertaining at clubs and parties. As a singer his voice attracted attention and he went to New York to study. World War I interrupted, stranding Smith in New York, so he went into vaudeville. Acting jobs followed and then back to vaudeville until 1929. During the 1930's, Smith went into radio, doing all kinds of character parts, from which he gradually returned to the stage. He appeared in such hits as *Dear Ruth* and *Death of a Salesman.* From the stage was a short step into films and he appeared in *Her Kind of Man, North Side 777, State of the Union, Street with No Name, Never Wave at a Wac,* and *Death of a Salesman,* in which he played Uncle Charlie, his favorite role in films. In October of 1965, Smith completed his 50th year in showbusiness.

WALTER SODERLING *(1872–Apr. 10, 1948)*

A veteran of the Dearborn and Hopkins stock companies which flourished in Chicago at the turn of the century, Walter Soderling brought years of stage experience to his roles as a character actor in motion pictures. Though he took no part in dramatics while attending Harvard, Northwestern and the University of Chicago, Soderling turned to the stage soon after completing his college education, and appeared in a long succession of Broadway successes with many of the notables of the theatre. Born in Milwaukee, Wisconsin, Soderling, after many years on the stage found his way into films. Though he preferred the stage to the screen he piled up an impressive list of screen roles including *Maid of Salem, St. Louis Blues, Mr. Smith Goes to Washington, Meet John Doe, The Master Race, One Foot in Heaven, I Married an Angel, Mark Twain,* and *Rhapsody in Blue.*

VLADIMIR SOKOLOFF *(1889–Feb. 15, 1962)*

Vladimir Sokoloff's face was well known to movie goers. He spent most of his acting career

Howard I. Smith, with Katharine Hepburn on set of State of the Union.

Walter Soderling

Vladimir Sokoloff

160

playing character roles of many nationalities. It is estimated he portrayed over 35 different nationalities during his fifty-year career. Sokoloff was born in Moscow and as a youth combined studies of philosophy and literature with study under Stanislavski. After leaving Russia, Sokoloff acted throughout Germany where he made his first film in 1925. In the 1930's he went to France to appear in motion pictures and returned to the United States in 1935 to make the film *The Life of Emile Zola*. Other film credits included *Road to Morocco, The Real Glory, Macao, For Whom the Bell Tolls, Two Smart People, The Baron of Arizona, Till We Meet Again*, and *To the Ends of the Earth*.

GALE SONDERGAARD (1899–   )

Although her appearance on the screen suggests an exotic background, Miss Sondergaard was born in Litchfield, Minnesota, of Danish-American parents, her father a professor at the University of Minnesota. It was in high school that Miss Sondergaard discovered her future belonged to the theatre. She completed her education at the University of Minnesota and also attended the Minnesota School of Dramatic Art. After receiving her college degree she joined a travelling Shakespearean company and later was a member of the famous Jesse Bonestelle's stock company in Detroit. From Detroit she went to New York under contract to the New York Theatre Guild. She appeared in a number of plays. Travelling with her husband, who was to become a motion picture director, Miss Sonder-

Gale Sondergaard, in The Letter.

gaard arrived in Hollywood. After several months of "freedom," Mervyn LeRoy decided she was just the type to play the role of Faith in *Anthony Adverse*. This was her first role in motion pictures, for which she won the Academy Award for Supporting Actress, the first time such a category was created. Some forty pictures followed over the years with many types of roles including *Maid of Salem, Seventh Heaven, The Story of Emile Zola, Juarez, Mark of Zorro, Road to Rio, The Blue Bird, The Letter, The Spider Woman*, and *Anna and the King of Siam*.

Ned Sparks, in George White's 1935 Scandals.

NED SPARKS (1883–Apr. 3, 1957)

Ned Sparks, the dour-faced comedian, was born in Ontario, Canada, and began his theatrical career at the age of seventeen, when he participated in the famed Klondike gold rush, billed as a "singer of sweet southern songs." For five years following the gold rush, Sparks passed through a period of carnivals, one-night stands and medicine shows, finally arriving in New York. In New York he gained fame as a comedian noted for his frozen-face delineations. After

161

heading the actors' strike against New York stage producers in 1918, which resulted in the establishment of Actors' Equity, he went to Hollywood in 1920. Sparks' first experience in films was in five Constance Talmadge feature comedies. After finally embarking upon a screen career, he continued the same type of roles which had made him famous on the stage. These included parts in *The Canary Murder Case, Blessed Event, 42nd Street,* and *Lady for a Day.*

LIONEL STANDER (1908–)

Lionel Stander, eccentric character comedian, was born in New York City. Stander received his education in a hit-and-miss fashion attending a number of schools. His theatrical career began when he was nineteen years old. He volunteered for a part in a play, but before the play opened, he was playing six roles. He decided acting was the career he had been looking for and subsequently appeared in scores of plays. Radio provided Stander with another opportunity to capitalize on his guttural dialect and he was featured on a number of radio programs. He made his debut as a screen actor in 1932 in a short subject, *Salt Water Daffy,* and was afterwards featured in seventeen other comedy shorts. His debut as a featured actor in full-length productions occurred in 1935 in *The Scoundrel.* He has played roles in *Page Miss Glory, Hooray for Love, The Gay Deception, Soak the Rich, The Milky Way, If You Could Only Cook, Mr. Deeds Goes to Town, Meet Nero Wolfe,* and *There Goes the Bride.* He gained a new audience with his role as Max in television's "Hart to Hart."

Arnold Stang

ARNOLD STANG (1926–)

Arnold Stang began his career when he dropped a postcard into a mailbox near his home in Chelsea, Massachusetts, requesting an audition with the *Horn and Hardart's Children's Hour.* He has been in show business ever since. Stang has worked in every phase of the entertainment industry. He began in the "Golden Age" of radio and when television moved in to engulf the big radio shows, he made the transition. Broadway productions like *Sailor Beware* led Stang to motion pictures. Usually cast as the curly-haired wise-cracking comic relief, the comic stooge proved himself a serious artist as well in his role of Sparrow in *The Man with the Golden Arm.* Other films include *Seven Days Leave, My Sister Eileen, Let's Go Steady, Hepcats, They've Got Me Covered, So This Is New York, The Expectant Father,* and more recently *The Wonderful World of Brothers Grimm,* and *It's a Mad, Mad, Mad World.*

Onslow Stevens

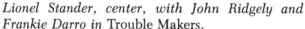

Lionel Stander, center, with John Ridgely and Frankie Darro in Trouble Makers.

HENRY STEPHENSON (1871–Apr. 24, 1956)
A native of Granada, British West Indies,
Stephenson was educated at Rugby in England.
He made his professional stage debut in London
and continued his theatrical career touring the
British provinces. He played on the New York
stage and toured the United States from 1901 to
1932 when he began making films. His first film
was *The Animal Kingdom* and others included
*Little Women, Mutiny on the Bounty, Of
Human Bondage, Oliver Twist, Captain Blood,
Little Lord Fauntleroy,* and *China Clipper.*

ONSLOW STEVENS (1871–Jan. 5, 1977)
Always in demand as a character actor, Onslow
Stevens had a rich theatrical and artistic
background. His parents were both of the stage
and his grandfather an English composer of note.
Born in Los Angeles, Stevens made his real stage
debut at the Pasadena Community Theatre in
Under the Roof in 1928. He did several hundred
plays for that organization. His entrance into pictures in 1931 was purely accidental. He was appearing in a Pasadena show while the leading
lady was called for a screen test at Universal. She
asked Stevens to help her out by playing opposite
her in a test. Both were given contracts. His first
important role was that of the harassed author
in *Once in a Lifetime.* He appeared in such films
as *Only Yesterday, The Three Musketeers,* and
Mother Lode.

Henry Stephenson, in The Adventures of Sherlock
Holmes.

*Paul Stewart, center, with Jack Webb and Alan
Ladd in* Appointment with Danger.

PAUL STEWART (1908–)
Paul Stewart had his eye on the theatre before
graduating from public school. By the time he
had completed his law course at Columbia
University, he was convinced that he was des-
tined to be an actor rather than a lawyer. His
first stage hit was made in *Subway Express.* Being a versatile actor, he varied his dramatic roles
with comedy work. During the summer seasons
he was active on the Straw Hat Circuit. In 1932
Stewart decided that radio offered greater opportunities and in no time secured work with the
top radio shows. Through membership in Orson Welles' Mercury Players he was brought to
Hollywood and films. His first important role
was in *Citizen Kane.* Following this he appeared
in *Johnny Eager, Mr. Lucky, Government Girl,
The Window, Champion,* and *Twelve O'Clock
High.*

FRED STONE (1873–Mar. 6, 1959)
Fred Stone, known as the "grand old man of the
American theatre," went into show business at
the age of ten with his brother Eddie, doing a
tight-rope act. Later he teamed with David
Montgomery and the pair became headliners in
minstrel and variety shows. Their first stage hit
was scored in *The Wizard of Oz* in which Stone

Fred Stone

was the original scarecrow. Among the musical shows in which Stone gained fame were *The Red Mill, Chin-Chin,* and *Criss-Cross.* For more than a half century he was a pillar of American musical comedy. Aside from his stage appearances, Stone was an active screen performer. He acted before the cameras as early as 1917 but his major work did not come until 1935. This was a film version of Booth Tarkington's *Alice Adams.* Among his other screen credits were *My American Wife, The Westerner, Life Begins in College, Trail of the Lonesome Pine, Grand Jury, Hideaway,* and *Quick Money.*

GEORGE E. STONE *(1903–May 26, 1967)*
Writers called him "Toothpick Charlie," "The Runt," "Society Max" and a score of other names epitomizing toughness and guile, but he began his career as a song-and-dance man for the Shuberts in New York. A friend of Damon Runyon, George Stone arrived in Hollywood in 1925 and his first role was the sewer rat in *Seventh Heaven.* That was the beginning of a lifetime career of notable characterizations on the screen which number more than 200. Among his many

George E. Stone, in Last of the Duanes.

screen credits were *Guys and Dolls, Some Like It Hot, Seventh Heaven, Tenderloin, The Racket, Strangers in the Night, My Buddy, Scared Stiff, Doll Face,* and *Untamed Breed.*

MILBURN STONE *(1904–Jun. 12, 1980)*
Milburn Stone became so well known as crusty Doc Adams on *Gunsmoke* it becomes difficult to imagine him as anyone else. He was born in Burrton, Kansas, and as a young man performed in little theater groups. He performed in a song and dance act in vaudeville, then on to Broadway and finally to films in 1935. In addition to the nearly 500 episodes of *Gunsmoke* he appeared in 100 films from 1935 to 1957. He won an Emmy in 1968 for his role as "Doc Adams". His films included *China Clipper, Crime School, Stunt Pilot, Enemy Agent, Frisco Lil, Sherlock Holmes Faces Death, Strange Confession, Branded, Black Tuesday* and *Smoke Signal.*

Milburn Stone with Julie Bishop in Strange Conquest.

LUDWIG STOSSEL *(1883–Jan. 29, 1973)*
Ludwig Stossel, born in Lockenhaus, Austria, received his education in Graz, Austria. Until 1938 he worked as an actor throughout Austria and Germany under such directors as Reinhardt, Jessner, Barnowsky, Preminger and Lothar. In

1938 he went to London and started in English motion pictures. After 1940 he was in Hollywood appearing in both motion pictures and television. He had featured parts in about 70 films including *The Climax, Bluebeard, House of Dracula, Miss Susie Slagle's, A Song Is Born, This Time for Keeps,* and *Escape Me Never.*

Ludwig Stossel

Glenn Strange

GLENN STRANGE *(1899–Sept. 20, 1973)*
Glenn Strange, born in Weed, New Mexico, started his theatrical career in radio in 1927. He began with CBS-KNX as a member of a western group known as the Arizona Wranglers. He continued there through 1934. During this period Strange did several films and numerous theatre appearances. Strange started motion picture work exclusively in 1935 as the sidekick of Dick Foran in a series of westerns. Later he went to heavy roles working with a number of stars. His favorite roles were as Frankenstein's monster in movies and Sam in the *Gunsmoke* television show. Among his numerous film credits were *Action in the North Atlantic, Red River, Great Sioux Uprising, Texas Carnival, Law of the Range, Knickerbocker Holiday, The Mad Monster, House of Frankenstein,* and *House of Dracula.*

ROBERT STRAUSS *(1913–Feb. 20, 1975)*
Strauss made his debut on the stage and then on into films. Born in New York he worked at many jobs–busboy, salesman–and then the Broadway stage. He appeared in *Detective Story, Stalag 17,* and *Twentieth Century.* Stock and touring

Robert Strauss

followed with *Here Comes Mr. Jordan, Season in the Sun* and *The Best of Steinbeck.* Strauss made his film debut in *Sailor Beware* and subsequently appeared in roles in *Act of Love, Attack, Jumping Jacks, Man with the Golden Arm, Seven Year Itch, Bridges at To-Ko-Ri,* and *Stalag 17,* in which he played Animal, his favorite role.

165

Gene Stutenroth, left, with Richard Travis in Alaska Patrol.

GENE STUTENROTH *(1903–July 19, 1976)*

Gene Stutenroth became interested in dramatics during his junior year in Minneapolis West High School. From then on he often appeared for little theaters. Later he joined a Pantages troupe as a juvenile. In summer he traveled with a carnival show. Traveling to Hollywood he won a break at the Mack Sennett studios. He appeared in several two-reel comedies. Small parts then came his way. Stutenroth decided he wasn't progressing and turned to the boxing game as a promoter and then to building pipe organs. But the entertainment field was in his blood and he went to New York in 1930, resuming little theater roles and summer stock. In 1943 he returned to Hollywood doing various types of roles in *Sherlock Holmes and the Spider Woman, The Strange Death of Adolf Hitler, Russia, Beyond the Pecos, The Fighting Guardsman, The Sudan,* and *Charlie Chan in the Secret Service.*

FRANCIS L. SULLIVAN *(1903–Nov. 19, 1956)*

Ponderous screen menace Francis L. Sullivan selected acting as his profession as soon as he was old enough to read Shakespeare. Born in London, Sullivan began his acting career at the age of 18, playing four parts in an Old Vic presentation of *Richard III*. During the next few years

Francis L. Sullivan

he created a number of character roles in Shaw plays and numerous Shakespearean plays. He made his motion picture debut in the British picture *The Missing Rembrandt*. After that he lent his talents to numerous English pictures, usually playing a menace. He did this so effectively that he was summoned to Hollywood. In 1934 Universal signed him to play Jaggers in *Great Expectations*, the role he repeated in the 1946 Rank production. Alternating between stage and screen, Sullivan's screen credits include *Caesar and Cleopatra, Joan of Arc, Broken Journey, The Man Within, Behave Yourself, Oliver Twist, My Favorite Spy,* and *The Citadel*.

Slim Summerville, in Rebecca of Sunnybrook Farm.

GEORGE SLIM SUMMERVILLE *(1892–Jan. 5, 1946)*

Slim Summerville, the portrayer of "hick" parts, was born in Albuquerque, New Mexico. He began his career in 1913 as one of Mack Sennett's original Keystone Kops. From then until the time of his death he was steadily before the cameras. It is estimated that he appeared in approximately 630 pictures, 80 being feature films, usually in comedy roles, but infrequently, as in *All Quiet on the Western Front*, in a serious role. Tall and thin, relying on blank stares and understatement for comic effect, Summerville was perhaps most popular during the 1930's. Included in his many film credits are *Tobacco Road, Jesse James, The Country Doctor, Way Down East, The Farmer Takes a Wife, Rebecca of Sunnybrook Farm*, and a series of comedies in which he was teamed with Zasu Pitts.

GRADY SUTTON (1908-)

Never having had a lesson in acting, Grady Sutton has had one of the most durable careers in Hollywood. Sutton worked his way through over 42 years of pictures, appearing at one time in every single picture on Hollywood Boulevard during one week. He entered movies by accident appearing as an extra in *The Mad Whirl*. He took to acting and didn't quit. From *The Mad Whirl* he went to work in a succession of Harold Lloyd's comedies. From there, he was teamed with W.C. Fields in a Mack Sennett two-reeler and later Fields' most memorable films. The epitome of the harassed clerk or floor walker, Sutton has appeared in such films as *The Man on the Flying Trapeze, Palm Springs, My Man Godfrey, Stage Door, Alexander's Ragtime Band*, and *My Wild Irish Rose*.

Grady Sutton, center, with Marie Wilson and Jean Parker in Flying Blind.

AKIM TAMIROFF (1899–Sept. 17, 1972)

Born in the Russian Caucasus, Tamiroff's future was obscure until he decided to become an actor. In 1918 he was one of four out of 500 selected for admission to the Moscow Art Theatre. In 1923 he came to America with a group to present several Russian plays and decided to stay. After several New York Theatre Guild productions and work in a Chicago nightclub he finally decided to try the movies. There followed long dull months of waiting, starving and capturing a stray role now and then which was only a brief bit at best. Then Henry Hathaway gave him a chance in *Lives of a Bengal Lancer*, in which he played a small but outstanding part. In 1934 he signed with Paramount and later appeared in numerous films, several under the direction of Cecil B. DeMille who considered Tamiroff "as one of the finest workmen as an actor" he ever encountered. Among his major film credits were *Gay Deception, Anthony Adverse, The General Died at Dawn, The Buccaneer, Union Pacific, The Way of All Flesh, Dangerous to Know, Northwest Mounted Police*, and *Topkapi*.

Akim Tamiroff, with George Raft in Outpost in Morocco.

VAUGHN TAYLOR (1911-)

Born in Boston, Massachusetts, where he received his education, Taylor had intended to become a certified public accountant. While attending Northeastern University he became interested in acting. He decided to become an actor but finished college first. After working as an accountant for a year he obtained a scholarship for the Leland Powers School of the Theatre. Money was scarce so he literally gave his blood to become an actor, receiving $20 or $25 a pint depending upon which hospital was buying. After graduation from Powers, Vaughn went to the Boothbay Playhouse in Maine. This was followed by stock experience with a Chautauqua group and radio announcing in Boston. From 1942–45 he served in the U.S. Army and was discharged with the rank of Captain. From 1946 until 1957 he worked almost entirely in live television appearing in over 400 live shows. Universal brought Taylor to Hollywood in 1950 for *Up-Front*. Subsequent films include *Francis Goes to the Races, Meet Danny Wilson, Back at the Front, It Could Be You*, and *This Could Be the Night*.

Vaughn Taylor

RAY TEAL *(1902–Apr. 2, 1976)*
Ray Teal, born of a non-theatrical family in Grand Rapids, Michigan, played the saxophone to work his way through college. Following

Ray Teal

graduation from the University of California, Teal did stage band conducting through 1936. Teal made his screen debut in 1938 in *Western Jamboree*. His favorite role was that of the sheriff on television in *Bonanza*. After his film debut he appeared in many Westerns and features including *Captain Kidd, Best Years of Our Lives, Joan of Arc, Northwest Passage, It Happens Every Spring, Redhead and the Cowboy, Montana Belle, Rogue Cop, Band of Angels*, and *Carrie*.

FRANK THOMAS *(1889–   )*
On film, Thomas has robbed more banks than the other well known St. Joseph, Missouri, resident, Jesse James. His acting career began with employment at the Van Dyke Stock Company, Lyric Theatre in St. Joseph, Missouri. This was followed by a number of company tours of the U.S. which eventually led to Broadway in 1913–14. Following a number of Broadway successes, Thomas was signed by RKO for motion pictures, appearing in a steady succession of films for this studio during 1935–37. From 1938

Frank Thomas, center, with Fred Stone and Owen Davis Jr.

through 1942 he free-lanced at all studios and became the busiest actor in Hollywood for two of those years, appearing in more pictures than any other actor. His film credits number over 160 films and include *A Man to Remember, The Ex-Mrs. Bradford, Vivacious Lady, The Last of the Bad Men, Lillian Russell, Brigham Young, Alexander Graham Bell, Ellery Queen, Gentlemen After Dark*, and *Rose of Washington Square*.

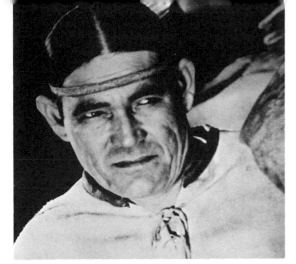

Chief Thundercloud

CHIEF THUNDERCLOUD (1899–Dec. 1, 1955)

Although his real name was Victor Daniels, he was a full-blooded Cherokee Indian. Born in Oklahoma, the oldest of nine children, he worked at all kinds of jobs until he started in pictures as double for stars and stunt man. Although mostly cast as a "heavy" he is best known for his portrayal of "Tonto" in *The Lone Ranger*. His films included *Geronimo, Typhoon, Northwest Mounted Police, Hudson's Bay, Western Union, Colt 45*, and *A Ticket to Tomahawk*.

GEORGE TOBIAS (1901–Feb. 27, 1980)

Veteran actor of the stage and screen, George Tobias began his acting career in his native New York. He made his debut in the Neighborhood Playhouse later joining the Provincetown Players. After doing many legitimate shows he moved to Hollywood where he free-lanced as an actor. He appeared in ten pictures during his first nine months in the film capital and then signed a contract with Warner Bros. Studios. His first picture was *Saturday's Children* followed by such films as *Torrid Zone, They Drive by Night,*

George Tobias

South of Suez, Sergeant York, Yankee Doodle Dandy, Mission to Moscow, This Is the Army, Thank Your Lucky Stars, Her Kind of Man, and *Sinbad the Sailor*.

SID TOMACK (1907–Nov. 12, 1962)

Sid Tomack was a native of Brooklyn, New York, and started his career as a vaudeville actor in the song-and-dance team of Sid Tomack and Reis Brothers. He was also a master of ceremonies at numerous Catskill Mountain resorts. Tomack migrated from New York to California appearing in character parts in a score of motion pictures and in several TV series. Among these were *The Thrill of Brazil, Framed, House of Strangers, Abandoned Woman, Somebody Loves Me*, and *The Joe Palooka Story*.

Sid Tomack, center, with Sumner Williams, John Derek, Mickey Knox and Jody Gilbert in Knock on Any Door.

ANDREW TOMBES (1889–May 4, 1976)

Andrew Tombes wanted to be an acrobat and spent his leisure as a youth around circus lots and vaudeville theaters. After completing grade and high schools, he matriculated at Phillips-Exeter becoming a star baseball player. From there he went into stock and finally to Broadway where he remained for 25 years. For seven years he

169

played in Shakespearean drama, alternating between comic and heavy roles. Then he was engaged for the *Ziegfeld Follies* and appeared in five of those productions. Will Rogers, one of his best friends, got him to Hollywood in 1936 to appear with him in *Doubting Thomas*, where he remained. His picture credits include *Weekend Pass, Patrick the Great, Murder in the Blue Room, Bring on the Girls, Make Way for Love, The Reckless Age, Something for the Boys, Can't Help Singing, Two Sisters from Boston, Going to Town*, and *Badman's Territory*.

Andrew Toombes, in Time Out for Romance.

Regis Toomey, in Voyage to the Bottom of the Sea.

REGIS TOOMEY (1902–   )
Regis Toomey's career numbers many "firsts." In 1928 he appeared with Chester Morris in *Alibi*, the first all-talking gangster melodrama

filmed. In 1931 he appeared opposite Clara Bow in *Kick In*, Miss Bow's first sound movie. Prior to his film debut in 1925 he toured England in George M. Cohan's *Little Nelly Kelly* during which severe laryngitis forced the end of his singing career and indirectly led him to Hollywood and a career in films. A native of Pittsburgh, Toomey became interested in dramatics while at the University of Pittsburgh where he graduated in 1921. His film debut followed a number of stage appearances when he was signed to a long-term contract by Paramount-Famous Players-Lasky. Except for the years on the Paramount roster, and a 1940–42 contract with Warner Bros., Toomey has worked as a free-lance actor, playing a great variety of roles. He has appeared in over 200 films including *Rich People, Illusion, Union Pacific, The High and the Mighty, Guys and Dolls, Boy with the Green Hair, Show Boat, Dakota Incident, The Big Sleep*, and *Warlock*.

MARY TREEN (1907–   )
Mary Treen was born in St. Louis, Missouri. She started her career as a dancer appearing in vaudeville, reviews, light opera, and musical comedy. Miss Treen started her film career in 1934 under contract to Warner Bros. and has continued in films and television to the present. Miss Treen's favorite role was one written for her in *I Love a Soldier* made by Paramount. Among her many other film credits are *Hot Tires, Happiness Ahead, Strange Impersonation, She Wouldn't Say Yes, The Stooge, Sailor Beware, The Caddy*, and *Birds and Bees*.

Mary Treen

IVAN TRIESAULT (1898–Jan. 3, 1980)

Ivan Triesault began his acting carer at the age of fourteen at the National Theatre in Tallinn, Estonia, the city of his birth. Triesault continued his studies and acted in London in the 1920's. This was followed by more study in New York and many plays on Broadway. In 1942 Triesault was brought to Hollywood by Warner Bros. to play in *Mission to Moscow*. Additional film credits included *Counter Attack, A Song to Remember, Notorious, Golden Earrings, To the Ends of the Earth, Kim, Jet Pilot*, and *The Bad and the Beautiful*. Triesault considered his favorite role to be that of the von Stroheim type director in *The Bad and the Beautiful*, and always found character parts to be stimulating and rewarding.

Ernest Truex

Ivan Triesault

ERNEST TRUEX (1889–June 27, 1973)

From gas jets in the footlights to television covered the acting career of Ernest Truex. He had a career of over 60 years of acting, with 48 opening nights on Broadway, ten in London, a long list of silent and talking motion pictures and over two hundred live TV show performances. Born in Kansas City, Truex began his career playing Hamlet in a kiddie show at the age of six. From that time on acting became his job in life. Usually cast as the wispy, henpecked husband or newlywed, he appeared in innumerable films such as *Whistling in the Dark, Warriors Husband, The Adventures of Marco Polo, Start Cheering, Freshman Year*, and *Swing, Sister, Swing*.

TOM TULLY (1908–Apr. 27, 1982)

Tom Tully, born in Durango, Colorado, planned a career in the navy when he was young. Falling short by only a single point to gain entrance into the Naval Academy, he enlisted as an ordinary sailor. After his days in the service he became a cub reporter on the Denver *Post*. However, the attraction of higher salaries in radio sent him to New York. His first opportunity came as a barking dog on the *Renfrew of the Mounted* radio show. This led to a speaking role later on the same program. Tully was to become a veteran of over 3000 coast to coast radio broadcasts. Broadway soon followed and after a period of flop plays a hit with revival of *Ah, Wilderness*. Tully followed this with successful runs in *The Time of Your Life* and *Jason* before he was brought to Hollywood to play in *I'll Be Seeing*

Tom Tully

171

You. Other films to follow were *Destination Tokyo, The Virginian, Scudda Hoo, Scudda Hay, Intrigue, June Bride, Tomahawk, Branded, The Caine Mutiny, Arrow in the Dust,* and *Love Me or Leave Me.*

HARRY TYLER *(1888–Sept. 15, 1961)*

Harry Tyler had an active theatrical career for sixty years, starting his professional career for Flo Ziegfeld in 1901 with Anna Held's Little Dutchess Company as a boy soprano. In 1910 he married Gladys Crolius and by 1912 they were launched in their own vaudeville act, one of the first man and woman nut acts, playing the Keith and Loew for twelve seasons. In 1925 he was back to the legitimate theatre and appearances in a number of plays. He arrived in Hollywood in 1929 to recreate for films his stage role of Eddie Allen in *The Shannons on Broadway.* Among other films in which he appeared and listed as his favorites were *Tobacco Road, Grapes of Wrath, The Quiet Man, The Last Hurrah,* and *Friends of Mr. Sweeney* with Charles Ruggles. Interestingly, Tyler never found satisfaction in acting in motion pictures. He missed the audience contact.

JO VAN FLEET *(1922–)*

Jo Van Fleet, an actress of considerable range, has appeared in less than a dozen films, frequently portraying women older than herself. She started as a character actress while at school and won a scholarship to the Neighborhood Playhouse in New York. Her first professional appearance was in the road company of *Uncle Harry* which starred Luther Adler. She then appeared on Broadway in *The Winter's Tale, The Whole World Over, The Closing Door, King Lear, Flight into Egypt,* and *Camino Real* directed by Elia Kazan. She won the Oscar as best supporting actress in 1955 for her first screen role as James Dean's mother in the film *East of Eden.* Her other films include *The Rose Tattoo,* as Susan Hayward's mother in *I'll Cry Tomorrow,* as Big Nose Kate in *Gunfight at OK Corral,* as a gun-toting mother in *The King and Four Queens,* and as an 80-year-old widow in her second film for Kazan, *Wild River.*

PHILIP VAN ZANDT *(1904–Feb. 15, 1958)*

Philip Van Zandt played more than 400 character roles in Hollywood. Born in Amsterdam, Holland, he began his theatrical career in 1927 and appeared in many stage plays in New York and on the road. He came to Hollywood in 1941 where his first role was in *These High Gray Walls.* Specializing in villainous roles, his film credits included *Somewhere in the Night, The Loves of Carmen, The Big Clock, Red, Hot and Blue, Cyrano de Bergerac, Yankee Pasha, Playgirl, Untamed, The Big Combo, Our Miss Brooks,* and *Around the World in 80 Days.*

EVELYN VARDEN *(1893–July 11, 1958)*

Evelyn Varden was a familiar character actress whose career began in childhood. Her first important role was as Mrs. Gibbs in Thorton Wilder's *Our Town.* Her other stage credits included *Russet Mantle* and *Candle in the Wind.* She was a longtime radio serialist and familiar player on live dramatic TV shows. Two of her most outstanding roles in films were in *Cheaper By the Dozen* and *The Bad Seed.*

HERB VIGRAN *(1910–)*

Herb Vigran, a native of Fort Wayne, Indiana, came to Hollywood in 1933 with an LL.B. from Indiana University, yet determined to get into the movies. His first time in front of a camera was in *Happy Landings* for Monogram playing a radio operator, for which he was paid ten dollars in those pre-Screen Actors Guild days. He went back to New York where he embarked on a very busy radio career interrupted by a stint in the service from 1943 to 1945. To his radio, TV, and movie career since World War II has been added the frequent use of Vigran's voice on "off-camera" commercials as well as his face on "on-camera" commercials. His favorite film role was with Dick Powell in *Susan Slept Here.* He also tremendously enjoyed his role as Dick Powell's bartender in Willie Dante shows on the "Four Star Television Playhouse." His many film credits include *Stranger on the Third Floor, Morning After, Sweet Rosie O'Grady, Ghost Ship, One Exciting Night, Monsieur Verdoux, All My Sons, Mr. 880, Murder, Mr. Malone, Half Angel, Three Guys Named Mike, Bedtime for Bonzo,* and *People in Love.*

THEODORE VON ELTZ *(1893–Oct. 6, 1964)*

Theodore Von Eltz planned to study for the

Harry Tyler

Evelyn Varden

Jo Van Fleet

Herb Vigran

Phillip Van Zandt, with James Stewart in The Jack-pot.

Theodore Von Eltz

173

medical profession but the theater attracted him at an early age. He was born in New Haven where his father was a professor of languages at Yale University. Von Eltz began his career on the New York stage in 1913. He appeared frequently in films, radio, and TV and was the narrator of Rachel Carson's *The Sea Around Us*. His last appearance was as Father Barbour in the television version of *One Man's Family*, an old radio favorite. His films included *Bermuda Mystery, Rhapsody in Blue, The Big Sleep*, and *Devil's Cargo*.

RAYMOND WALBURN (1887–July 26, 1969)
Raymond Walburn was born in Plymouth, Indiana. He arrived in California in 1906. After working at various jobs, he made his debut at the Liberty Theatre in Oakland. Other stock engagements followed and four years later he crashed New York in a production of *Mary Jane's Pa*. The following twenty-three years were packed with plays in which he was featured. Between engagements on Broadway he played stock and took time out for service in World War I. Walburn's film career began in 1934 under contract to Columbia. He remained in Hollywood for 21 years, making 87 films for every major studio. He retired in 1955 only to return to Broadway in 1962 in *A Funny Thing Happened on the Way to the Forum*, staying with the company for 18 months. His film credits include *Count of Monte Cristo, Mr. Deeds Goes to Town, Craig's Wife, Louisiana Purchase, Dixie, State of the Union*, the *Henry* series, *Riding High, She Couldn't Say No*, and *The Spoilers*.

H.B. WARNER (1875–Dec. 21, 1958)
Henry Byron Charles Stewart Warner was born in England to a family renowned for three generations on the English stage. He made his first appearance on the stage at the age of seven with his father. Many stage roles followed and in 1905 he came to the United States playing leading roles in many of the favorite productions of the stage. Beginning in 1924, Warner's career was devoted exclusively to the screen. His greatest role and success was as Christ in C.B. DeMille's *King of Kings*. He subsequently appeared in over 130 films generally in the later years as a featured player. Among these many

H. B. Warner, *with Maria Ouspenskaya in* The Rains Came.

films were *Here Comes the Groom, Sunset Boulevard, Prince of Thieves, It's a Wonderful Life, Crossroads, The New Moon, The Rains Came, Mr. Smith Goes to Washington, You Can't Take It with You, Kidnapped*, and *Lost Horizon*.

ROBERT WARWICK (1878–June 6, 1964)
Robert Warwick, born Robert Taylor Bien in Sacramento, California, appeared for many years on the Broadway stage and in motion pictures and later, on television. Early in life he studied singing in Paris returning to the United States for an operatic career which he abandoned. He became an understudy in Clyde Fitche's play *Glad of It* in 1903. Many parts on Broadway followed, after which Warwick quit

Robert Warwick, *right, with John Hamilton, S. Z. Sakall and Randolph Scott in* Sugarfoot.

Raymond Walburn in Rise and Shine.

the stage for screen, playing romantic leads for Paramount and heading his own picture company for a short time. After service in World War I, Warwick remained in pictures for a year and then returned to the stage in a number of successful productions through 1935. Following 1935, he appeared again in films, among them were *A Tale of Two Cities, Romeo and Juliet, Mary of Scotland, The Prince and the Pauper, The Life of Emile Zola, Adventures of Robin Hood, Devil's Island, Elizabeth and Essex, Juarez, Tennessee Johnson,* and *Salome.*

LUCILLE WATSON (1879–June 24, 1962)

Lucille Watson was one of stage and screen's best known character actresses. Her career ran from the stage of 1900 to present day motion pictures and television. Her first major triumph in New York was as Maggie in *The Girl with the Green Eyes* in 1902. She went to Hollywood in 1934 for a decade of films, and for the last 20 years appeared in New York plays and television. Born in Quebec, Canada, she specialized in British character roles in such films as *The Bishop Misbehaves, What Every Woman Knows, Watch on the Rhine, Till We Meet Again, Never Say Goodbye,* and *The Razor's Edge.*

Lucille Watson

Minor Watson, left, with Charles Halton and Esther-Howard in The Young People.

MINOR WATSON (1889–July 28, 1965)

Minor Watson, born in Alton, Illinois, made his professional debut on a stage in Brooklyn in 1911. It took eleven years of stock performances around the nations to get to Broadway. His first Broadway role was in *Why Men Leave Home.* His Broadway career began to decline in the 1930's and with motion pictures offering more opportunities he went to Hollywood in 1933. "I'm a stage actor at heart and by profession," Watson said "I was a movie star by necessity and a desire to eat." In motion pictures he was cast in repeated roles of authority–as a judge, Army officer, or successful rancher. Among his many films are *The Jackie Robinson Story, Guadalcanal Diary, The Big Shot, Mr. 880, As Young as You Feel, My Son John,* and *Mr. District Attorney.*

HOWARD WENDELL (1908–Aug. 11, 1975)

Born in Johnstown, Pennsylvania, Wendell attended Ohio University, majoring in drama. There followed an apprenticeship at the Cleveland Playhouse and five seasons of directing in community theatres in Pennsylvania, then on to New York and Broadway. Wendell made his first film in 1951, *Affair in Trinidad,* and

Howard Wendell, left, with Henry Daniell in The Four Skulls of Jonathan Drake.

followed it with 28 others. Among them were *You for Me, By the Light of the Silvery Moon, Gentlemen Prefer Blondes, Prince Valiant, Athena, Never Say Goodbye, It Happened to Jane,* and *Stranger in My Arms.*

JOHN E. WENGRAF *(1897–May. 4, 1974)*

Born in Vienna, the son of a prominent theater critic, Wengraf received dramatic training in the finest school in Vienna. He began his career in 1920 at one of Vienna's suburban repertory theaters. There followed several seasons at the Vienna Volkstheater. In 1924 he appeared in various theaters in Germany and at the age of 26 began directing. With the rise of Hitler, Wengraf went to London where he appeared in the first live B.B.C. television productions as well as films. In 1941, Wengraf made his Broadway stage debut and from there into films in Hollywood in 1942. He subsequently appeared in over 100 motion pictures including *Lucky Jordan, Sahara, Mission to Moscow, The Seventh Cross, Weekend at the Waldorf, Hotel Berlin, The Razor's Edge,* and more recently *Judgment at Nuremberg,* and *Ship of Fools.*

JESSE WHITE *(1919–   )*

Touching all major corners of stage, screen and television have made White a "household face" to the general public. Born in Buffalo, New York, White got his show business "bug" while attending grade school in Akron, Ohio. His first employment was in night club dates in and around Cleveland. In 1942 he went to New York on a vacation where he landed a part in *The Moon Is Down.* A whole series of flops followed, eventually leading to his biggest break in *Harvey.* In 1950 *Harvey* and Hollywood called and since then he has remained to continue in motion pictures and television. He has appeared

John Wengraf

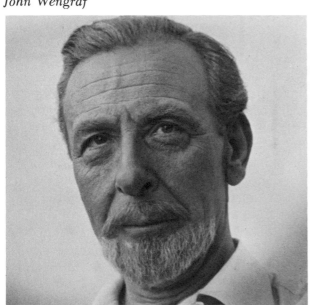

Jesse White, in Bedtime for Bonzo.

in over 55 motion pictures including *Marjorie Morningstar*, *The Bad Seed*, *Designing Woman*, *Back from Eternity*, *Death of a Salesman*, and *Not as a Stranger*. In recent years he has become famous as the "lonely Maytag repairman" in television commercials.

Lee "Lasses" White, in Mississippi Rhythm.

LEE "LASSES" WHITE *(1888–Dec. 16, 1949)*

"Lasses" White, once one of the nation's top minstrel men, went to California in 1940 to retire and ended up in motion pictures. A native of Willis Point, Texas, White started out as a stagehand in Dallas, Texas. For years he was with top minstrel shows. He played most of the vaudeville circuits and tent shows. In motion pictures he was known chiefly as a western character comedian with Tim Holt and others. White's pictures included *Cyclone on Horseback*, *Sergeant York*, *Rolling Tumbleweed*, *The Roundup*, *The Outlaw*, and *Scattergood Baines*.

Sammy White, right, with Louise Henry and Phil Regan in The Hit Parade.

SAMMY WHITE *(1894–Mar. 3, 1960)*

Sammy White, born Sammy Kwait in Providence, Rhode Island, spent his early years in vaudeville as a member of the team of White and Puck. He later appeared on the Broadway stage in such hits as *Showboat* and *The Girl Friend*. In 1936 he appeared in a film version of *Show Boat*, his first film. He continued in and out of vaudeville, films and eventually motion pictures during the rest of his career. Among his film credits are *Cain and Mabel*, *Swing Your Lady*, *711 Ocean Drive*, *The Half-Breed*, *The Bad and the Beautiful*, and *The Helen Morgan Story*.

DAME MAY WHITTY *(1865–May. 29, 1948)*

For more than sixty-two years, Dame May was an important theatrical figure and ranked as one of the first ladies of the British and American stages. Born in Liverpool, England she made her London stage debut in 1882. Until 1885 she was at the St. James Theatre, chiefly as an understudy. Then, at the age of twenty, she went on tour with a stock company. There followed many distinguished years on the stage. She received her title in 1918 for her services to Britain during World War I. Though she appeared in a film in 1914 it was in 1937 that her real film career was launched. After that time she appeared in such films as *Thirteenth Chair*, *The Lady Vanishes*, *Raffles*, *Bill of Divorcement*, *Suspicion*, *Mrs. Miniver*, *Mme. Curie*, *Lassie Come Home*, *Green Dolphin Street*, *This Time for Keeps*, and *The Sign of the Ram*.

MARY WICKES *(1912–   )*

Miss Wickes' birthplace was St. Louis, Missouri, where her parents were prominent in social and civic affairs. She attended college at Washington University in St. Louis, majoring in English and Political Science. With no speech or acting training, Miss Wickes learned to act by acting. She played theatrical stock in the East, beginning the same month she graduated from college at the age of eighteen, then went on to Broadway and later films and television. At the age of eighteen she was playing a sixty-year-old role in New York. Miss Wickes' first film was as the nurse in *The Man Who Came to Dinner*. Other films have included *Now Voyager*, *Mayor of 44th Street*, *June Bride*, *By the Light of the Silvery*

Dame May Whitty with Teresa Wright in Mrs. Miniver.

Mary Wickes

FRANK WILCOX *(1907–Mar. 3, 1974)*
The son of a doctor, Frank Wilcox intended to follow in his father's footsteps, but circumstances forced him to abandon his plans. He entered the oil business only to become interested in the Resident Theatre in Kansas City, where he worked for several seasons. In 1934, Wilcox went to California to visit his father and decided to move there the next year. After organizing the Pomona Theatre Guild he enrolled at the Pasadena Playhouse where he was finally tabbed by a talent scout from Warner Bros. His picture credits included *Across the Pacific, Mark Twain, North Star, Night Editor, Cass Timberlane, Gentleman's Agreement, Samson and Delilah,* and *All the King's Men.*

Moon, On Moonlight Bay, White Christmas, Destry, Half a Hero, and *I'll See You in My Dreams.*

Frank Wilcox, right, with Richard Martin and Tim Holt in The Mysterious Desperado.

Guinn "Big Boy" Williams

Rhys Williams, in How Green Was My Valley.

ductions on the legitimate stage and summer stock, Williams appeared in such films as *Mrs. Miniver, The Corn Is Green, The Inspector General, The Farmer's Daughter, The Hills of Home, Blood on the Sun, The Spiral Staircase, The Imperfect Lady,* and *Lightning Strikes Twice.*

GUINN (BIG BOY) WILLIAMS *(1900–June 6, 1962)*

Williams carved a career in westerns as a dull-witted comic relief type. An authentic Texas cowboy, a rarity on the Hollywood western scene, he attended North Texas State College and performed as a rodeo rider before going to Hollywood to work in silent films. The nickname "Big Boy" was given him by Will Rogers whom he met on a movie set. Williams starred in 34 westerns in the 1920's and continued to play western character parts and "heavies" in non-western films during the remainder of his career. His last picture was *Comancheros,* released in 1961. IIis many other screen credits included *The Desperadoes, Badmen of Tombstone, Stations West, Swamp Water, My Man,* and *Private Worlds.*

RHYS WILLIAMS *(1897–May 28, 1969)*

Born in Wales, Williams was originally brought to Hollywood as a technical director and dialect coach for the production of *How Green Was My Valley.* He impressed the director so much he was signed for the role of Dai Bando, the prize fighter. The role remained a favorite of Williams. After appearing in a number of pro-

Dave Willock, and Dorothea Kent in Pin-Up Girl.

DAVE WILLOCK *(1909–   )*

Dave Willock was born in Chicago, Illinois, to a non-theatrical family. He gained early acting experience while attending the University of Wisconsin. In 1931–35 he appeared in vaudeville as part of the team "Willock and Carson" playing all the major circuits with the late Jack Carson. Willock also appeared on radio from 1931–1945 on various stations and shows. He made his film debut in 1939 in *Good Girls Go to Paris* and has since appeared in over 200 pictures. One of his first parts was as a bell-hop and during a period of a year or so played 42 bellhops, elevator boys, or pages. From there he went on to reporters, photographers, and an assortment of military types. Among his many film credits are *The Fleet's In*, *Let's Face It*, *Chicago Deadline*, *Pin-up Girl*, *Wing and a Prayer*, *Yankee Doodle Dandy*, and *the Fabulous Dorseys*.

Chill Wills, right, with Jack Holt in Loaded Pistols.

CHILL WILLS (1902–Dec. 15, 1978)
The state of Texas' unofficial ambassador to the movie capital was born in Seagoville, Texas. Chill got his name because he was born on the hottest July 18th ever recorded in Seagoville and his parents decided to name him in contrast to the high temperature of that day. Chill began his professional career with the Harley Sadler Tent Show in West Texas. By the age of twelve he had appeared before half of Texas. Before he finally made his way to the West Coast, he had appeared in every vaudeville theater in the south and midwest, and had performed in more than 20 plays with various stock companies. He was discovered for movies while filling a singing engagement at the popular Trocadero. After being signed he appeared in numerous films including *Boom Town*, *Leave Her to Heaven*, *See Here, Private Hargrove*, *The Yearling*, *Tulsa*, *Kentucky Rifle*, *The Alamo*, and *Giant*. He was the voice of Francis, the talking mule, in several films.

Charles Winninger, in Woman Chases Man.

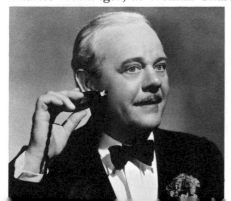

CHARLES WINNINGER (1884–Jan. 27, 1969)
Born near Athens, Wisconsin, Winninger was given a musical education by his father and in 1893 became a part of the Winninger Family Novelty Company which his father formed. Starting during Chicago's World Fair, the troupe traveled successfully throughout the country for several seasons. In 1909 after having left the troupe, Winninger arrived in New York where he got the part of a German comedian in the *Yankee Girl Company*. He scored a hit and eventually toured with the show. He continued on the stage until 1915 when he was signed to act in comedy films made on the Universal lot. He returned to the stage again and successfully appeared in vaudeville, plays and musical comedies. In 1930, Winninger return to motion pictures subsequently appearing in such films as *Showboat*, *Three Smart Girls* (favorite role), *Flying High*, *Coney Island*, *State Fair*, *Give My Regards to Broadway*, *Hers to Hold*, *Inside Story*, *Father Is a Bachelor*, and *Perilous Journey*.

ROLAND WINTERS (1904–   )
Roland Winters, the third actor to play Charlie Chan, began his career in his native Boston in a stock company. In 1923, after two seasons of stock, he got a part in the New York stage production of *The Firebrand*. When the show closed he returned to stock playing two seasons. Too big to play juveniles and too young to play straight leads he became a character man. In 1932, Winters entered radio in Boston and moved to New York radio in 1938 appearing on such shows as Kate Smith's, Kay Kyser's and "The Aldrich Family." Winters was signed by Monogram Pictures in 1947 to the Charlie Chan role. In addition to the Chan pictures his credits include *Come By My Love*, *Operation Malaya*, *After Midnight*, *The Bail Bond Story*, *13 Rue Madeleine*, *West Point Story*, *Follow the Sun*, *So Big*, and *She's Working Her Way Through College*.

Roland Winters, with Elvis Presley in Follow That Dream.

ESTELLE WINWOOD (1883–1984)
London-born, Estelle Winwood was an actress of imaginative intelligence who learned her art in the Liverpool Repertory Company. After appearing in the classical dramas and working under Shaw and Galsworthy she went on to star on Broadway where she made her debut in 1921 in *The Circle*. Broadway stage fame brought movie offers and a motion picture and television career as an outstanding character actress. She played the barmaid in the Van Johnson movie *23 Paces to Baker Street*, Leslie Caron's godmother in *The Glass Slipper*, the churchwoman asking for donation in *The Misfits* with Marilyn Monroe and Clark Gable, and Debbie Reynold's housekeeper in *This Happy Feeling*.

Estelle Winwood with Zero Mostel in The Producers.

JOSEPH WISEMAN (1919–)
Joseph Wiseman, who was born in Montreal, got his theatrical start when he joined an Italian acting company in New York. He went on to play with such leading actresses as Hayes, Bankhead, Cornell and Gordon, in such plays as *Antony and Cleopatra* and *The Lark*. Active on the stage, in television and motion pictures,

182

Wiseman is best known to moviegoers as a villain and he has demonstrated his fine acting ability in such films as *Detective Story*, *Viva Zapata*, and *The Unforgiven*.

Joseph Wiseman, center, with William Bendix and Kirk Douglas in Detective Story. *In the background, Russell Evans and Howard Joslin.*

GRANT WITHERS (1905–Mar. 27, 1959)
Born in Pueblo, Colorado, Grant Withers, a former salesman for an oil company and newspaper reporter, went to California in the early 1920's as a reporter for the Los Angeles *Record*. Later his experience in newspapers earned him several roles in pictures. Withers created a sensation in 1930 when he eloped with actress Loretta Young, then a seventeen-year-old Wampas Baby Star. A film star in the 1920's Withers became a character actor as sound took over Hollywood. His many film credits include *Fort Apache*, *Tripoli*, *Fighting Kentuckian*, *Lady Godiva*, *My Darling Clementine*, *The Trespasser*, *Wyoming*, *Tycoon*, *Yellow Rose of Texas*, and *Blackmail*.

Grant Withers

Cora Witherspoon, with George Barbier in On the Avenue.

CORA WITHERSPOON *(1890–Nov. 17, 1957)*
An actress for more than 50 years, Miss Witherspoon was born in New Orleans, where she launched her acting career. She made her New York debut when only seventeen, playing a 70-year-old woman in *The Concert*. She appeared in numerous films including *Marie Antoinette, Picadilly Jim, Dark Victory, Just for You, Colonel Effingham's Raid, The Mating Season, Over 21,* and *First Time*.

IAN WOLFE *(1896–)*
Born in Canton, Illinois, Wolfe made his Broadway debut with Lionel Barrymore in *The Claw*, and was featured in many other productions of that period including *Lysistrata* and *The Lower Depths*. He appeared with Katherine Cornell in *The Age of Innocence* and *The Barretts of Wimpole Street*. This latter play brought him to the attention of Irving Thalberg and Hollywood. He was brought to Hollywood for the same role in the 1934 film version. He has since been featured in over 200 films and 60 leading television shows.

Ian Wolfe, in Wonderful World of the Brothers Grimm.

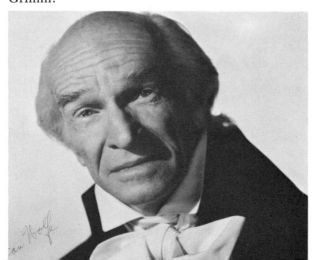

Among his many film credits are parts in *Mutiny on the Bounty, The Wonderful World of the Brothers Grimm, Witness for the Prosecution, Seven Brides for Seven Brothers, The Prince and the Pauper, Clive of India,* and *the Emperor's Candlesticks*.

HARRY WOODS *(1889–Dec. 28, 1968)*
Harry Woods became an actor after earning a comfortable living as a millinery salesman. Alternating between the business world and acting, Woods finally moved to Hollywood to try the films. He finally made it into films and appeared in the first Technicolor film ever produced, *The Viking*. Woods, generally featured as a heavy, appeared in over 200 pictures, dying violently in most of them. Most of his deaths have been by gunfire, but he has varied them by being trampled to death by elephants, killed by lightning, and by snake bite. His many pictures include *Code of the West, Westward Bound, Monkey Business, The Adventures of Mark Twain, Nevada, Tall in the Saddle, West of the Pecos,* and *Thunder Mountain*.

Harry Woods, with Edmond O'Brien, Harry Seymour at the piano and Viveca Lindfors in Backfire.

WILL WRIGHT *(1894–June 19, 1962)*
A native of San Francisco, Wright was a newspaper reporter, in vaudeville, on the New York stage and on radio before entering films. He worked on the *Gang Busters* radio series before coming to Hollywood. A long-time char-

Will Wright, right, with Robert Walker in
Vengence Valley.

acter actor, Wright appeared in such movies as
*Blue Dahlia, Man with the Golden Arm, Court
Martial of Billy Mitchell,* and *These Wilder
Years.*

MARGARET WYCHERLY (1881–June 6, 1956)
Born in London, Margaret Wycherly made her
stage debut in London in 1898. Thereafter she
toured in stock before coming to Broadway. Miss
Wycherly appeared on the New York stage
almost every season, appearing in such productions as *Tobacco Road* and *The Thirteenth
Chair.* Following her success on the Broadway
stage, Miss Wycherly became active in both films
and television. Among her film credits are
*Richard III, Sergeant York, Forever Amber,
Loves of Carmen,* and *President's Lady.*

*Margaret Wycherly with Virginia Mayo and James
Cagney in* White Heat.

184

ROLAND YOUNG *(1887–June 5, 1953)*

Roland Young, one of the most famous and versatile of all screen comedians, received his acting training at the London Academy for Dramatic Art. In films, Young made whimsy his trademark, and gained fame in his stock role of the somewhat bewildered and droll fellow whose style of drawing room comedy was to belittle himself with fluttering mannerisms. He appeared in over a hundred films, and was probably best known for the series of three *Topper* movies. In 1945, he appeared with Cornelia Otis Skinner in a radio series, *William and Mary*. On television he played the part of "William," a suburban husband. His films, in addition to the *Topper* series, included *Ruggles of Red Gap, Forever and a Day, David Copperfield, The Philadelphia Story, Tales of Manhattan, Fog Bound* as the timid burglar, *Her Private Life, Madam Satan, One Hour with You, Pleasure Cruise,* and *And Then There Were None.*

Roland Young, in Give Me Your Heart.

BLANCHE YURKA *(1887–June 6, 1974)*

Blanche Yurka was born in St. Paul, Minnesota, and spent most of her career on the stage in

Blanche Yurka with Barbara Stanwyck and Gilbert Roland in The Furies.

Ibsen, Shakespearean, and Greek plays. She was regarded as one of the foremost interpreters of the classics on the American stage. She made her screen debut in 1935 when MGM brought her to Hollywood to play the role of Madame DuFarge in *A Tale of Two Cities*. This was a role that had been turned down by Nazimova, who instructed a mutual friend to have Miss Yurka go after the role. Her other pictures included *Queen of the Mob, Escape, City for Conquest, Lady for a Night, Pacific Rendezvous, A Night to Remember, The Song of Bernadette, The Bridge of San Luis Rey, One Body too Many, The Southerner,* and *The Furies*.

GEORGE ZUCCO *(1886–May 27, 1960)*

George Zucco was best known for his villainous roles in motion pictures. A native of Manchester, England, he began his career in 1908 and appeared in vaudeville in New York in 1913. He returned to England to play leading roles in London stage productions and in 1935 played Disraeli opposite Helen Hayes in Gilbert Miller's New York production of *Victoria Regina*. His first screen role recreated his Broadway part in *Autumn Crocus*. His other films included *House of Frankenstein, Sudan, Confidential Agent, Captain from Castile, Moss Rose, Where There's Life, Joan of Arc,* and *David and Bathsheba*.

George Zucco

PART 2
NON-BIOGRAPHICAL
SECTION

JOHN ABBOTT (1905–   )
b. London. *The Shanghai Gesture, Anna and the King of Siam, Madame Bovary, Humoresque,* and *Sombrero.*

WALTER ABEL (1898–   )
b. St. Paul, Minn. *Three Musketeers, Steel Jungle, Holiday Inn, 13 Rue Madeleine,* and *So This Is Love.*

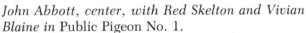
John Abbott, center, with Red Skelton and Vivian Blaine in Public Pigeon No. 1.

Walter Abel

EDDIE ACUFF *(1908–Dec. 17, 1956)*
b. Caruthersville, Mo. *Petrified Forest, Notorious Lone Wolf, Timber Trail, Song of Idaho, Blondie* series, *Singing Marine,* and *Ladies in Distress.*

Philip Ahn, right, with Gabe Dell and Florence Rice in Let's Get Tough.

Eddie Acuff, with Pennie Singleton in Blondie's Secret.

PHILIP AHN *(1905–Feb. 28, 1978)*
b. Los Angeles, Calif. *General Died at Dawn, Cobra Strikes, Macao, Wind to Java, Battle Zone,* and *Love Is a Many Splendored Thing.*

LUIS ALBERNI *(1886–Dec. 23, 1962)*
One Night of Love, What Price Glory, Anthony Adverse, and *Santa Fe Trail.*

ERVILLE ALDERSON *(1882–Aug. 4, 1957)*
Jungle Princess, Square Shooter, Jesse James, To the Last Man, Career Woman, and *The Mighty Treve.*

LUTHER ADLER *(1903–   )*
Wake of the Red Witch, Loves of Carmen, Desert Fox, House of Strangers, and *Under My Skin.*

Luis Alberni

Luther Adler

Erville Alderson, with Clark Gable in To Please a Lady.

JOHN ALEXANDER (1897–July 13, 1982)
b. Newport, Ky. *Arsenic and Old Lace, Fancy Pants, Cass Timberlane, Jolson Story,* and *Marrying Kind.*

John Alexander, second from left, with Grant Mitchell, Josephine Hull, Jack Carson and Edward McNamara in Arsenic and Old Lace.

MURRAY ALPER (1904–   )
b. New York. *Seven Keys to Baldpate, Saboteur, Highway Dragnet, Big Tip Off,* and *On the Town.*

LEON AMES (1903–   )
b. Portland, Ind. *Meet Me in St. Louis, Velvet Touch, Date with Judy, Moon Is Blue, On Moonlight Bay, By the Light of the Silvery Moon,* and on TV, *Life with Father.*

Leon Ames

STANLEY ANDREWS (1891–June 23, 1969)
The Crusades, Nevada, Alexander's Ragtime Band, Kentucky, Cocoanut Grove, and *The Buccaneer.*

Stanley Andrews, center, with Hugh Beaumont and Harriet Hilliard in Canal Zone.

189

Murray Alper, right, with Bob Cummings in Let's Live a Little.

HARRY ANTRIM *(1884–Jan. 18, 1967)*
b. Chicago, Ill. *Ma and Pa Kettle, Heiress, Johnny Allegro, I'll See You in My Dreams,* and *Thelma Jordan.*

Harry Antrim, with Van Heflin in Gunman's Walk.

ROBERT ARMSTRONG *(1890–April 20, 1973)*
b. Saginaw, Mich. *Mighty Joe Young, Shady Lady, Return of the Bad Men, Paleface,* and *Captain China.*

Robert Armstrong

Benny Baker, center, with Lynn Overman and Edward Everett Horton in Wild Money.

BENNY BAKER *(1907–   )*
b. St. Joseph, Mo. *Inspector General, My Girl Tisa, Touchdown Army, Hotel Haywire, Blonde Trouble,* and *Big Broadcast of 1936.*

Walter Baldwin, with Dorothy Adams, Mary Murphy and Jennifer Jones in Carrie.

WALTER BALDWIN *(1889–Jan. 27, 1977)*
Devil Commands, Come to the Stable, Best Years of Our Lives, Unsuspected, Special Agent, and *Sing While You Dance.*

191

ROBERT BARRAT *(1889–Jan. 7, 1970)*
b. New York City. *Sea of Grass, Life of Emile Zola, Trail of the Lonesome Pine, Mary of Scotland, Magnificent Doll,* and *Fabulous Texan.*

Robert Barrat, in Mountain Justice.

JAMES BARTON *(1890–Feb. 19, 1962)*
b. Gloucester, N.J. *Shepherd of the Hills, Lifeboat, Yellow Sky, Daughter of Rosie O'Grady, Here Comes the Groom,* and *Golden Girl.*

James Barton, with Bing Crosby in Here Comes the Groom.

ALBERT BASSERMAN *(1867–May 15, 1952)*
b. Mannheim, Germany. *Dr. Ehrlich's Magic Bullet, Foreign Correspondent, Red Shoes, Strange Holiday, Dispatch from Reuters, Rhapsody in Blue,* and *Searching Wind.*

Albert Basserman, left, with Richard Carlson and Marion Martin in Fly by Night.

ALAN BAXTER *(1908–May 8, 1976)*
b. Cleveland, Ohio. *Trail of Lonesome Pine, Abe Lincoln in Illinois, Santa Fe Trail, Winged Victory, Setup,* and *Close-Up.*

Alan Baxter.

192

Noah Beery, Jr., with Martha O'Driscoll in Under Western Skies.

Noah Beery Sr.

NOAH BEERY JR. *(1915–)*
b. New York City. *Road Back, Doolins of Oklahoma, Outside the Law, Two Flags West, Tropic Zone, Story of Will Rogers,* and *Jubal.*

NOAH BEERY SR. *(1882–April 1, 1946)*
b. Kansas City, Mo. *David Harum, Sweet Adeline, Our Fighting Navy, Bad Man of Brimstone,* and *Girl of the Golden West.*

LEON BELASCO *(1902–)*
b. Odessa, Russia. *Swing Parade, For the Love of Mary, Bagdad, Love Happy, Call Me Madam,* and *Cuban Fireball.*

WILLIE BEST *(1916–Feb. 27, 1962)*
Little Miss Marker, The Littlest Rebel, Mummy's Boys, Racing Lady, Super Sleuth, Goodbye Broadway, and *Vivacious Lady.*

BILLY BEVAN *(1887–Nov. 26, 1957)*
b. Orange, Australia. *A Tale of Two Cities, Girl of the Golden West, The Lost Patrol, Lloyds of London, Another Dawn, Slave Ship,* and *The Sheik Steps Out.*

Leon Belasco, right, with Florence Marly and Leonid Kinsky in Gobs and Gals.

Billy Bevan, with Ramon Navarro in The Sheik Steps Out.

Willie Best, as Jughead in Goodbye Broadway.

194

Oliver Blake, right, with Zachary Charles in Ma and Pa Kettle at the Fair.

Fortunio Bonanova, right, with Bing Crosby and Rise Stevens in Going My Way.

OLIVER BLAKE (PRICKETT) (1905–)
b. Centralia, Ill. Senator Was Indiscreet, Ginger, Conflict, I Married an Angel, Wake Up and Dream, and Guilty.

FORTUNIO BONANOVA (1895–April 2, 1969)
b. Palma de Mallorca. Citizen Kane, Black Swan, Adventures of Don Juan, September Affair, Moon Is Blue, Going My Way, and Whirlpool.

WADE BOTELER (1888–May 7, 1943)
b. Santa Ana, Calif. Ambush, You Only Live Once, Valley of the Giants, Human Cargo, Charlie Chan at the Circus, Billy the Kid Returns, and It Can't Last Forever.

Wade Boteler, second from left, with Dan Wolheim, Ed Pawley and Humphrey Bogart in The Oklahoma Kid.

HENRY BRANDON (1912–)
Killer at Large, Buck Rogers, Beau Geste, The Paleface, War Arrow and Vera Cruz.

Al Bridge, second from right, with Randolph Scott, Jock Mahoney and John Ireland in The Doolins of Oklahoma.

Henry Brandon, left, with John Merton in Drums of Fu Manchu.

AL BRIDGE *(1891–Dec. 27, 1957)*
Two Gun Justice, Borderland, Partners of the Plains, Western Gold, Springtime in the Rockies, Crime School, and *Down in Arkansas.*

CHARLES D. BROWN *(1887–Nov. 25, 1948)*
b. Council Bluffs, Iowa. *Barefoot Boy, It Happened One Night, Island in the Sky, Up the River, Algiers, Duke of West Point,* and *The Crowd Roars.*

Charles D. Brown, center with cigar, with William Lundigan, Lee Phelps, Jeff Corey and Art Dupois in Follow Me Quietly.

196

TOM BROWN (1913–)
b. New York City. *A Lady Lies, Duke of Chicago, Swing That Cheer, Maytime, Navy Blue and Gold, In Old Chicago*, and *Rose Bowl*.

Tom Brown, left, with Tyrone Power and Don Ameche in In Old Chicago.

Wally Brown, with Randolph Scott in Westbound.

WALLY BROWN (1904–Nov. 13, 1961)
b. Malden, Mass. *Come to the Stable, Notorious, Family Honeymoon, High and the Mighty, Adventures of a Rookie*, and *Seven Days Ashore*.

Paul Bryar, third from left, with Gene Nelson, Steve Cochran and Frank Lovejoy in She's Back on Broadway.

PAUL BRYAR (1910–)
b. New York City. *Gas House Kids, Robin Hood in Texas, Under My Skin, Three on a Ticket*, and *Chinese Ring*.

BILLIE BURKE (1885–May 14, 1970)
b. Washington, D.C. *Father of the Bride, Dinner at Eight, Wizard of Oz, The Man Who Came to Dinner, Topper*, and *Everybody Sing*.

Billy Burke, right, with Edna May Oliver in Parnell.

James Burke

JAMES BURKE (1886–May 23, 1968)
b. New York. *College Humor, Treasure Island, Ruggles of Red Gap, Dead End, Dawn Patrol, Beau Geste*, and *Ellery Queen* series.

197

PAUL E. BURNS *(1881–May 17, 1967)*
b. Philadelphia, Pa. *Night Editor, My Pal Trigger, Sing While You Dance, Johnny Allegro, Look for the Silver Lining,* and *Montana.*

MARIETTA CANTY *(   )*
b. Hartford, Conn. *Father of the Bride, I Don't Care Girl, My Foolish Heart, Home Sweet Homicide,* and *Searching Wind.*

Maurice Cass, seated, with The Ritz Brothers in Life Begins in College.

Marietta Canty, right, with Julia Dean, Thurston Hall and Laura Elliot in Girls School.

Nora Cecil, with Victor Jory

MAURICE CASS *(1884–June 9, 1954)*
b. Vilan, Russia. *Exposed, The Baroness and the Butler, Two for Tonight, Pepper, This Is My Affair, Sunset Trail,* and *A Desperate Adventure.*

NORA CECIL *(1879–   )*
b. England. *Big Town, Two Sisters From Boston, Find the Lady,* and *No Leave, No Love.*

SPENCER CHARTERS *(1875–Jan. 25, 1943)*
b. Duncannon, Pa. *Jesse James, Three Blind Mice, Inside Story, Mr. Deeds Goes to Town, Checkers, Mountain Music,* and *Banjo on My Knee.*

CLIFF CLARK *(1889–Feb. 8, 1953)*
Mountain Music, Kentucky, Time Out for Murder, Cocoanut Grove, Inside Story, and *Mr. Moto's Gamble.*

WALLIS CLARK *(1882–Feb. 14, 1961)*
b. Essex, England. *It Happened One Night, Mutiny on the Bounty, Parole, Easy Money, Big Business,* and *The Higgins Family.*

Paul Burns, right, with Paul Hurst and Wallace Beery in Barbary Coast Gent.

Spencer Charters, left, with Claire Trevor and Donald Woods in Big Town Girl.

Cliff Clark, left, with George Cooper in Flaming Fury.

Wallis Clark, right, with Lester Dorr, Marsha Hunt and Warren Hull in Star Reporter.

Stanley Clements with Gloria Henry in Hot News.

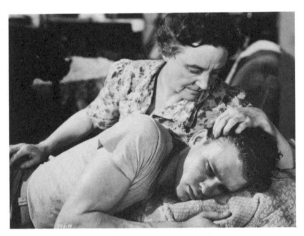

Patricia Collinge, with John Ericson in Teresa.

STANLEY CLEMENTS *(1926–Oct. 16 1981)*
b. Long Island, N.Y. *Going My Way, Racing Luck, Off Limits, Robbers Roost, Pride of Maryland,* and *Tall, Dark and Handsome.*

CHESTER CLUTE *(1891–April 2, 1956)*
The Great Garrick, The Wrong Road, Rascals, Change of Heart, Pardon Our Nerve, and *Living on Love.*

PATRICIA COLLINGE *(1892–April 10, 1974)*
b. Dublin, Ireland. *The Little Foxes, Casanova Brown, Washington Story, Teresa,* and *Shadow of a Doubt.*

Eddie Collins, in Alexander's Ragtime Band.

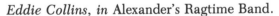

Chester Clute, center, with Don Ameche and Claudette Colbert in Guest Wife.

EDDIE COLLINS *(1883–Sept. 1, 1940)*
In Old Chicago, Alexander's Ragtime Band, Little Miss Broadway, Penrod and His Twin Brother, *and* Kentucky Moonshine.

ELISHA COOK JR. *(1907–)*
b. San Francisco, Calif. *The Maltese Falcon, Casanova Brown, The Long Night, Shane, Cinderella Jones, Dillinger, The Big Sleep, I the Jury, *and* Rosemary's Baby.*

Elisha Cook, Jr., in Black Zoo.

ROBERT COOTE *(1909–Nov. 26, 1982)*
b. London, England. *Sally in Our Alley, Forever Amber, Red Danube, Scaramouche, Prisoner of Zenda,* and *The Ghost and Mrs Muir.*

Robert Coote, center, in Gunga Din.

HARRY CORDING *(1891–Sept 1, 1954)*
b. New York City. *Mrs. Parkington, Sudan, San Antonio, Fortunes of Captain Blood, Demetrius and the Gladiators,* and *Cripple Creek.*

Harry Cording, center, with Robert Bice, Judy Nugent and Virginia Huston in Night Stage to Galveston.

Jeff Corey, in Lady in a Cage.

JEFF COREY *(1914–   )*
b. New York City. *All That Money Can Buy, The Killers, Joan of Arc, Bagdad, Rawhide, Bright Leaf,* and *Red Mountain.*

Lloyd Corrigan, with Jane Withers in High School.

LLOYD CORRIGAN *(1900–Nov. 5, 1969)*
b. San Francisco. *Ghost Chasers, Son of Paleface, Dancing in the Dark, Return From the Sea, Rainbow Round My Shoulder,* and *Hidden Guns.*

202

DICK CURTIS *(1902–Jan. 3, 1952)*
b. Newport, Ky. *Spook Town, Song of Arizona, Girl Crazy, King Kong, The Shadow, Adventure in Sahara,* and *Rawhide.*

Frankie Darro, right, with Dick Furcell, in Tough Kid.

Dick Curtis, right, with Charles Starrett in The Stranger from Texas.

FRANKIE DARRO *(1918–Dec. 25, 1976)*
b. Chicago, Ill. *Tugboat Annie, Wild Boys of the Road, Little Men, The Payoff, Juvenile Court,* and *Tough Kid.*

FRANK DARIEN *(1876–Oct. 20, 1955)*
b. New Orleans, *Big Executive, Cimarron, Little Colonel, Grapes of Wrath, Claudia and David, Bad Bascomb,* and *Magic Town.*

Frank Darien, right, with Barton MacLane in Prison Break.

William B. Davidson with Jane Bryan in Marked Woman.

WILLIAM B. DAVIDSON *(1888–Sept. 28, 1947)*
Fog Over Frisco, St. Louis Kid, On Trial, Dust Be My Destiny, My Little Chickadee, The Farmer's Daughter.

George Davis, carrying tray, with Gino Corrado, June Vincent and Warren Douglas in Secrets of Monte Carlo.

Hal K. Dawson with Jane Withers.

GEORGE DAVIS (1889–April 19, 1965)
b. Amsterdam, Holland, *Hunted Men, You Can't Have Everything, Thin Ice, The Black Cat, The Baroness and the Butler,* and *Always Goodbye.*

HAL K. DAWSON (1896–   )
Keep Smiling, Second Honeymoon, On Again-Off Again, Cafe Metropole, Love and Hisses, and *Dr. Socrates.*

Julia Dean, second from left, with Thurston Hall and Laura Elliot in Girls School.

JULIA DEAN (1878–Oct. 18, 1952)
b. St. Paul, Minn. *Nightmare Alley, Curse of the Cat People, Out of the Blue, Magic Town, Emperor Waltz,* and *Experiment Perilous.*

EDGAR DEARING (1893–Aug. 17, 1974)
b. Ceres, Calif. *Big Noise, The Rainmakers, Thanks for Everything, Little Orvie, Strange Affair,* and *Cross Country Romance.*

Edgar Dearing, center, with Hugh Herbert and Charles Ray.

Rosemary DeCamp, with Donald Woods in 13 Ghosts.

ALBERT DEKKER *(1905–May 5, 1968)*
Dr. Cyclops, Wyoming, Gentleman's Agreement, Two Years Before the Mast, Cass Timberlane, East of Eden, and *Great Garrick.*

BILLY DeWOLFE *(1907–March 5, 1974)*
b. Wollaston, Mass. *Miss Susie Slagle's, Blue Skies, Tea for Two, Call Me Madam, Dear Wife,* and *Perils of Pauline.*

ALAN DINEHART *(1886–July 17, 1944)*
Dante's Inferno, Born to Dance, Love on a Budget, Second Fiddle, Sweet Rosie O'Grady, Oh, What a Night.

Ted DeCorsia, right, with Dean Jones in Handle With Care.

ROSEMARY DeCAMP *(1914–   )*
Cheers for Miss Bishop, Rhapsody in Blue, The Merry Monahans, Yankee Doodle Dandy, and *Strategic Air Command.*

TED DeCORSIA *(1905–April 11, 1973)*
The Naked City, A Place in the Sun, The Steele Jungle, Slightly Scarlet, Baby Face Nelson, and *Nevada Smith.*

Albert Dekker

205

Billy DeWolfe, right, with Florence Bates and S. Z. Sakall in Lullaby of Broadway.

TOM DUGAN (1889–March 7, 1955)
b. Dublin, Ireland, *Halfpast Midnight, Lights of New York, Good News, Texas, Crashout,* and *A Woman's Man.*

EDDIE DUNN (1896–May 5, 1951)
Rascals, Bermuda Mystery, Call Northside 777, Dead Man's Eyes, Big Punch, and *Checkered Coat.*

RALPH DUNN (1902–Feb. 19, 1968)
b. Titusville, Pa. *Laura, The Hairy Ape, Dick Tracy, Great Plane Robbery, The Jade Lady,* and *Singing Guns.*

CLIFF EDWARDS (1895–July 17,1971)
b. Hannibal, Mo. *Salute for Three, Good News, Girl of the Golden West, Bad Man of Brimstone* and *Fun and Fancy Free.*

Alan Dinehart

Eddie Dunn, with John Ireland in I Shot Jesse James.

Tom Dugan, right, with Kane Richmond and Barbara Read in The Shadow Returns.

Ralph Dunn, right, with Dick Foran and Abbott and Costello in In the Navy.

SARAH EDWARDS *(1881–Jan. 7, 1965)*
Hollywood Hotel, Welcome Home, Dark Angel,
The Golden Arrow, Early to Bed, We're on the
Jury, and *Women Are Like That.*

GILBERT EMERY *(1875–Oct. 28, 1945)*
b. Naples, N.Y. *House of Rothschild, Clive of*
India, Cardinal Richelieu, Let's Live Tonight,
Magnificent Obsession, and *The Life of Emile*
Zola.

RICHARD ERDMAN *(1925–)*
b. Enid, Okla. *Bengazi, Janie, Cry Danger,*
Happy Time, Stalag 17, and *Francis in the Navy.*

LEON ERROL *(1881–Oct. 12, 1951)*
b. Sydney, Australia. *Joe Palooka, Cocktails for*
Two, Alice in Wonderland, Never Give a Sucker
an Even Break, Panamericana, and many short
subjects.

Gilbert Emery

Richard Erdman, left, with Allen Jenkins in Wild
Harvest.

Leon Errol, with Zasu Pitts in Finn and Mattie.

Cliff Edwards

Sarah Edwards, left, with Arthur Loft and Sidney
Toler in Charlie Chan in the Secret Service.

207

HERBERT EVANS (1882–Feb. 10, 1952)
b. London, Eng. *Bringing Up Father, Pardon My Past, Abroad with Two Yanks, Speedy,* and *The Prodigal.*

Herbert Evans, with monocle, with Gregory Peck and Frank Morgan in The Great Sinner.

VERNA FELTON (1890–Dec. 14, 1966)
b. Salinas, Calif. *Cinderella, The Gun Fighter, Little Egypt, New Mexico, Buccaneer's Girl,* and *Alice in Wonderland.*

PAUL FIX (1902–Oct. 14, 1983)
b. Dobbs Ferry, N.Y. *High and the Mighty, Giant, Bad Seed, Mail Order Bride,* and *To Kill a Mockingbird.*

Verna Felton

Paul Fix

JAMES FLAVIN (1906–April 23, 1976)
b. Portland, Me. *Naked Street, Follow the Sun, Tars and Spars, Nora Prentiss, Cloak and Dagger, Mr. Roberts,* and *Fighter Attack.*

SAM FLINT (1882–Oct. 24, 1980)
b. Guinette County, Ga. *State Police, Broadway Bill, Chained, Florida Special, Diamond Jim Brady,* and *Mrs. Wiggs of the Cabbage Patch.*

James Flavin, left, with Stanley Clements in Hot News.

Sam Flint, as doctor, in Snowfire.

Francis Ford, right, with Charles Grapewin in Tobacco Road.

JAY C. FLIPPEN *(1899–Feb. 3, 1971)*
b. Little Rock, Ark. *East of Sumatra, Wild One, Lady from Texas, Bend of the River, Far Country, Kismet,* and *Oh You Beautiful Doll.*

FRANCIS FORD *(1882–Sept. 5, 1953)*
b. Portland, Me. *Sun Shines Bright, High Tide, Hangover Square, Driftwood, Quiet Man,* and *Toughest Man in Arizona.*

VICTOR FRANCEN *(1888–Nov. 18, 1977)*
Mission to Moscow, Madame Curie, Desert Song, San Antonio, In Our Time, Confidential Agent, and *Adventures of Captain Fabian.*

Victor Francen

Jay C. Flippen

Howard Freeman, with William Powell in Take One False Step.

Willie Fung, third from left, with Broderick Crawford, Andy Devine and Keye Luke in North to the Klondike.

ETIENNE GIRARDOT (1856–Nov. 10, 1939) b. London, Eng. *Professor Beware, The Great Garrick, The Road Back, Seven Seas, Arizona Wildcat, There Goes My Heart,* and *Go West, Young Man.*

BERNARD GORCEY (1888–Sept. 11, 1955) (Father of Leo Gorcey). *Fighting Fools, Bowery Bombshell, Jinx Money,* and *Joan of Paris.*

MARY GORDON (1882–Aug. 23, 1963) *Lady Behave, Kidnapped, Bride of Frankenstein, Waterfront, Mary of Scotland, Stage Struck,* and *Laughing Irish Eyes.*

Steven Geray

Etienne Girardot, with Jack Haley.

HOWARD FREEMAN (1899–Dec. 11, 1967) b. Helena, Mont. *Mexicana, You Came Along, Cass Timberlane, Long Night, Scaramouche, Turning Point,* and *Million Dollar Mermaid.*

WILLIE FUNG (1896–April 16, 1945) b. China. *One Way Ticket, The General Died at Dawn, White Hunter, Lost Horizon, Sinners in Paradise,* and *Too Hot to Handle.*

STEVEN GERAY (1904–Dec. 26, 1973) b. Uzhored, Czechoslovakia. *Man at Large, Cornered, Little Egypt, Big Sky, Call Me Madam, French Line, Knock on Wood,* and *Daddy Long Legs.*

Bernard Gorcey, center, with Gabe Dell, William Benedict, Benny Bartlett, David Gorcey in Trouble Makers.

Mary Gordon, right, with Brenda Joyce in The Missing Head.

JONATHAN HALE *(1891–Feb. 28, 1966)*
Call Northside 777, Alice Adams, Scandal Sheet, Let's Go Navy, Steel Trap, and *Blondie* series.

PORTER HALL *(1888–Oct. 6, 1953)*
b. Cincinnati, Ohio. *Miracle on 34th Street, Plainsman, Unconquered, Wells Fargo, Arkansas Traveler, Story of Louis Pasteur,* and *Tom Sawyer.*

Reed Hadley

Robert Greig, left, with John Howard and Marsha Hunt in Easy to Take.

ROBERT GREIG *(1879–June 27, 1958)*
b. Melbourne, Australia. *Lloyds of London, Algiers, Rose Marie, Easy to Take, Trouble in Paradise, The Moon and Sixpence,* and *Clive of India.*

REED HADLEY *(1911–Dec. 11, 1974)*
b. Petrolia, Texas. *Captain from Castile, House on 92nd Street, Dallas, A Southern Yankee, Iron Curtain,* and *Panhandle.*

Jonathan Hale, right, with Andrew Toombes and Warner Oland in Charlie Chan at the Olympics.

Porter Hall

211

JOHN HAMILTON *(1887–Oct. 15, 1958)*
Seventh Heaven, Rose of Washington Square, Violence, Song of My Heart, Law of the Golden West, and *Wife Wanted.*

WALTER HAMPDEN *(1879–June 11, 1955)*
Hunchback of Notre Dame, Reap the Wild Wind, All About Eve, and *The Vagabond King.*

JOHN HARMON *(   )*
King of Alcatraz, Gambling Ship, Devil's Island, and *King of the Underworld.*

HARRY HARVEY *(1901–   )*
b. Indian Territory, Okla. *A Tree Grows in Brooklyn, Leave It to Henry, Romance of Limberlost, Robbers of the Range,* and *Pride of the Yankees.*

PAUL HARVEY *(1882–Dec. 5, 1955)*
House of Rothschild, Late George Apley, Fountainhead, Riding High, Dreamboat, Sabrina, and *High Society.*

John Harmon, left, with Dorothy Malone and Mark Stevens in Jack Slade.

John Hamilton, left, with Milburn Stone and Stanley Waxman in The Judge.

Harry Harvey, right, with Raymond Burr in Unmasked.

Walter Hampden, right, with Charles Boyer and Leo G. Carroll in The First Legion.

RAYMOND HATTON *(1887–Oct. 21, 1971)*
b. Red Oak, Iowa. *Hunchback of Notre Dame, Treasure of Ruby Hills, Big Killing,* and numerous westerns.

Paul Harvey, right, with Jed Prouty in the Jones Family picture Love on a Budget.

Harry Hayden, center with Herbert Ashley and Richard Dix in Here I Am a Stranger.

Raymond Hatton

Richard Haydn, with Jerry Lewis in Money from Home.

HARRY HAYDEN (1882–July 23, 1955)
Barbary Coast Gent, Big Noise, Colonel Effingham's Raid, Unfinished Dance, Judge Steps Out, and *Beautiful Blonde from Bashful Bend.*

RICHARD HAYDN (1907–   )
Charley's Aunt, And Then There Were None, Cluny Brown, Singapore, Forever Amber, Dear Wife, and *Her Twelve Men.*

GEORGE "GABBY" HAYES (1885–Feb. 9, 1969)
b. Wellsville, N.Y. Featured in many westerns.

HOLMES HERBERT (1882–Dec. 26, 1956)
Dr. Jekyll and Mr. Hyde, The Invisible Man, Lloyds of London, The Black Doll, Sherlock Holmes in Washington, Johnny Belinda.

EARLE HODGINS (1893–April 14, 1964)
Crime of the Century, Borderland, Range Defenders, Hills of Old Wyoming, Partners of the Plains, and *Border Caballero.*

George "Gabby" Hayes

Arthur Hohl

Holmes Herbert with Louise Allbritton in Danger in the Pacific.

ARTHUR HOHL (1889–March 10, 1964)
b. Pittsburg, Pa. *Monsieur Verdoux, Down to the Sea in Ships, Salome, Where She Danced, Love Letters, It Happened on Fifth Avenue,* and *The Eve of St. Mark.*

STERLING HOLLOWAY (1905–   )
b. Cedartown, Ga. *Alice in Wonderland, Death Valley, Beautiful Blonde from Bashful Bend, Walk in the Sun,* and *Sioux City Sue.*

Earle Hodgins, with Alice Fleming in San Antonio Kid.

Sterling Holloway, in Doubting Thomas.

Olin Howlin

ROBERT HOMANS (1877–July 27, 1947) b. Malden, Mass. *Shantytown, Merry Monahans, Rogues Gallery, Over the Wall, River Gang,* and *Beyond the Pecos.*

OLIN HOWLIN (1886–Sept. 19, 1959) b. Denver, Colo. *Them, Home Sweet Homicide, Tenderfoot, Wistful Widow of Wagon Gap,* and *Gobs and Gals.*

JOSEPHINE HULL (1886–March 12, 1957) b. Newton, Mass. *Solid Gold Cadillac, Arsenic and Old Lace, Harvey,* and *Lady from Texas.*

Robert Homans, right, with Edward Everett Horton in Stand Up and Sing.

Josephine Hull, with Cecil Kellaway in Harvey.

Roger Imhof, in Drums Along the Mohawk.

Selmer Jackson, with Helen Westcott in Alaska Patrol.

ROGER IMHOF *(1875–April 15, 1958)*
b. Rock Island, Ill. *There Goes the Groom, David Harum, Ever Since Eve, Life Begins at Forty, Farmer Takes a Wife,* and *San Francisco.*

SELMER JACKSON *(1888–March 30, 1971)*
Alexander's Ragtime Band, Gambling Ship, Down in Arkansas, Federal Bullets, The Westland Case, and *Off the Record*

SAM JAFFE *(1893–March 24, 1984)*
Lost Horizon, Gunga Din, Gentlemen's Agreement, The Asphalt Jungle, The Day the Earth Stood Still and *The Dunwich Horror.*

DEAN JAGGER *(1903–)*
Western Union, 12 O'Clock High, It Grows on Trees, Executive Suite, White Christmas, Elmer Gantry.

Dean Jagger in Bad Day at Black Rock.

SI JENKS *(1876–Jan. 6, 1970)*
Kentucky Moonshine, Rawhide, Tom Sawyer, Detective, Captain January, and *The Outcasts of Poker Flat.*

217

am Jaffe in Ben-Hur

Si Jenks, with Jerry Colonna in Kentucky Jubilee.

ROSCOE KARNS *(1891–Feb. 6, 1970)*
b. San Bernardino, Calif. *It Happened One Night, Something Always Happens, My Son the Hero, Navy Way, They Drive by Night, Win That Girl,* and *Flying Ensign.*

Roscoe Karns

KURT KASZNAR *(1913–Aug. 6, 1979)*
b. Vienna, Austria. *My Sister Eileen, Anything Goes, Last Time I Saw Paris, Valley of the Kings, Happy Time,* and *Kiss Me Kate.*

ROBERT EMMETT KEANE *(1883–July 2, 1981)*
It Happens Every Spring, Circumstantial Evidence, Rogues Gallery, Roses Are Red, Bermuda Mystery, and *Public Opinion.*

BARRY KELLEY *(1908–   )*
b. Chicago, Ill. *New York Confidential, South Sea Woman, Love That Brute, Wabash Avenue, Asphalt Jungle,* and *Knock on Any Door.*

FRED KELSEY *(1884–Sept. 2, 1961)*
b. Sandusky, Ohio. *Hans Christian Andersen, Donovan Affair, On Trial, Subway Express, O. Henry's Full House,* and *Racing Blood.*

DOUGLAS KENNEDY *(1915–Aug. 10, 1973)*
b. New York City. *Strange Lady in Town, Sitting Bull, Sea of Lost Ships, Last Train from Bombay, The Way of All Flesh,* and *Northwest Mounted Police.*

Kurt Kasznar, center, with George Murphy and Billy Gray in Talk About a Stranger.

JOSEPH M. KERRIGAN *(1884–April 29, 1964)*
b. Dublin, Ireland. *The Wild North, My Cousin Rachel, 20,000 Leagues Under the Sea, Call Northside 777, Treasure Island, Wilson, Big Bonanza,* and *Spanish Main.*

Robert Emmett Keane, right, with Tim Ryan and Joan Davis in Kansas City Kitty.

Barry Kelley

Douglas Kennedy, left, with George Montgomery in Indian Uprising.

Fred Kelsey, right, with Jane Withers in Angel's Holiday.

MILTON KIBBEE *(1896–April 17, 1970)*
The Case of the Black Cat, River Lady, Old Fashioned Girl, Polo Joe, Trouble Chasers, and *Vacation Days.*

J. M. Kerrigan, left, with Victor McLaglen, Reginald Denny and Boris Karloff in Lost Patrol.

Charles King, center, with Black Jack O'Shea and Roy Barcroft in Riders of the Rio Grande.

Henry Kolker, with John Howard, in Let Them Live.

Martin Kosleck, center, with Richard Basehart in Hitler.

Milton Kibbee, center, with William Haade and Ross Latimer in Three Desperate Men.

CHARLES KING *1895–May 7, 1957)*
b. Hillsboro, Texas. *Wild Horse Canyon, Sing Cowboy Sing, The Lawless Nineties, Outlawed Guns, Son of the Border, Strawberry Roan,* and *Guns and Guitars.*

220

HENRY KOLKER *(1870–July 15, 1947)*
Baby Face, Adventures of Marco Polo, Invincible, Last Days of Pompeii, Maid of Salem, Conquest, and *Union Pacific.*

MARTIN KOSLECK *(1907–   )*
b. Barkotse, Pommern. *Nurse Edith Cavell, Bombers Moon, Hitler Gang, The Spider, Mummy's Curse, Assigned to Danger,* and *Smuggler's Cove.*

FRANK LACKTEEN *(1895–July 8, 1968)*
b. Kubber-Ilias, Asia Minor. *Amazon Quest, Moonlight and Cactus,* and *Frontier Gal.*

JESSIE ROYCE LANDIS *(1904–Feb. 2, 1972)*
b. Chicago, Ill. *Mr. Belvedere Goes to College, The Swan, My Foolish Heart, It Happens Every Spring,* and *To Catch a Thief.*

SAM LEVENE *(1906–Dec. 28, 1980)*
Three Men on a Horse, Yellow Jack, Crossfire, Three Sailors and a Girl, Brute Force, and *Destination Unknown.*

GEORGE LLOYD *(1897–   )*
b. Hobart, Tasmania. *Devil's Island, San Quentin, The Big Noise, Mr. Wong, Detective, Slight Case of Murder,* and *Freckles.*

Jessie Royce Landis, right, with James Darren and Cindy Carol in Gidget Goes to Rome.

Sam Levene, left, with Marty Milner in Sweet Smell of Success.

Frank Lackteen, with Lois Hall in Daughter of the Jungle.

George Lloyd, fourth from left, with Paulette Goddard, Burgess Meredith, Max Wagner, George Davis and Al Hill in All's Well That Ends Well.

Emmett Lynn, with Wild Bill Elliott.

Noel Madison

J. Farrell MacDonald and Polly Ann Young in The Last Alarm.

Edwin Maxwell, center, with Marie Wrixon and Terry Frost in Waterfront.

Eily Malyon with Lloyd Corrigan in She-Wolf of London.

Horace MacMahon

Sean McClory

Matt McHugh, left, with Otto Kruger in Exposed.

EMMETT LYNN *(1897–Oct. 20, 1958)*
b. Muscatine, Iowa. *The Robe, Here Comes Trouble, Apache War Smoke, Bluebird, Town Went Wild,* and *Hollywood and Vine.*

J. FARRELL MacDONALD *(1875–Aug. 2, 1952)*
b. Waterbury, Conn. *Beautiful Blonde from Bashful Bend, Web of Danger, In Old Cheyenne, My Darling Clementine,* and *Whispering Smith.*

HORACE MacMAHON *(1907–Aug. 17, 1971)*
Ladies in Distress, Fast Company, Exclusive, Navy Blue, The Wrong Road, and *When G-Men Step In.*

NOEL MADISON *(1897–Jan. 6, 1975)*
b. New York City. *Man with 100 Faces, Little Caesar, Manhattan Melodrama, Journal of Crime, Missing Girls,* and *Nation Aflame.*

EDWIN MAXWELL *(1890–Aug. 13, 1948)*
b. Dublin, Ireland. *Night Key, Jazz Singer, Duck Soup, The Crusades, Come and Get It, Mystery Liner,* and *Slave Ship.*

EILY MALYON *(1879–Sept. 26, 1961)*
b. London, Eng. *She Wolf of London, On Borrowed Time, Rasputin, Little Minister, Tale of Two Cities, Young Tom Edison,* and *Secret Heart.*

SEAN McCLORY *(1924–   )*
b. Dublin, Ireland. *Long Gray Line, Daughter of Rosie O'Grady, Quiet Man, Botany Bay, Diane,* and *Moonfleet.*

MATT McHUGH *(1894–Feb. 22, 1971)*
b. Connellsville, Pa. *Dark Corner, The Escape, It Happened in Flatbush, Jones Family in Hollywood,* and *Yesterday's Heroes.*

Margaret McWade, left, with Elizabeth Risdon and Irene Dunne in Theodora Goes Wild.

Lafe McKee, with Johnny Mack Brown.

MARGARET McWADE (1872–April 1, 1956)
Mr. Deeds Goes to Town, Danger—Love at Work, Love in a Bungalow, Wings Over Honolulu, and *Let's Make a Million.*

JOHN McINTYRE (1907–)
b. Spokane, Wash. *The Kentuckian, Far Country, President's Lady, Yellow Mountain, Winchester '73,* and *Francis.*

LAFE McKEE (1872–Aug. 10, 1959)
b. Morrison, Ill. *Rawhide, Rustlers of Red Gap, Cross Fire, West of the Divide, Knight of the Plains,* and *Gun Justice.*

ROBERT McKENZIE (1880–July 8, 1949)
Stars Over Arizona, Comin' Round the Mountain, Stone of Silver Creek, Rebellion Hideaway, and *Sing Cowboy Sing.*

GEORGE MEEKER (1904–)
b. Brooklyn, N.Y. *Marie Antoinette, The Westland Case, Broadway Bill, Country Doctor, Ever Since Eve, Only Yesterday,* and *Career Woman.*

JOHN MERTON (1901–Sept. 18, 1959)
Gang Bullets, Colorado Kid, Knight of the Plains, Range Defenders, Three Mesquiteers, and *Two Gun Justice.*

TORBEN MEYER (1884–May 22, 1975)
b. Copenhagen, Denmark. *Unfaithfully Yours, Mighty McGurk, Sin of Harold Diddlebock, Beautiful Blonde from Bashful Bend,* and *Mr. Twilight.*

Robert McKenzie, second from left, with Brandon Tynan, Walter Pidgeon and Hank Bell in The Girl of the Golden West.

John McIntyre, right, with Van Johnson and William Phipps in Scene of the Crime.

George Meeker.

Torben Meyer, right, with Burt Lancaster in Judgment at Nuremberg.

JOHN MILJAN *(1893–Jan. 24, 1960)*
b. Lead City, S.D. *Border G-Man, Whirlpool, Mississippi, Sutters Gold, The Plainsman,* and *North of Nome.*

GAVIN MUIR *(1909–May 24, 1972)*
b. Chicago, Ill. *O.S.S., Calcutta, Sherlock Holmes in Washington, Eagle Squadron, Prince of Thieves,* and *Unconquered.*

BERNARD NEDELL *(1893–Nov. 23, 1972)*
b. New York City. *Exposed, Man from Chicago, Heat Wave, Shadow Man, Mr. Moto's Gamble, First Offense,* and *The Code.*

John Miljan, right, with J. Carrol Naish in Forced Landing.

John Merton, center, with Linda Stirling and Tom Steele.

Gavin Muir, center, with Ray Milland and Barry Fitzgerald in California.

Bernard Nedell, in They All Come Out.

George Offerman Jr., left, with John Alvin, Edward Ryan, John Campbell, James Cardwell and Thomas Mitchell in The Fighting Sullivans.

Jay Novello

JAY NOVELLO (1904–Sept. 2, 1982)
Port Said, Hotel Berlin, Girl from Havana, Two Gun Sheriff, Sleepytime Gal, and Chicago Kid.

Dave O'Brien

DAVE O'BRIEN (1912–Nov. 8, 1969)
b. Big Springs, Tex. Little Colonel, Devil Bat, Texas Ranger, and many Pete Smith shorts.

GEORGE´ OFFERMAN JR. (1917–Jan. 14, 1963)
b. Chicago, Ill. Old Gray Mayor, Action in the North Atlantic, The Sullivans, House of Rothschild, and Calling Dr. Kildare.

LYNNE OVERMAN (1887–Feb. 19, 1943)
b. Maryville, Mo. Union Pacific, Murder Goes to College, Jungle Princess, Nobody's Baby, True Confession, Men with Wings, and Ride a Crooked Mile.

SARAH PADDEN (1881–Dec. 4, 1967)
Wonder of Women, Range Law, Prince of Players, Dude Goes West, Summer Storm, Dakota, and Homicide.

JACK PENNICK (1895–Aug. 16, 1964)
b. Portland, Oregon. Cocoanut Grove, Submarine Patrol, The Virginian, Tugboat Annie, Under Two Flags, and Navy Blues.

BARBARA PEPPER (1915–July 18, 1969)
b. New York City. Sea Devils, Winterset, Three Sons, Foreign Correspondent, Brewster's Millions, and Unmasked.

Lynne Overman, in Hotel Haywire.

Sarah Padden, left, with Anne Nagel in Should a Girl Marry?

RALPH PETERS (1902–June 5, 1959)
Tough Kid, Swing It, Professor, The Great Gambini, Outlaws of Sonora, and Wanted by the Police.

LEE PHELPS (1893–March 9, 1953)
The Gladiator, Crash Donovan, Lefthanded Law, Long Shot, and Palm Springs.

VICTOR POTEL (1889–March 8, 1947)
b. LaFayette, Ind. Outside the Law, Yellow Dust, Border Romance, Three Godfathers, Song of the Saddle, and Western Gold.

Jack Pennick, with Kate Smith.

MARJORIE RAMBEAU (1889–July 7, 1970)
b. San Francisco, Calif. A Man Called Peter, Her Man, Strictly Personal, East of the River, Tobacco Road, Salome Where She Danced, and Forever Female.

Barbara Pepper

GEORGE H. REED (1866–Nov. 6, 1952)
b. Georgia. Home in Indiana, Kentucky, Green Pastures, Swanee River, Sporting Blood, and The Buccaneer.

FRANK REICHER (1875–Jan. 19, 1965)
b. Munich, Germany. House of Frankenstein, Mr. District Attorney, The Great Mystic, The Shadow Returns, and Yankee Fakir.

227

Ralph Peters, right, with Harlan Tucker and William Powell in Take One False Step.

Lee Phelps, left, with Max Hoffman Jr. and Ralph Bellamy in Brother Orchid.

Victor Potel, right, with Alan Curtis.

George H. Reed, right, with Van Johnson and Lionel Barrymore in Dr. Gillispie's New Assistant.

Marjorie Rambeau, right, with Dennis O'Keefe and Gale Storm in Abandoned.

Frank Reicher, right, with Dennis O'Keefe in Unexpected Father.

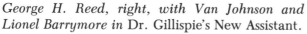

Jack Rice, left, with Jack Holt and Lee Phelps in Crime Takes a Holiday.

Charles Richman, second from left, with James Gleason, William Powell, Jean Arthur and Eric Blore in The Ex-Mrs. Bradford.

John Ridgely, left, with MacDonald Carey in South Sea Sinner.

Bert Roach, with Jack Haley.

Willard Robertson, right, with Ida Lupino in Deep Valley.

JACK RICE *(1893–Dec. 14, 1968)*
b. Grand Rapids, Mich. *Weekend Pass, Crazy House, Her Lucky Night, Meet Me on Broadway, So This Is Washington,* and *Mr. Smith Goes to Washington.*

CHARLES RICHMAN *(1870–Dec. 1, 1940)*
Devil's Island, Adventures of Tom Sawyer, Life of Emile Zola, Becky Sharp, Parole, and *Cowboy and the Lady.*

JOHN RIDGELY *(1909–Jan. 17, 1968)*
b. Chicago, Ill. *Outcasts of Poker Flat, Greatest Show on Earth, Place in the Sun, Arsenic and Old Lace,* and *Big Sleep.*

BERT ROACH *(1891–Feb. 16, 1971)*
b. Washington, D.C. *The Jade Lady, Bedside Manner, Perils of Pauline, Sensations of 1945,* and *Man from Rainbow Valley.*

WILLARD ROBERTSON *(1886–April 5, 1948)*
The Cisco Kid, Tugboat Annie, Here Comes the Navy, The Last of the Mohicans, Jesse James and *Sitting Pretty.*

DEWEY ROBINSON *(1898–Dec. 11, 1950)*
b. New Haven, Conn. *Black Market Babies, Forged Passport, Countess of Monte Cristo, The Shadow, The Jade Lady,* and *Pardon My Past.*

SELENA ROYLE *(1904–April 23, 1983)*
b. New York City. *Gallant Journey, Night and Day, Cass Timberlane, Joan of Arc, Branded, Mrs. Parkington,* and *Till the End of Time.*

CHRISTIAN RUB *(1887–April 14, 1956)*
b. Austria. *You Can't Take It with You, Parole, Mr. Deeds Goes to Town, Cafe Metropole, No Greater Glory,* and *One Hundred Men and a Girl.*

Dewey Robinson, with Joan Blondell and Glenda Farrell in We're in the Money.

Selena Royle, with Thomas Mitchell in The Fighting Sullivans.

Christian Rub.

TIM RYAN *(1899–Oct. 22 1956)*
Brother Orchid, Sarong Girl, Hit Parade of 1943, Fargo, Crazy Over Horses, and *Stand By for Action.*

RALPH SANFORD *(1899–June 20, 1963)*
b. Springfield, Mass. *Girl on the Spot, Winner Take All, French Leave, Sioux City Sue, Shaggy,* and *Linda Be Good.*

Tim Ryan with Elyse Knox in Forgotten Women.

Ralph Sanford, center, with Charles Kemper and Walter Catlett in Kid Nightingale.

JOE SAWYER *(1901–April 21, 1982)*
Johnny Dark, Curtain Call at Cactus Creek, Naughty Nineties, Red Skies of Montana, Frisco Kid, and *Man of Iron.*

SYD SAYLOR *(1895–Dec. 21, 1962)*
b. Chicago, Ill. *Cheaper by the Dozen, Jackpot, Union Pacific, Abe Lincoln in Illinois, Three of a Kind, Tall Texan,* and *Snake Pit.*

ROBERT SHAYNE *(1908–   )*
b. Yonkers, N.Y. *Shine on Harvest Moon, Prince of Pirates, Welcome Stranger, Mr. Skeffington, Christmas in Connecticut,* and *Murder Is My Beat.*

ANN SHOEMAKER *(1891–Sept. 18, 1978)*
b. New York City. *Wallflower, Alice Adams, Stranded, Magic Town, Above Suspicion,* and *Return of the Whistler.*

ALISON SKIPWORTH *(1863–July 5, 1952)*
b. London, Eng. *Night Angel, High Pressure, Tonight or Never, Strictly Unconventional,* and *Oh for a Man.*

Syd Saylor, left, with Jack Overman, Jimmy Ames, William Haade, Tyrone Power and Gene Tierney in The Wonderful Urge.

Joe Sawyer, in The Traveling Saleswoman.

Robert Shayne, right, with Gene Autry and Barbara Britton in Loaded Pistols.

ABRAHAM SOFAER *(1896–)*
b. Rangoon, Burma. *His Majesty O'Keefe, Bhowani Junction, Sinbad, Elephant Walk,* and *Rembrandt.*

CHARLES STEVENS *(1893–Aug. 22, 1964)*
b. Solomonsville, Ariz. *San Antonio, Lives of a Bengal Lancer, The Gaucho, The Virginian, Son of His Father,* and *The Iron Mask.*

HOUSELEY STEVENSON *(1879–Aug. 6, 1953)*
b. London, Eng. *Knock on Any Door, Kidnapped, Sierra, Colorado Territory, Lady Gambles,* and *Dark Passage.*

AL "FUZZY" ST. JOHN *(1892–Jan. 21, 1963)*
b. Santa Ana, Calif. *Frontier Scout, Trail Dust, Outcasts of Poker Flat, Sing Cowboy Sing, Knight of the Plains,* and *Call of the Yukon.*

Abraham Sofaer, with Elizabeth Taylor in Elephant Walk.

Ann Shoemaker, right, with Victor Jory and Gloria Grahame in A Woman's Secret.

Alison Skipworth, with Warren William in Satan Met a Lady.

Charles Stevens in Blood and Sand.

Al "Fuzzy" St. John, with Buster Crabbe in Panhandle Trail.

CARL STOCKDALE (1874–March 15, 1953)
b. Worthington, Minn. *Along the Rio Grande, Lost Horizon, Oliver Twist, China Bound,* and *Thundering Frontier.*

Carl Stockdale, seated second from left, with Donald Kirke, Harry Davenport, and Dorothy Appleby in Paradise Express.

Lewis Stone, in You're Only Young Once *with Fay Holden, Cecilia Parker, Sara Haden and Mickey Rooney.*

Houseley Stevenson, left, with Humphrey Bogart in Knock on Any Door.

LEWIS STONE (1879–Sept. 13, 1953)
b. Worcester, Mass. *Madame X, Big House, Treasure Island, State of the Union, Grand Hotel,* and *Hardy Family* series.

HARRY STRANG (1892–April 10, 1972)
Submarine Patrol, Two Gun Justice, Come on Leathernecks, The Purple Vigilantes, and *Mr. Moto Takes a Vacation.*

LEONARD STRONG (1908–Jan. 23, 1980)
Back to Bataan, We Were Strangers, Anna and the King of Siam, Bombardier, and *Blood on the Sun.*

Harry Strang, left, with Elizabeth Patterson, Dickie Moore and Margaret Sullavan in So Red the Rose.

Frank Sully with Janet Leigh in Bye Bye Birdie.

Leonard Strong, center, with Richard Widmark, Don Taylor, Casey Adams, Ross Bagdasarian and Darryl Hickman in Destination Gobi.

FRANK SULLY *(1908–Dec. 17, 1975)*
b. St. Louis, Mo. *Naked Street, Grapes of Wrath, Killer Shark, Silver Lode, My Sister Eileen,* and *Escape to Glory*

CLINTON SUNDBERG *(1906–)*
b. Appleton, Minn. *The Caddy, Toast of New Orleans, Undercurrent, Hucksters, Easter Parade, Good Sam,* and *Command Decision.*

Clinton Sundberg, with Tallulah Bankhead in Main Street to Broadway.

LYLE TALBOT *(1902–)*
b. Brainard, Neb. *Up in Arms, One Body Too Many, Gamblers Choice, Steel Cage, Star of Texas,* and *The Jackpot.*

FORREST TAYLOR *(1883–Feb. 19, 1965)*
Painted Trail, Headin' for the Rio Grande, Arizona Days, and *Heroes of the Hills.*

ERNEST THESIGER *(1879–Jan. 14, 1961)*
b. London, Eng. *Caesar and Cleopatra, Jassy, Colonel's Lady, Winslow Boy, Man in the White Suit, Magic Box,* and *Man with a Million.*

Lyle Talbot, in Heat Lightning.

Forrest Taylor

ZEFFIE TILBURY *(1863–July 22, 1950)*
Federal Bullets, Hunted Men, Gorgeous Hussy, Maid of Salem, Last Days of Pompeii, and *Give Me Your Heart.*

HENRY TRAVERS *(1874–Oct. 18, 1965)*
b. Ireland. *Reunion in Vienna, Death Takes a Holiday, Madam Curie, Dragon Seed, Yearling,* and *Beyond Glory.*

ARTHUR TREACHER *(1894–Dec. 14, 1975)*
b. Brighton, Sussex, Eng. *Viva Villa, Mme. DuBarry, David Copperfield, National Velvet, Star Spangled Rhythm,* and *Midnight Kiss.*

Ernest Thesiger, right, with Dean Stockwell and Wendy Hiller in Sons and Lovers.

Henry Travers, left, with Virginia Weidler and Fay Holden in I'll Wait For You.

Zeiffie Tilbury with Milburn Stone in Federal Bullets.

Arthur Treacher in Splendor.

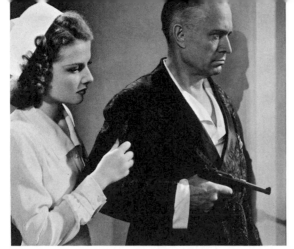

Charles Trowbridge, with Ann Sheridan in The Patient in Room 18.

Luis Van Rooten, center, with Sid Tomack and Chester Morris in Boston Blackie's Chinese Venture.

CHARLES TROWBRIDGE *(1882–Oct. 30, 1967)*
b. Vera Cruz, Mexico. *The Great Lie, Ten Gentlemen from West Point, Sweetheart of the Fleet, Gorgeous Hussy, Captains Courageous, That Certain Woman, Key Witness,* and *Mr. District Attorney.*

MINERVA URECAL *(1884–Feb. 26, 1966)*
Frontier Scout, Oh Doctor, Start Cheering, Prison Nurse, Exiled to Shanghai, The Go Getter, Wake Up and Dream, and *The Trap.*

DOROTHY VAUGHAN *(1889–March 15, 1955)*
b. St. Louis, Mo. *Fighting Fools, Egg and I, Annapolis Farewell, Town Went Wild, Sweet and Low Down,* and *Bishop's Wife.*

Minerva Urecal in The Ape Man.

Dorothy Vaughan, right, with Phil Brito and Virginia Welles in Square Dance Katy.

LUIS VAN ROOTEN *(1906–June 17, 1973)*
b. Mexico City, Mex. *Across the River, Hitler Gang, Two Years Before the Mast, Beyond Glory, Night Has a Thousand Eyes,* and *Lydia Bailey.*

WALLY VERNON *(1904–March 7, 1970)*
Alexander's Ragtime Band, Mountain Music, Sharpshooters, Happy Landing, Kentucky Moonshine, and *This Way Please.*

Wally Vernon, with Dana Andrews in Sailor's Lady.

William Von Brincken, left, with Fay Wray and Grant Withers in Navy Secrets.

EMMETT VOGAN (1893–Nov. 13, 1969)
The Beloved Brat, The Big Noise, Sergeant Murphy, Female Fugitive, Let's Get Married, and San Quentin.

WILLIAM VON BRINCKEN (1881–Jan. 18, 1946)
b. Flensburg, Ger. Espionage, Prisoner of Zenda, Life of Emile Zola, International Crime, and Bulldog Drummond in Africa.

MURVYN VYE (1913–Aug. 17, 1976)
b. Quincy, Mass. Golden Earrings, Road to Bali, Escape to Burma, Connecticut Yankee, Destination Gobi, and Green Fire.

EDDY WALLER (1889–Aug. 19, 1977)
Far Country, Jesse James, Grapes of Wrath, Love, Honor and Oh-Baby, Make Haste to Live, and Man Without a Star.

Emmett Vogan, second from left, with Roy Gordon, Lane Chandler and Gene Autry in Riders of the Whistling Pines.

Murvyn Vye

Eddy Waller, center, with Willard Robertson and Evelyn Keyes in Renegades.

HENRY B. WALTHALL (1878–June 17, 1936)
Viva Villa, Abraham Lincoln, Scarlet Letter, The Barrier, Single Wives, and *Laughing at Life.*

Pierre Watkin, with Susan Hayward in Tulsa.

Henry B. Walthall, in Dante's Inferno.

ANTHONY WARDE (1908–Jan. 8, 1975)
The Affairs of Annabel, Come on Leathernecks, Escape by Night, and *Mr. Moto Takes a Vacation.*

PIERRE WATKIN (1887–Feb. 3, 1960)
Stage Door, Sea Devils, The Californian, Green Light, Dangerous to Know, The Chaser, and *Dangerous.*

BEN WELDEN (1901–   )
b. Toledo, Ohio. *Hidden Guns, Search for Danger, It's in the Bag, Sorrowful Jones, All Ashore,* and *Steel Cage.*

Ben Welden, right, with Paul Guilfoyle in The Missing Corpse.

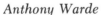

Anthony Warde

DICK WESSEL (1913–April 20, 1965)
They Made Me a Criminal, Slim, In Spite of Danger, Arson Gang Busters, and *Borrowing Trouble.*

HELEN WESTLEY (1875–Dec. 12, 1942)
b. Brooklyn, N.Y. *Heidi, Alexander's Ragtime Band, Captain Hurricane, Death Takes a Holiday, Zaza, Showboat,* and *Cafe Metropole.*

Dick Wessel, right, with Dean Jones and Susan Pleshette in The Ugly Dachshund.

CHARLES WILLIAMS *(1898–Jan. 4, 1958)*
b. Albany, N.Y. *Doll Face, Dude Goes West, End of the Road, Heldorado, Grand Canyon,* and *Identity Unknown.*

Peter Whitney, right, with Jan Merlin and Kent Taylor.

Helen Westley, with Slim Summerville in Rebecca of Sunnybrook Farm.

Guy Wilkerson

Charles Williams

PETER WHITNEY *(1916–March 30, 1972)*
b. Long Branch, N.J. *Spy Ship, Underground, Hotel Berlin, Three Strangers, Big Heat, Black Dakotas,* and *Last Frontier.*

GUY WILKERSON *(1899–July 8, 1971)*
Yodelin' Kid from Pine Ridge, Mountain Justice, and *Paradise Express.*

239

Matt Willis

MATT WILLIS *(1914–   )*
Behind Prison Walls, Return of the Vampire, Louisiana Hayride, Forever Yours, Strange Voyage, and *Corporal Hargrove.*

NORMAN WILLIS *(1903–   )*
b. Chicago, Ill. *San Antonio, Mary Burns, Fugitive, Apology for Murder, Johnny Come Lately,* and *In Old New Mexico.*

CHARLES WILSON *(1894–Jan. 7, 1948)*
b. New York. *Song of Love, The Night Hawk, Showboat, The Glass Key, Woman in Distress, Roaring Timber,* and *Pennies from Heaven.*

DOUGLAS WOOD *(1880–Jan. 13, 1966)*
b. New York City. *Because of Him, Tomorrow Is Forever, Voice of the Whistler, Two Blondes and a Redhead,* and *It Had to Be You.*

Charles Wilson, left, with Richard Cromwell in Name the Woman.

Douglas Wood with Gloria Stuart in The Prisoner of Shark Island.

Norman Willis, left, with Charles Starrett in Outlaws of the Panhandle.

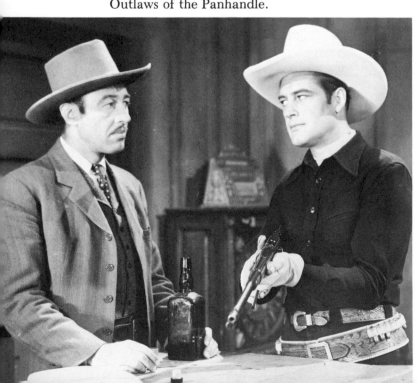